Underground Building Design
Commercial and Institutional Structures

John Carmody
Architect and Research Coordinator

Dr. Raymond Sterling, P.E.
Associate Professor and Director

Underground Space Center
University of Minnesota

 VAN NOSTRAND REINHOLD COMPANY
NEW YORK   CINCINNATI   TORONTO   LONDON   MELBOURNE

Library of Congress Catalog Card Number 83-6925
ISBN 0-442-28687-2 (cl)
ISBN 0-442-28686-4 (pb)

Printed in the United States of America
Designed by John Carmody

Published by Van Nostrand Reinhold Company Inc.
135 West 50th Street
New York, New York 10020

Van Nostrand Reinhold
480 Latrobe Street
Melbourne, Victoria 3000, Australia

Van Nostrand Reinhold Company Limited
Molly Millars Lane
Wokingham, Berkshire RG11 2PY, England

16   15   14   13   12   11   10   9   8   7   6   5   4   3   2   1

Library of Congress Cataloging in Publication Data
Main entry under title:

Underground building design.

  Bibliography: p. 256
  Includes index.
  1. Underground construction.   2. Earth Sheltered
houses   3. Buildings—Energy conservation. I. Carmody,
John. II. Sterling, Raymond. III. University of
Minnesota (Minneapolis-St. Paul Campus). Underground
Space Center.
TA712.U45 1983 721 83-6925
ISBN 0-442 28687-2
ISBN 0-442-28686-4 (pbk.)

Graphics, page layout, and cover design were done by John Carmody with assistance from Mark Heisterkamp and Katherine Carmody. Many of the drawings in chapters 3 through 8 were contributed by the architects of the buildings selected as case studies. Additional drawings throughout the book were prepared by the people mentioned above. The cover drawing is a section perspective of the Civil and Mineral Engineering Building at the University of Minnesota (see chapter 4). BRW Architects, Inc. of Minneapolis, Minnesota, designed the building and prepared the cover drawing.

Preface

In past centuries, natural caves have been inhabited, space has been carved out of rock or soil, and earth has been used as a building material. These indigenous solutions to the need for shelter have resulted partially from a lack of other building materials and technology. Such shelters have, however, offered a number of advantages such as protection from climatic extremes and natural disasters as well as security and defense against enemies.

Although many more options exist in construction today, many problems also exist. Urban areas are overcrowded and often do not provide an acceptable overall environment; moreover, conservation of fossil fuel energy for heating and cooling buildings will be increasingly important in the future. Underground buildings present opportunities not typically available in conventional structures to resolve some of these problems. Considered suitable only for very specialized sites and circumstances by many planners and designers prior to the 1970s, underground structures have, in fact, been built for a wide variety of reasons. Rather than being limited by their subsurface location, underground buildings have exhibited a diverse range of design approaches.

As interest in underground space use increases and more underground commercial and institutional structures are built, there emerges a better understanding of the particular design issues and technical considerations inherent in underground buildings. The main purpose of this book is thus to assemble and synthesize current information on the design and construction of underground buildings. It is hoped that this information will enable planners, policy-makers, potential developers and building owners to better understand the advantages and disadvantages of underground space along with its numerous and varied applications. In addition, the book is intended to clarify key design issues for architects while providing numerous case studies and technical information.

It is not the intention of the authors to suggest that an underground building represents the best solution for each situation. A subsurface structure is not suitable for many sites, functions and building programs. The underground alternative, however, deserves to be considered when conditions are appropriate and this book is intended to help design and evaluate this option.

The eight chapters and two appendices included in the book present information related to underground building design in three forms—general information, case studies, and technical information. The first two chapters provide a general overview of underground buildings including their basic characteristics as well as key design considerations. In chapters 3 through 8, case studies of twenty-three underground buildings are presented. Organized by building type, these chapters provide general design information as well as technical data on the buildings. Reflecting the diversity of underground buildings in existence, the case studies are divided into libraries, educational institutions, office and commercial buildings, manufacturing and storage facilities, visitor and interpretive centers, as well as special use facilities. Less common building types are included in the last group such as a monastery, a university fieldhouse, a convention center, and a prison. In the appendices, information is presented in two areas of particular concern—life safety and fire protection in underground buildings, and below-grade waterproofing.

Contents

Acknowledgments

This book represents the culmination of several years of research on the design and construction of underground buildings. Such an effort has only been made possible through the support, contributions, and cooperation of a number of people and organizations. The primary funding for the research was provided by the Legislative Commission on Minnesota Resources, which has shown foresight in supporting a series of research projects in the fields of underground space use and energy conservation.

The authors particularly wish to thank Dr. Charles Fairhurst, whose efforts have led to the establishment of the Underground Space Center at the University of Minnesota. Without his vision of the many facets and applications of underground space, research projects such as this book would never have been realized. As Chairman of the Department of Civil and Mineral Engineering, Dr. Fairhurst has also played a major role in bringing about one of the most innovative underground structures built to date—the Civil and Mineral Engineering Building at the University of Minnesota, which is presented in chapter 4.

Among the contributors to this book, two people in particular were responsible for providing useful technical information. Brent Anderson of Division 7, Inc., Minneapolis, provided much of the information that is incorporated in the evaluation of below-grade waterproofing methods contained in Appendix B. Dan Kallenbach of Setter, Leach, and Lindstrom, Inc., Minneapolis, provided original material on fire protection issues for underground buildings found in Appendix A.

In addition to these major contributions, many individuals provided advice and support throughout the project. Discussions with Peter Herzog of Associated Energy Consultants as well as Dr. George Meixel, Jr. and Louis Goldberg of the Underground Space Center staff were helpful in clarifying energy use issues in large buildings. Conversations with Ken Labs of Undercurrent Design and Michael Barker of the American Institute of Architects led to the final selection of case studies included in the book.

The production of the book has required the time and talents of many people. In particular, Linda Rathjen of Van Nostrand Reinhold Company provided much needed editorial advice and assistance. Additional editing of the text was done by Jean Rice. Many of the drawings in the book and the keylining were done by Mark Heisterkamp, Katherine Carmody, and Raquel Derrenberger. The extensive typing and retyping of the text was done by Arlene Bennett with assistance during early stages of the project from Penny Bader and Andrea Spartz.

Finally, we would like to thank the architects and owners of the twenty-three buildings that appear as case studies in the book. A significant amount of time and energy was required to provide the authors with drawings, photographs, and detailed information about the buildings. It is impossible to list all the people who were of assistance in the various architecture firms that designed the buildings or in the organizations that own and operate the structures. The architecture firms and building owners, however, are listed at the end of each case study.

Legislative Commission on Minnesota Resources

B-46 STATE CAPITOL   ST. PAUL, MINNESOTA 55155   (612) 296-2406

ROBERT E. HANSEN
EXECUTIVE DIRECTOR

To the Citizens of Minnesota and the United States

    The Legislative Commission on Minnesota Resources welcomes the appearance of this latest book by the Underground Space Center. The Commission maintains a very active interest in the potential for earth sheltered buildings and deep underground space development. Visits by Commission members in 1977 to underground facilities in Scandinavia and within the United States stimulated both the initiation of the Underground Space Center and the funding of a series of three research projects. The results of the first two projects, Earth Sheltered Housing Design and Earth Sheltered Community Design, have already been published and widely disseminated. This volume on non-residential underground building design completes the series.

    What started in 1977 with a solely Minnesota focus has been broadened to provide information for the wide ranges of climate experienced within the United States and in other regions of the world.

    The Legislative Commission on Minnesota Resources is pleased to have had a key role in these developments as part of its mission to encourage the wise use or preservation of Minnesota's resources. Questions concerning underground space uses should be directed to Ray Sterling, Director, Underground Space Center, 790 Civil & Mineral Engineering Building, 500 Pillsbury Drive, S. E., Minneapolis, MN 55455 (612) 376-5341.

Sincerely,

Representative Fred C. Norton,
Chairman
Legislative Commission
on Minnesota Resources

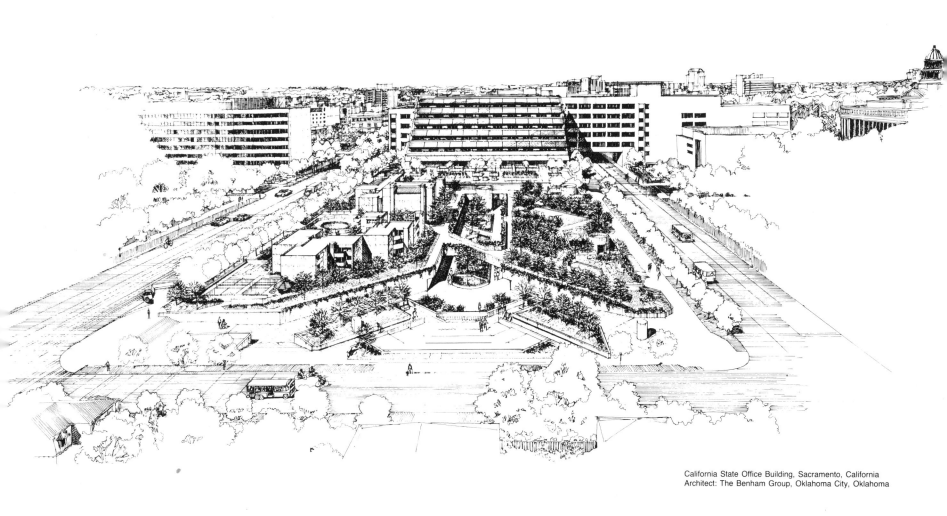

California State Office Building, Sacramento, California
Architect: The Benham Group, Oklahoma City, Oklahoma

Chapter 1: Characteristics of Underground Space

Introduction

In this chapter, the basic characteristics of underground buildings are presented in four sections—types of space, advantages, disadvantages, and appropriate uses. Types of space are defined to establish a vocabulary of terms and to indicate the widely varying characteristics of individual spaces which may all be grouped under the category of underground buildings.

In the second section of the chapter are the general advantages associated with underground space in comparison with conventional aboveground buildings. These diverse advantages form the rationale for deciding to place structures partially or completely below the surface. In some cases a unique site or a particular characteristic of underground space will be the overriding concern leading to the selection of an underground design. In most cases, however, there are multiple reasons for building underground based on a number of interrelated advantages.

The third section includes a discussion of the most generally perceived disadvantages of underground space compared with conventional above-grade buildings. Considering the wide range of benefits presented in the previous section, the intention in including these disadvantages is to provide a balanced perspective on underground buildings as well as indicate areas of special concern in their design. Most general advantages and disadvantages of underground buildings are strongly related to the function of the space. A disadvantage such as limited natural light and view may be a significant concern for office space but inconsequential for an auditorium. For this reason the last section of the chapter includes an analysis of the appropriate use of underground space.

Types of Underground Space

Mined Space

Although underground buildings are often discussed as a general category with certain advantages and disadvantages, many types of underground space with widely varying characteristics exist. One clear distinction usually drawn is between mined space and earth sheltered (cut-and-cover) space. Mined space is excavated through limited points of access from the surface either through vertical shafts or horizontal tunnels. Often it is excavated in self-supporting rock or soil but is restricted to suitable geological conditions. Mined space is usually deeper and thus more isolated from the surface than earth sheltered space.

Historically many forms of shelter were carved into rock or self-supporting soil as a means of protection from the elements or to provide self-defense. Such developments can be found on every inhabited continent, often in places with climatic extremes where few other building materials were available. In northern China an entire community lives underground in mined space (see fig. 1-1). Carved out of the self-supporting loess soil, this space near the surface is used for housing, but other functions, such as storage, occur in deeper mined space. In contrast to historical developments, few modern examples of mined space exist for purposes other than utilities, defense, and subway systems in the United States. Two notable exceptions, however, are the extensive industrial and warehouse complex carved out of limestone near Kansas City, Missouri, and the deep-mined space being developed for laboratories and offices in a soft sandstone layer beneath the University of Minnesota campus in Minneapolis. These projects are discussed in detail in chapters 4 and 6.

Cut-and-Cover/Earth Sheltered Space

Buildings that are placed into the soil near the surface and are designed to support the soil represent the other major category of underground space. The vast majority of all underground spaces fall into this group. Examples range from small housing

1-1: Underground Village in China

Drawing by Mark Heisterkamp based on a photograph from *Architecture Without Architects* [1.1].

structures to very large multiuse commercial, transit, and industrial complexes. Essentially, near-surface buildings are constructed in the same way that surface buildings are; the surrounding earth is not a structural part of the building as it is with mined space. This type of near-surface development is often referred to as cut-and-cover, reflecting the construction process involved. Near-surface underground development is also referred to as earth sheltered. Cut-and-cover/earth sheltered spaces are not limited to completely below-grade structures that are isolated from the surface. Many variations are discussed below. Figure 1-2 illustrates different types of space proposed for the University of Minnesota campus. At least in the unique geology of this particular campus, deep-mined space and cut-and-cover space can be combined. In many cases near-surface space is combined with above-grade space.

Relationship to Grade

Beyond the general classification of deep-mined and near-surface space, underground space can be divided into more specific categories in a number of ways. Generally, the key factor that characterizes underground buildings is their relationship to the surface. Based on a classification system developed by Ken Labs, structures placed on flat sites can be divided into bermed and subgrade [1.2]. The floor level of a bermed structure is at or slightly below existing grade, with earth built up around the building (see fig. 1-3). Such a building is not "invisible," as the berms are architectural forms that define the space on the site. On-grade access and a more balanced cut-and-fill ratio are advantages of bermed structures. Subgrade structures are placed completely below the existing grade. By permitting continuity of the grade level, the presence of the

building is far less apparent. On sloping sites the distinction between bermed and subgrade is less apparent and less relevant. Buildings are set into the hillside, submerging them on one side and exposing them on the other. This use of sloping sites is unique to earth sheltered buildings and presents many advantages, described later in this chapter.

In addition to defining bermed and subgrade space, a second distinction can be made between buildings that have earth covering both the roof and walls versus those with earth against only the walls, using a conventional roof. This may seem to be a subtle variation since the earth cover is usually two feet or less in thickness and does not affect the form of the buildings in any significant way. Some definite structural, cost, energy-use, and aesthetic differences are associated with earth-covered roofs, however, and the

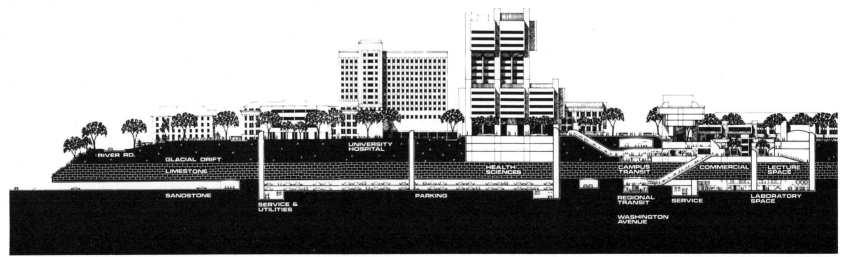

1-2: Mined Space Combined with Cut-and-Cover Space

Drawing by John Carmody illustrates potential development on University of Minnesota campus.

A: Bermed on Flat Site

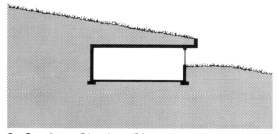

B: Subgrade on Flat Site

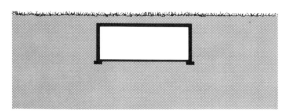

C: Set into Sloping Site

1-3: Building Types Based on Relationship to Grade

distinction is important to make. Both designs are considered underground or earth sheltered; earth covered is simply a further classification within that category.

Relationship to Surface through Openings

Underground structures can be further categorized by the types of openings used to reach the surface. The four classifications developed by Labs are *chamber, atrium, elevational,* and *penetrational* designs [1.2]. These different types can result in fundamentally different building forms and feelings of enclosure. The chamber is completely windowless (see fig. 1-4). Most mined construction results in spaces that fall in the chamber category. The atrium or courtyard type can provide an open feeling with much natural light, but views are inwardly oriented. Elevational designs offer an outward view in one direction, whereas penetrational designs have openings in several directions. It is interesting to note that in their pure form elevational structures appear to be most appropriate for sloping sites, whereas all the other types are more suitable to flat sites. In reality most buildings are usually not built in these pure diagrammatic forms but have elements of two or more types in the same structure. Especially in larger buildings with multiple functions, it is not uncommon to have deeper chamber-type spaces for some functions, other spaces around an atrium near the surface, and perhaps elevational openings if the site is sloping.

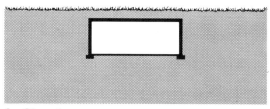

A: Chamber

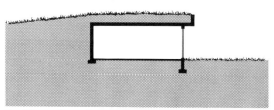

B: Atrium

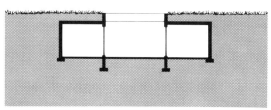

C: Elevational

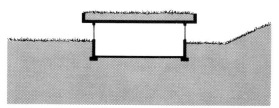

D: Penetrational

1-4: Building Types Based on Openings to the Surface

Advantages of Underground Space

Although the advantages listed in this section are diverse, nearly all are directly or indirectly related to the obvious fact that underground space is isolated from the surface to some extent. It is this isolation that results in a number of benefits for the surface environment as well as the activities that are placed underground.

As indicated in the previous discussion, underground construction includes buildings with widely varying characteristics. The degree of integration with earth, the structural systems, materials, relation to the outside, construction costs, and actual energy use can vary somewhat just as they would with any other broad classification of building type. Thus, in enumerating the advantages of earth sheltering, some basic assumptions must be made about the most important and likely characteristics of underground structures. It must be remembered, however, that these characteristics and the advantages associated with them apply in varying degrees and sometimes may not apply at all in a particular case.

Limited Visual Impact

Partially or completely underground buildings are less visible than conventional buildings, which can be an advantage in a number of situations. For example, an underground building can preserve the character of sensitive sites with natural beauty where the intrusion of man-made building forms may be considered undesirable. Many park buildings and wildlife interpretive centers are built into the earth for this reason. In a similar way, an underground building is often an appropriate solution for an area with a special historical character in which an above-grade contemporary building would be disruptive. This is one reason why many newer buildings on university campuses are built underground, including libraries, student unions, and bookstores at universities such as Cornell, Yale, Harvard, Michigan, and Minnesota. A recently completed underground addition to a library at Cornell University is shown in figure 1-5.

The advantage of reduced visibility is not limited to special or unique sites. In some instances a business or institution will choose an earth-integrated building in order to project an image that is environmentally harmonious and conserving of natural resources. More commonly, however, buildings are placed below the surface because they are undesirable aboveground; the overall surface environment can benefit greatly when certain functions are made less visible. Industrial and storage buildings, utilities, transit systems, and parking garages are often placed underground because they are quite massive in appearance and are often considered unattractive. Cut-and-cover space near the surface has varying degrees of visibility depending on the amount of exposure for entrances, courtyards for light and view, and any above-grade elements. Mined space, on the other hand, can have almost no visible forms on the surface except an occasional point of access.

1-5 (opposite): Uris Undergraduate Library, Cornell University, Ithaca, New York; Gunnar Birkerts and Associates, architect; photograph by Timothy Hursley, The Arkansas Office.

Preservation of Surface Open Space

Closely related to the advantage of low visibility for underground buildings is the preservation of open space on the surface. By placing a building below grade and allowing the roof to remain as a park or plaza area, no open space is lost. This advantage is particularly important in very built-up areas, such as urban commercial centers or college campuses, where it is desirable to preserve as much remaining open space as possible. Not only is open space desirable for recreation, but it can relieve the feeling of density and allow greater access to sunlight and view for existing above-grade buildings. The most common examples of preserving open space by building underground are individual buildings such as the Pusey Library at Harvard University (see chapter 3) that are surrounded by above-grade structures.

In addition to these limited special circumstances, underground space use can contribute to the preservation of surface open space in a broader and more extensive manner. Mined space, for example, can occur under large areas with virtually no disruption to the surface. By placing large areas of manufacturing, storage, or other appropriate functions beneath the surface, as exemplified by developments in Kansas City, Missouri, substantial areas of surface land are available for other uses. This has broad implications for the preservation of agricultural land as well as recreational wilderness.

Efficient Land Use

The use of underground or earth sheltered space has a number of important implications with regard to efficient land use. When most or all of the functions in a building are placed below grade, the surface is available for other uses. This creates the possibility of greater density of development without some of the negative aspects associated with overly built-up environments. As indicated previously, the rooftop of an underground building can be used for open space, allowing for expansion in areas that are too heavily built-up to permit additional above-grade buildings. It is also possible to develop some of the surface space for a use other than open space, resulting in a lower total land requirement for the project. Walker

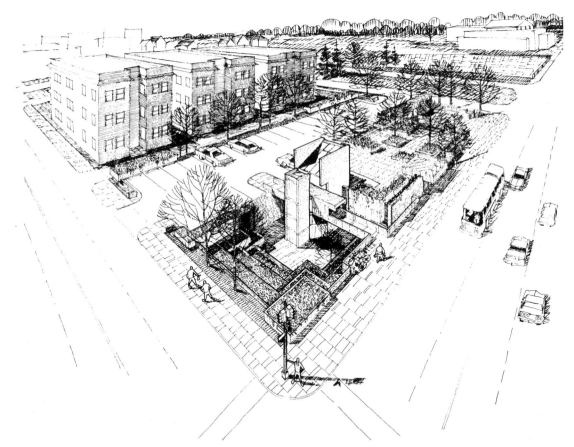

1-6: Walker Community Library, Minneapolis, Minnesota

Architect: BRW Architects, Inc.

Community Library in Minneapolis (fig. 1-6) was built on a smaller site than would be required for a conventional building because the library is underground and parking covers part of the roof. In other examples the rooftops of underground schools are often used for playgrounds. This can result in substantial savings in land costs and permit the use of sites that are too small for conventional construction.

Another advantage of underground space related to land-use efficiency is the ability to exceed normal setback and lot coverage requirements. Usually underground portions of buildings that exceed these requirements do not violate the intentions of the zoning ordinances, which are to limit density and provide open space or buffer space between buildings. Assuming that no other circumstances prevent the acquisition of a zoning variance, a partially or completely underground building can be built on a smaller parcel of land than required for an above-grade building. An example of this is the Holaday Circuits Building, a manufacturing facility in Minnetonka, Minnesota which was permitted to exceed zoning setbacks with the underground portions of the building (see chapter 6).

Among the advantages of underground space discussed in this chapter are isolation from surface noise and the low visual impact of subsurface structures. Because of this isolation from the surface, normally incompatible land uses can be placed in closer proximity. For example, functions requiring quiet such as schools, libraries, or housing can be placed near noisy freeways, airports, or manufacturing facilities if either the quiet or the noisy function is placed below grade. For examples where housing and

manufacturing or storage facilities are adjacent, it is considered necessary to provide a buffer, which may require a substantial amount of land (see fig. 1-7). If the industrial facility is placed underground, however, the buffer zone is unnecessary, and in fact, the rooftop of the facility may even be suitable as open space for the housing. The implications for saving land resulting from this ability to locate incompatible functions in closer proximity are not limited to reducing buffer zones between these activities. It also becomes

possible to use sites within urban areas that have been previously considered undesirable because of their proximity to noisy or unattractive land uses. This use of undesirable sites in central locations generally results in more compact development with inherent efficiencies in utility and road systems.

An important characteristic of buildings that are integrated into the earth is the ability to build on steeply sloping sites. In some cases an earth sheltered building designed

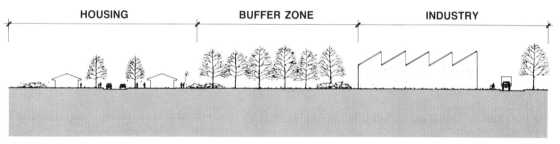

A: Conventional Planning for Housing and Industry

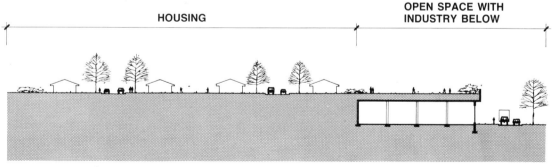

B: Underground Industry Combined with Conventional Housing

1-7: Land Use Implications for Housing and Industry

to step down a hillside can be built on slopes exceeding 50 percent (27 degrees) providing the correct site and soil conditions are present. Such buildings are particularly suitable for functions that require light and view to most spaces, such as offices or housing. In fact, if it is desirable to provide solar access for heating to most of the spaces, as it is with housing in many climate regions, a greater density can be achieved on a south-facing slope than on flat land [1.3]. Since steep slopes (over 20 percent) are often considered undesirable for conventional construction, this ability to use sloping land results in more efficient overall land use. Not only can hilly sites be used more extensively, but sloping sites in dense urban areas that were previously considered unusable can now be developed. As with other undesirable infill sites, this can contribute to more compact and thus more efficient development patterns.

In this discussion most of the concepts and examples related to land-use efficiency pertain to underground buildings near the surface. Where it is possible to create mined space, an entirely new and separate layer of development can be provided without occupying any additional land except near access points. This layer of mined space can be created under densely developed areas on the surface with little disruption, as shown in figure 1-8. Not only can extensive amounts of space be created without requiring additional land, but unique and efficient functional relationships could be developed, such as housing on the surface with workplaces in the mined space below, or commercial uses on the surface with manufacturing, storage, and service below. Clearly, such relationships can create

compact, efficient development patterns within urban areas while preserving agricultural and recreational land by reversing the trend toward sprawling development.

Efficient Circulation and Transportation

An advantage of underground space development that is closely related to the various land-use efficiencies discussed in the previous section is the efficient circulation and transportation systems that result. Increased densities and more compact development generally can be served more efficiently by mass transit systems. Mass transit systems in mined space also have the unique advantage of being able to serve heavily built-up areas with minimal disruption to the surface.

Since underground space development provides unique opportunities for mixing housing and workplaces, the length of trips and thus the time and energy expended for transportation can be reduced. Likewise, placement of commercial, manufacturing, and storage functions in closer proximity can reduce the costs and energy required to move materials.

In addition to these overall efficiencies in transportation, pedestrian circulation between buildings and activities can generally be made more efficient with more compact development. Often underground buildings on crowded campuses not only use land efficiently while providing open space, but provide indoor walkways connecting the surrounding buildings without interfering with pedestrian and vehicular circulation on the surface.

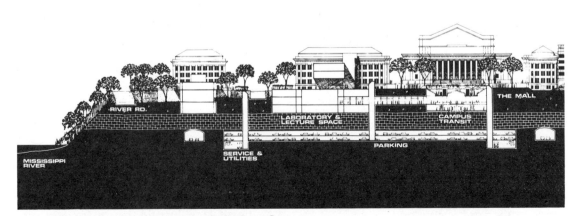

1-8: Mined Space Beneath Existing Structures

Environmental Benefits

The potential aesthetic benefits of earth sheltered structures have been a major attraction for many architects and planners. Well-designed earth sheltered buildings can blend unobtrusively with the surrounding earth and become part of the natural landscape. In addition to the positive aesthetic effects on the environment, underground buildings provide other opportunities to improve or enhance the natural environment, particularly in urban areas.

Architect Malcolm Wells, an underground advocate and designer of many earth-covered structures, cites several ecological contributions made by buildings covered by earth and vegetation [1.4]. In dense conventional developments the great area of hard surfaces and rooftops contributes to poor water runoff patterns and results in much rainwater being carried off in the storm sewer system. An earth-covered roof can retain more water on the site to maintain existing water tables and can reduce the requirements for storm sewers in these denser areas.

A second benefit can be the revitalization of the natural landscape that results simply from increase in the amount of plant and animal habitat in a given area. Water and air quality are enhanced and the soil is enriched by allowing the natural ecological processes to occur within the boundaries of a built environment. Toward this purpose Wells uses mulch on his earth-covered roofs and allows the natural wild plants and animals to take over. It can be argued that building in harmony with nature in this manner results in benefits associated with the psychological well-being of the inhabitants. As discussed in the section on land-use efficiencies, underground buildings have the ability to use otherwise undesirable land and make a positive contribution to the total environment. An excellent example of this is an office Malcolm Wells built on a barren piece of land adjacent to a freeway. The underground design resulted in a quiet, private place to work, while the natural vegetation of the land was beautifully restored.

In a general sense, earth sheltered construction has the potential to enhance the environment in ways not possible with above-grade buildings. Each structure, through conservation of existing natural landscape, can positively contribute to various problems of ecological imbalance that threaten us. Most of the potential environmental advantages discussed here are most applicable to structures with earth-covered roofs that are extensively landscaped. A building with earth-covered walls and a conventional roof may be aesthetically pleasing, but it cannot blend into and preserve the natural landscape as completely as a totally covered building. The aesthetic and environmental effects mentioned are particularly applicable in the context of larger subsurface developments where a reasonable impact on the overall community environment can be made.

Energy Use Reduction/Climate Control

Subsurface structures have unique characteristics that result in some potential energy-conservation benefits. The word potential must be emphasized for two reasons: some of the benefits are not yet easily quantified, and the degree to which energy is conserved can vary greatly depending on the individual design and the climate.

Most of the benefits listed below relate to the direct contact of the structure with the earth. Generally, the greater the percentage of surface area in contact with the earth and the deeper the structure penetrates into the earth, the more the structure will benefit from these effects in terms of energy conservation. For many functions, however, direct access to grade and window openings are required for a variety of psychological, physiological, and safety reasons that are reflected in building codes. Thus, energy-related benefits are tempered by the requirement for openings, as well as by the structural costs of supporting extensive earth loads at greater depths. Nevertheless, many of the benefits can be achieved to some degree in buildings near the surface that are only partially in contact with the earth. Mined space, with its greater depth and lack of openings to the surface, provides the most complete isolation from the exterior climate.

reduced infiltration

For building surfaces in contact with the earth, infiltration is completely eliminated, resulting in both heating and cooling load reduction. In addition, if the exposed surfaces of the structure are located away from the prevailing winter winds, the berms can divert wind over and around the structure to reduce infiltration through these areas. Although most nonresidential functions require mechanical ventilation systems, the lack of infiltration underground permits the ventilation to be well controlled, and heat-exchange devices can operate efficiently when outside air is required.

reduced heat loss through envelope in winter

It is generally assumed that heat loss resulting from conduction will be minimized through surfaces that are in contact with the earth at a reasonable depth below grade. Below-grade ground temperatures are more moderate than above-grade air temperatures, and in most climates below-grade temperatures reach reasonable stability at depths greater than 10 feet (see fig. 1-9 for temperatures for the Minneapolis-St. Paul area). Ground temperatures will generally approximate the annual average air temperature in warm climates and be a few degrees warmer than the annual average temperature in areas with significant winter snow cover. Urban areas also have higher local ground temperatures.

Although the thermal resistance of earth is not great compared with the thermal resistance of typical insulation materials, the large mass of earth results in a significant reduction and delay in heat exchange with the surface, which in turn results in a net benefit during extremely cold periods. It is important to note that in most climates these temperature moderation effects are more significant at depths greater than 4 to 6 feet. Areas of the structure with smaller amounts of earth cover need supplemental insulation to improve the isolation of the building from the outdoor climate.

On the other hand, mined space, which can be 100 feet or more beneath the surface (as it is in both Kansas City and Minneapolis), presents conditions of very constant temperature and humidity. This can be a definite advantage for certain functions that demand a carefully controlled climate, such as laboratories, computer rooms, document storage, or cold storage.

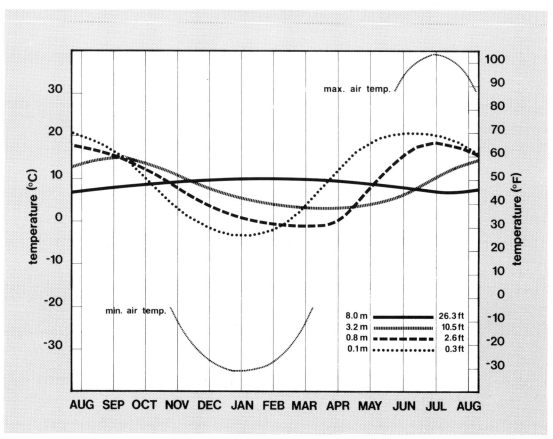

1-9: Annual Temperature Fluctuations—Minneapolis, Minnesota

Chart based on information from R.K. Maxwell [1.5].

increased earth cooling potential in summer

For most climates in the United States, ground temperatures at depths of 2 feet or greater are lower than the temperatures required for comfort in summer. Thus, when air temperatures within the space of the building exceed the ground temperatures, heat is transferred from the space to the surrounding ground. This occurs both by conduction through the envelope and radiation from warmer objects in the space to cooler wall and floor surfaces. Insulation, which separates the interior space from the earth, reduces this cooling effect. Cooling potential is very dependent on the ground temperatures surrounding a building which is affected not only by climate but other factors such as ground cover, soil moisture content, and heat from adjacent buildings.

reduced heat gain

Earth-covered roofs and earth-bermed walls reduce radiant heat gain from the sun. The massive earth can absorb a considerable amount of radiation before it reaches the envelope. In climates with cool summer nights, the earth may release the heat to the cooler air by conduction and to the night sky by radiation. A very important component in reducing heat gain from radiation is the use of plant materials. In the process of evapotranspiration, plants can effectively cancel out most, if not all, of the incoming radiation from the sun. This process requires a sufficient level of moisture in the ground to enable the plants to grow. Finally, since the window area of most underground buildings is minimized by design, a major source of heat gain in many conventional buildings is reduced considerably.

dampened daily temperature fluctuations

The large mass of the earth surrounding the space delays and dampens the effect of rapid fluctuations in temperature and typical day-night temperature swings. In addition, because many earth sheltered structures are constructed primarily of concrete and are insulated on the outside, the resultant large mass inside the insulated envelope further stabilizes inside temperature fluctuations. The most significant effect of this phenomenon is that peak loads are reduced, resulting in smaller requirements for heating and cooling equipment. Total energy consumption is also reduced to some degree, depending on the exact climate characteristics and on whether the building is in the heating or the cooling season.

A final effect associated with reduced temperature fluctuations is that temperatures may remain relatively stable for many days with no heat input. This can be a great benefit during a power outage, especially for a building situated in a remote location. For example, highway rest area buildings, which are isolated and not constantly occupied, contain plumbing that is subject to freezing. Such buildings in Minnesota have been designed with earth sheltering to take advantage of the more stable temperatures it provides (see chapter 7). The slow response to changing energy inputs also may enable use of off-peak heating and cooling energy at lower rates from the utility company. Moreover, intermittent energy sources such as passive solar systems for heating or nighttime ventilation for cooling can work effectively with lower storage requirements than needed for conventional construction.

seasonal temperature lag in ground

As indicated in the chart of ground temperatures (fig. 1-9), at greater depths temperature fluctuations on a seasonal basis are not only dampened, but are also delayed. This presents the potential for saving heating energy because the warmer ground temperatures from summer are carried into the fall and winter, thus reducing heating needs during the early months of the heating season. Conversely, the cooler ground temperatures of the winter, which are carried into the spring and summer, reduce cooling loads. Of course, mined space is often so deep that seasonal temperatures do not fluctuate at all—the temperature remains constant, approximating the annual average air temperature.

impact of occupancy patterns on energy-related benefits

Many of the energy-related benefits discussed above are associated with heat transfer through the exterior skin of the building. The relative importance of the exterior envelope of the building in terms of heating and cooling loads depends on the occupancy patterns and use of the structure. For functions with a relatively high number of people, ventilation requirements are greater and usually internal heat gain from lights, people, and machines are increased as well. Thus, the functions that can benefit to the greatest extent by being underground are those with low to moderate occupancy levels. These include warehouses, cold storage, archives, laboratories, recreational facilities, parking, and some offices and libraries. It is important to note, however, that even if heat transfer through the exterior envelope of a building is not large relative to ventilation and internal heat gains, it may still represent a substantial amount of energy. In addition, as ventilation and lighting systems become more energy efficient, the relative importance of energy transfer through the exterior skin will increase.

Not only the number of people in a space, but also the patterns or timing of that occupancy, affect energy used. Some buildings must be operated 100 percent of the time, whereas others have sporadic or intermittent use. The majority of nonresidential functions are typically occupied 30 to 50 percent of the time (eight to twelve hours per day). Buildings must be heated or cooled to within the human comfort zone only when they are occupied. Also, ventilation is only required when people are present. In most cases it is inefficient and inadvisable to run heating and cooling systems only when people are present in conventional buildings. It is possible, however, to let temperatures drift somewhat outside of the comfort zone. Assuming it is desirable to minimize energy use when buildings are unoccupied, underground buildings offer some potential advantages to be exploited. As previously discussed, underground buildings respond very slowly to changes in temperature. This slow response, caused by storage of heat in the building and soil mass, can be used effectively in reducing nighttime and weekend energy use when the building is unoccupied. For example, in the winter the mechanical systems can be shut off at night. The temperature will drift downward very slowly until heat is reintroduced in the morning. A similar pattern can be used on weekends as long as mechanical systems are started several hours before people begin using the space again.

Protection from Natural Disasters

Structures that are substantially surrounded by and covered with earth are more protected from a variety of natural disasters than conventional structures are. In some areas of the country subject to frequent high winds, hail storms, and tornadoes, earth sheltered housing is gaining popularity largely because of the protection it affords. Underground buildings also provide greater protection from earthquakes. Assuming an underground building is not located directly over a geological fault, it is likely to sustain less damage than an above-grade building during an earthquake if properly designed. Earthquake resistance is generally enhanced below ground because the amplitude of the vibration decreases with depth into the ground when distant from the epicenter of the quake and also because the building is not being shaken only through its foundations, which introduces large shear forces. The building still needs to be well reinforced, and particular attention should be paid to the connection of a heavy earth-covered roof to the remainder of the building.

Fire Protection

Most underground structures are built of concrete surrounded by soil or, in the case of mined space, rock caverns. These inherently fireproof materials provide a great degree of fire protection and prevent the spread of any fires to or from other buildings. Underground buildings are consequently likely to sustain less fire damage, and this fact has been reflected in lower insurance rates in some cases. Subsurface space is therefore suitable for storage of valuable or irreplaceable

materials or records. The isolation from the surface also makes underground space appropriate for the storage of volatile or flammable fuels or other liquids.

In spite of the fireproof nature of underground buildings, however, materials within the buildings may still be combustible. Since these structures often have fewer openings to the surface and the path of exit for occupants is upward rather than downward, some unique life safety problems may arise. Careful design and consultation with building code authorities is necessary (see Appendix A).

Civil Defense

Many of the characteristics that provide protection from natural disasters in underground buildings can contribute to safeguarding occupants from man-made destruction, attacks, and nuclear fallout if the buildings are properly designed. The degree of protection depends on the amount of earth and structure between the space and surface, as well as the number and size of any openings to the surface. Mined space, at greater depths and with fewer connections to the surface than cut-and-cover construction, would represent the best conditions for protection. Of course, to provide maximum protection, entries and ventilation systems would have to be specially designed as well.

Historically, as well as in the present time, civil defense has been one of the leading motivations for developing underground space. Since this is not a constant use, however, the most cost-effective situation occurs when the space is used for other purposes with civil defense being a secondary benefit. This allows efficient use of the space while keeping the space well-maintained if and when it is needed for civil defense. Subway systems in Europe were an excellent example of this dual use in World War II.

Security

Because of its isolation from the surface, substantial fireproof construction, and limited points of access, underground space can be considered more secure than conventional buildings. One benefit of building schools underground is the limited vandalism that can occur when most of the building is not exposed to the surface. With limited points of entry, surveillance is easier, resulting in fewer break-ins. This is a particularly appealing feature for the storage of important records, manuscripts, or critical materials such as emergency food and fuel supplies. Storage of important records is one of many uses in the extensive mined space development in Kansas City. Just as the surrounding earth mass and heavy concrete construction can keep unwanted intrusions out of a space, it can also serve to keep people in. A recent example of an earth-integrated design utilizing this benefit is the Minnesota Correctional Facility at Oak Park Heights (see fig. 1-10).

Isolation from Noise and Vibration

The large earth mass surrounding most underground buildings, as well as the limited exposure to the surface, dampens or completely eliminates noise and vibration. Isolation from noise and vibration can be desirable for two reasons. First, the function to be enclosed may require quiet and isolation from the surrounding

1-10: Minnesota Correctional Facility, Oak Park Heights, Minnesota; Winsor/Faricy Architects, Inc.; photograph by Saari and Forrai.

environment. A unique example of the advantage of isolation underground occurs in specialized laboratory and manufacturing facilities that require a minimal amount of vibration. Mined space was created for the Brunson Instrument Company in Kansas City, Missouri, specifically because of the need for isolation from surface vibrations in the manufacture of precision instruments. A second reason is that the function itself creates undesirable noise and the outside environment would benefit from any reduction in the noise. Manufacturing facilities or transit systems are examples of such undesirable functions. The necessity

for isolation in a particular building is naturally linked to its surroundings. Physical separation may not be required for a library in a quiet setting or a factory near a freeway. As previously discussed, the ability to place normally incompatible functions in close proximity and to use sites that are otherwise undesirable by building underground can result in generally more efficient land use. The relative effectiveness of this isolation from noise and vibration is enhanced in buildings that are deeper with minimal openings to the surface.

Maintenance

Another advantage of earth covering the walls and/or roof of a structure is reduction in maintenance. This lower maintenance requirement is based on some assumptions about the type and nature of earth sheltered buildings. It is assumed that the structure is made of long-life materials, primarily concrete. Moreover, high-quality waterproofing and insulation products requiring little or no replacement or maintenance should be used below grade. One contributing factor to the long life of an earth-covered structure is the protection of various materials from the wide temperature variations and freeze-thaw cycles that occur under exposed conditions in many climates. The protection from ultraviolet degradation given to building materials by the earth is another important contribution to the longer life of building materials.

It should be noted, however, that overall reduced maintenance costs are influenced by many variables and details in the building design. For example, a poor choice or application of waterproofing material or inadequate drainage can cause water problems that will quickly outweigh any maintenance savings. Likewise, earth-covered roofs and berms can be planted with a low-maintenance ground cover materials or be landscaped with lawns and gardens requiring extensive and costly watering and care.

Cost Efficiencies with Cut-and-Cover Space

It is difficult to generalize about initial construction costs for underground space in comparison with above-grade structures.

Cost comparisons indicate a wide range of variation, from the underground alternative costing less to it costing considerably more than conventional construction. These variations occur because of differences in the type or quality of buildings being compared, the percentage of the total cost that the building shell represents in a particular case, and most important the specific site conditions. Basically, though, the technology, materials, and methods of construction are similar for underground cut-and-cover structures and conventional structures.

In spite of these limitations, a few general cost areas can be identified as being potentially advantageous or disadvantageous for underground buildings. For most larger scale commercial and institutional buildings, the exterior finishing costs (brick, metal, glass) are usually reduced in underground structures. For a high-quality building on a university campus, these cost savings can be substantial, but for a less expensive warehouse, the difference may be minimal. Another potential area for savings is a reduction in the size of mechanical equipment necessary for heating and cooling. The various areas of potentially increased initial costs are discussed in the following section on disadvantages.

Cost Efficiencies for Mined Space

Creating mined space is a fundamentally different process than conventional construction either above or below grade. Costs associated with mining of the rock are subject to a number of variables including the type of rock to be extracted, the available rock layer that forms the roof, and the type of access (horizontal or

shaft). Some of the costs of mining can be offset if the extracted material can be sold. For example, in Kansas City, the limestone that is extracted to form the space is marketable, reducing the cost of creating the space. Although there is not necessarily a profitable market for the sandstone mined beneath the Minneapolis-St. Paul metropolitan area, the ease of mining this softer rock makes costs of creating the space relatively low. In the Minneapolis-St. Paul area creating access to the mined layer with shafts through the harder limestone layers above is a very significant component of the total cost. Thus, providing horizontal access from bluffs is very important in reducing costs.

Aside from these variables affecting the actual cost of mining the space, some cost advantages are associated with this type of construction. A structural shell is unnecessary because the rock is substantially self-supporting, so the major costs are in finishing the space. Likewise, no costs are related to exterior building finishing except for at the points of access. A related cost benefit of mined space is limited disruption of the surface during construction except for the minimal areas required for shaft access.

Finally, there are some cost advantages related to the height of the space and the length of clear spans that can be created. The height and span of the space that can be mined out safely are determined by the geology and sometimes the depth of the water table. In the Minneapolis-St. Paul area, it is presently considered safe to mine spans up to 60 feet with a height of 25 feet in the sandstone layer, providing suitable conditions exist. In terms of cost, this means that there is no incremental cost for larger spans (up to 60 feet) and heights (up to 25 feet) compared with smaller ones. In fact, it is easier and therefore a little less expensive to work in larger spaces. This can be an advantage for a number of functions that require spans and heights of this size, for example, laboratories, recreational spaces, warehouses, and manufacturing facilities. It is also a suitable size for railway, mass transit, parking, and vehicular access. The drawback to this situation is that the maximum safe span and height cannot be exceeded under any circumstances without significant changes in structural design, possibly making costs prohibitive.

Reduced Life Cycle Costs

Evaluating the life-cycle costs of a building is a means of determining the total cost of a building to its owner over the real or economic life of the structure. In addition to initial construction and financing costs, life-cycle costs include operating costs, such as energy use, maintenance, and insurance. It has been demonstrated in many cases that an underground building can have a lower life-cycle cost than a comparable above-grade building even if its initial construction costs are somewhat higher. This is primarily due to the reduced energy and maintenance costs and, in some cases, reduced insurance costs as well. In addition, it can be argued in some cases that an underground structure will have a longer useful lifetime than some types of above-grade construction.

Although it is possible to say that life-cycle cost analysis appears to favor underground buildings in a general sense, very specific figures must be approached with some caution. Life-cycle costs are based on a

number of interrelated assumptions, some of which—future energy costs for example—are impossible to predict accurately. Also, underground buildings, like above-grade buildings, actually have a wide range of energy and maintenance costs. Regardless of these limitations, however, the life-cycle costs of underground buildings can have a number of factors in their favor. In addition, underground space offers many benefits to the community and the environment as a whole that are not accounted for in a typical life-cycle cost analysis, including preservation of surface open space, more efficient land use and transportation, aesthetic and environmental enhancement, and reduced energy imports.

Disadvantages of Underground Space

Clearly, the fact that underground buildings are more isolated from and less exposed to the surface presents some design problems. The extra cost of resolving these difficulties along with other technical problems can present drawbacks compared with above-grade construction. Rarely, however, do the drawbacks constitute absolute obstacles. Assuming that taking advantage of the benefits of building underground is desirable, design and technical innovations can overcome the constraints. The ability to successfully resolve the inherent difficulties of designing subsurface space is clearly demonstrated by the wide range of case studies presented later in this book.

It is interesting to note that some of the greatest drawbacks to the use of underground space are not physical or technical in nature but are psychological. The idea of placing a public function underground is often met with resistance, even though similar functions already occur in windowless spaces or basements of conventional buildings. Although such attitudes can present a real drawback for some projects that require public approval, the negative reactions usually diminish or disappear once a well-designed project is actually constructed and used. As stated for the advantages of underground buildings, the uses and characteristics of subsurface space vary widely. Thus, the disadvantages discussed in this section are based on assumptions about typical situations but should not be universally applied.

Limited Opportunities for View and Natural Light

When a building is placed partially or completely below grade so that a substantial area of the wall surface is earth covered, provision of natural light and outside view limits design options. Although this constraint for underground buildings can be overcome to some extent by the use of courtyards, skylights, and other openings for buildings that are near the surface, fewer alternatives in plan arrangements are available compared with conventional structures. For mined space the problem is more extreme, although design innovations such as solar optics—in which light and view from the surface can be transferred by means of lenses—have promising potential.

Although access to natural light and view are considered psychologically and physiologically beneficial, it does not follow that they are required continuously or for all types of activities. Very few buildings must have windows in every space. Private offices and hospital patient rooms would seem the most unacceptable without windows—perhaps because they are small spaces in which a great deal of time is spent. Larger spaces in which inwardly focused activities take place and where less time is spent, such as stores or libraries, do not generally require windows. For some functions, of course, windows are completely undesirable, as in a theater where they would be a distraction or in a warehouse where they are unnecessary with so few people.

Access and Circulation Limitations

Assuming that most major pedestrian and vehicular circulation occurs at the surface level, access or circulation to underground spaces by people and vehicles can present design constraints. The degree to which this poses a problem depends on the proximity to the surface of the underground space, specific site conditions, and the access requirements for the intended use of the building. Naturally, access problems are most easily resolved in bermed buildings at the surface or spaces that are only one to two levels beneath the surface where ramps, stairs, and courtyards can easily provide pedestrian access that differs little from conventional buildings. Buildings set into sloping sites provide the best opportunities for direct horizontal access by people or vehicles. In deeper mined space, access problems can be difficult and costly if the space can only be entered through long vertical shafts. Excellent access can be provided to deep space, however, if horizontal access tunnels can be constructed in a nearby bluff. Figures 1-11 and 1-12 illustrate various types of access for underground space.

The function of a building determines the access requirement and thus the type and extent of the problems encountered by placing the structure underground. Pedestrian access in some form is a requirement for virtually all subsurface uses. A few functions, such as shopping centers, classrooms, auditoriums, theaters, churches, and sports stadiums, require adequate access and circulation for large numbers of people, often all moving at the same time. This implies large entrances

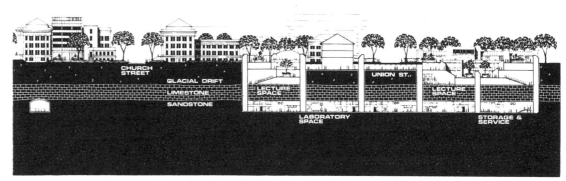

1-11: Mined Space with Vertical Access

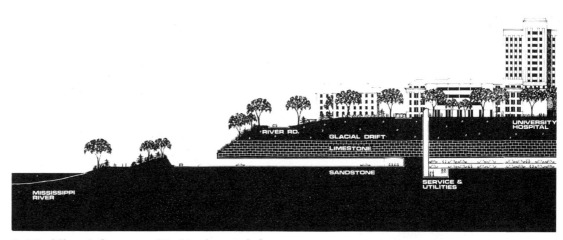

1-12: Mined Space with Horizontal Access

and corridors or lobbies, along with ramps, escalators, or at least large stairways for vertical circulation. Although many of these high-occupancy functions are suitable in underground space, they should be located near the surface to minimize costly and extensive vertical circulation. Most other functions, such as laboratories, indoor recreation, manufacturing, warehouses, and even some offices, museums, and libraries, do not have high-occupancy levels and frequent coming and going. Thus, major entrances, corridors, and means of conveyance are often not required. Usually elevators and stairways are adequate, making access less of a limitation when these functions are placed underground.

Direct vehicular access is provided to buildings mainly for the movement of goods and services. For buildings such as warehouses, factories, and of course, parking garages, vehicular access is a major requirement. Unless the structure is located near the surface, or on a sloping site permitting horizontal access, an underground location can present major problems. Costly, large ramps for vehicles or extensive vertical movement of goods to a surface loading dock would be required. For virtually all other functions, at least a minor degree of vehicular access is required for routine maintenance functions and occasional movement of goods. Since this can be handled with elevators for below-grade buildings just as it is for above-grade buildings, vehicular service access is less of a restriction for most functions. In addition to vehicular access for service purposes, many buildings must provide vehicular access and parking for the users of the building. If a building is totally underground, the major exterior image could be a parking lot and

recognition of the main building entrance and loading dock may be more difficult for a visitor.

Limited Visibility

One of the advantages of underground buildings discussed in the previous section was their limited visual impact. Although this characteristic can be a benefit in a number of situations, it can be a drawback in some others. For example, commercial functions, particularly stores, must be visible from the road to attract business; moreover, to attract pedestrian customers, individual stores often depend on display windows. A completely underground store would have to be very noticeable, designed to attract attention. A larger complex of retail shops with internal pedestrian circulation, such as a regional shopping center, could more easily be placed partially or even completely underground since the displays and exposure of individual stores would be no different than they would be in a conventional shopping mall. Using a building to create a positive image for a business or institution is another situation where public visibility is required. Office buildings, churches, and museums, for example, may require a symbolic architectural form that simply cannot be achieved with a completely underground structure.

Negative Psychological Reactions

Some people have a strongly adverse reaction when earth sheltered or particularly underground buildings are mentioned. Many people have never seen well-designed buildings of this type but

nevertheless have conscious or subconscious negative feelings about them. Several reasons have been suggested for this phenomenon. One is the association with death and burial; another, the fear of collapse or being trapped. Also, people may associate underground spaces with poorly designed and ventilated basements, which are damp and unpleasant. Finally, feelings of claustrophobia may occur. Although the true physiological effects of being underground depend on a number of variables, the negative psychological reactions associated with going below the surface must be recognized. The problem can best be dealt with by alleviating much of the source of these fears through careful design (see chapter 2).

Site Restrictions

While underground buildings in their many forms can be adapted to a wide variety of site conditions, a few site characteristics can cause special problems for subsurface construction. Soil conditions can be a limitation for both above- and below-grade buildings, but poorly draining soils are a particular problem below grade. In addition, expansive clay soils can place additional pressure on an underground structure. Sites with bedrock near the surface will be less feasible for below-grade cut-and-cover construction than for conventional buildings because of the difficulty and cost of blasting in the rock. The location of the water table below grade represents a major restriction for underground construction as well.

For underground buildings near the surface, adjacent building foundations may present problems if the subsurface structure is to be placed at a lower level

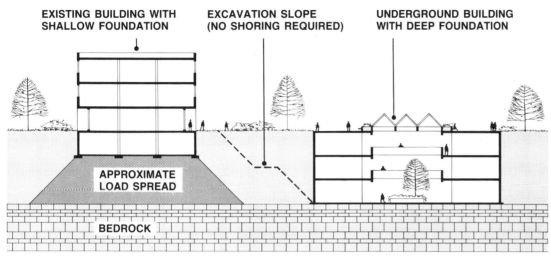

EXISTING BUILDING WITH SHALLOW FOUNDATION

EXCAVATION SLOPE (NO SHORING REQUIRED)

UNDERGROUND BUILDING WITH DEEP FOUNDATION

APPROXIMATE LOAD SPREAD

BEDROCK

1-13: Buildings Separated to Avoid Interference with Existing Foundation

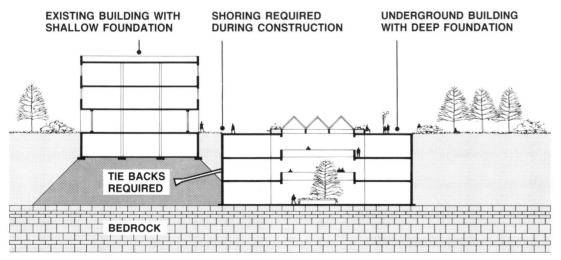

EXISTING BUILDING WITH SHALLOW FOUNDATION

SHORING REQUIRED DURING CONSTRUCTION

UNDERGROUND BUILDING WITH DEEP FOUNDATION

TIE BACKS REQUIRED

BEDROCK

1-14: Buildings in Close Proximity Requiring Shoring and Tie Backs

than the existing building foundations (figs. 1-13 and 1-14). In mined space the restrictions are somewhat different. Generally, existing buildings on the surface have little effect on the feasibility of mined space. The major determining factors for mined space are the geology and the location of the water table. Access from a bluff also has a major influence on feasibility. Many of the site restrictions for cut-and-cover and, to some extent, mined space, can be overcome technically; however, the cost may not be acceptable.

Water Problems

Generally, a below-grade building has a greater potential for water leakage problems than a typical above-grade structure does. This is particularly true if the underground structure is partially beneath the subsurface water table. Construction below the water table is rare, however. A disadvantage in selecting waterproofing products is that long-term performance records do not exist or are difficult to find for many of the vast array of systems available.

Although the cost of a good-quality waterproofing system can be relatively high, the costs and problems associated with the repair of a leaking building are usually far worse. One of the inherent difficulties in repairing a water leak underground is that with many systems the water can travel from the original source of the leak and emerge at different points in the structure, making leaks difficult to locate. When a leak is located, it can be an expensive job to remove the soil to repair it. These potential problems serve to emphasize the importance of carefully selecting and applying waterproofing below grade. Additional information on waterproofing systems is included in Appendix B.

Increased Structural Requirements

The relatively great weight of earth on flat roofs, combined with the lateral earth pressures on buried walls (these pressures increase with depth in soil), require heavier and more expensive structures. This economic limitation is one reason why some underground structures are not placed more deeply or extensively into the subsurface environment.

Some building types, because of the nature of their functions, require relatively large spans and high spaces. Auditoriums, theaters, churches, and other large gathering places are notable examples, along with most indoor recreation facilities such as tennis courts or swimming pools. Several functions including laboratories, factories, warehouses, museums, and some offices, do not inherently require large spans and high spaces but may require them in some situations because flexibility is desired, not because any one activity requires so much space.

Generally, spaces that require large spans and heights can be built below grade just as they can above grade, so this is not an absolute physical constraint. Larger spaces may be proportionately more costly for completely below-grade buildings, however, particularly those with earth on the roof. This is simply because of the structural costs of large spans supporting relatively heavy earth loads as well as high walls resisting the large lateral pressures from the earth. In some cases the use of curvilinear shell structures may

alleviate this problem by providing a more efficient means of supporting heavy earth loads. In deep-mined space where natural rock forms the roof, the limitations and economic implications of spans depend on the characteristics of the local geology. Often a moderate span of 40 to 60 feet can be achieved at no greater structural cost than shorter spans; it may be virtually impossible to safely exceed certain limits, however.

Energy-Related Limitations

In addition to energy-related benefits, underground buildings have potential limitations. Although the energy-related limitations of underground buildings represent a possible reduction in the overall benefits of these structures, they need not negate the benefits entirely. First, neither benefits nor limitations are quantified here, and both can exist to varying degrees. Second, the effect of the potential limitations depends on specific climate conditions as well as on the individual design of the structure. After the potential limitations are identified, it may be possible to design the structure to minimize the effects of the drawbacks while maintaining the positive benefits.

impact of ventilation rate on benefits

One of the basic characteristics relating to energy use in buildings is the ventilation rate required by the building code to provide a healthy, pleasant environment. The amount of fresh outside air that must be brought into a building is a function of the number of people occupying it. Thus, higher rates are required for functions such as auditoriums, theaters, and classrooms that have a high concentration of people.

Many offices and shopping centers also require relatively high rates. Libraries and museums are quite variable in the number of people that typically use the space, but often the concentration is not as great as in the spaces listed above, making more moderate rates possible in some cases. A few functions, such as a parking garage in an enclosed space or a manufacturing process that emits undesirable odors and fumes, may require higher ventilation rates as well.

A high ventilation requirement does not present any unusual constraints for underground buildings. That is, if a building is placed below the surface, fresh air can be supplied mechanically just as it is for most above-grade nonresidential buildings. If energy conservation is one of the main reasons for locating a building underground, however, then the ventilation requirement has certain implications.

Many of the energy-saving benefits of underground buildings are associated with minimizing both transmission and infiltration losses through the exterior skin of the building. In buildings with high ventilation rates, the skin losses are a less significant portion of the total load and the effect of building underground for energy saving is somewhat diminished when large amounts of outside air must be introduced into the building. It should not necessarily be inferred, however, that there are no energy-related benefits to placing buildings with high ventilation rates underground. The losses attributed to ventilation can be reduced significantly by heat-exchange devices. Also, code requirements for ventilation may continue to be reduced in the future in the interest of energy conservation. With these changes the losses through the skin of the building may become a more significant portion of the load and the relative benefits of energy savings underground will be enhanced. Buildings with low to moderate ventilation rates should be able to take maximum advantage of energy-conserving benefits below grade.

impact of internal heat gain on benefits

The primary energy concern with many nonresidential buildings is cooling rather than heating, even in very cold climates. This is because of relatively high amounts of internal heat gain from lights, people, and machines in the spaces. Functions with very high levels of occupancy, such as auditoriums and theaters, experience high internal loads from people alone when they are in full use. Other functions, such as offices, stores, and classrooms, have medium to high concentrations of people combined with constant general lighting, resulting in relatively high internal heat gains. Libraries and museums have a more variable occupancy than the other functions mentioned above, but they often have high lighting levels so internal heat gain may be problem, although not as significant as in other cases. Churches do not present the same problems, even though they have a high occupancy, because the space is not used very long or very often. Machines used in manufacturing as well as in offices can also contribute to high internal heat gain. It is difficult to generalize about factories and offices in this respect since they can contain widely differing types and numbers of machines.

High internal heat gains do not necessarily represent more problems for underground buildings than they do for aboveground

buildings. Conventional mechanical systems can be used to cool spaces with excessive internal heat gains. As previously stated, some of the major energy-conserving benefits of underground buildings are associated with reducing losses through the skin of the building. It is also true that heat gains from the sun and warmer outside air are reduced, especially when window openings are minimized and earth and vegetation are placed on the roof. Nevertheless, these advantages of underground space do not directly alleviate the problem of excessive internal heat gain.

Similar to buildings with high ventilation rates, either outside air must be introduced, which diminishes the energy-saving effect of the underground envelope, or mechanical air-conditioning must be used, which requires substantial amounts of energy. The generally cooler walls of a buried structure do absorb some heat from the space and assist in cooling the building; however, the capacity for dealing with high and constant internal loads from larger buildings may not be available, especially if there is a low surface-to-volume ratio in the building. Thus, as with buildings requiring high ventilation rates, those with high internal heat gains do not benefit as much from placement underground as buildings with low to moderate gains. The relative benefits of placing a building with high occupancy levels underground are likely to be enhanced as more energy-efficient lighting systems and office machines that produce lower levels of heat are designed.

requirements for openings

A windowless chamber buried in the earth is unsuitable for many functions. The

various requirements for access, window openings, and other exposed portions of the building envelope diminish the area of the envelope in contact with the ground, as well as the depth of the structure. Access must occur from grade, and windows, courtyards, and other openings are most easily designed in structures that are only partially set into the earth. Numerous openings on various sides of a structure break the continuity of the earth mass surrounding the building, thereby diminishing the energy-conserving benefits related to structure-earth contact.

slow response

Although the mass of the concrete structure within the envelope and the surrounding earth mass are assets in many ways, they result in a structure that cannot respond rapidly to changed conditions. This means that some energy-conserving strategies, such as night thermostat setback, may not work effectively or may work only with an unsatisfactory time lag. Also, problems may occur in adjusting quickly to unusual or extreme loads such as overheating from a large crowd in a theater or an auditorium.

lack of useful ground temperatures

Ground temperatures are related to annual climate conditions. During both heating and cooling seasons, a lack of useful ground temperatures can diminish the benefits of a structure's contact with the earth. The parts of the country requiring the most heat have the lowest ground temperatures, and the regions with the greatest cooling requirements have the highest ground temperatures. Because the moderating influence of the ground temperature is useful during periods of extreme temperature fluctuations, the most significant benefits are likely in climates that have the greatest daily and seasonal temperature fluctuations.

drawbacks of seasonal time lag in temperatures

Although ground temperatures are often more favorable than the outside temperatures throughout the year, they can be less favorable at certain points in the seasonal cycle. For example, in a cold climate, the ground at a depth of 10 feet reaches its lowest temperature in spring. Although this time lag is beneficial in the summer, it is detrimental in the spring because the air temperatures, which are warming faster than the ground, would result in a lower heating requirement for the building if it were above grade. In a warm climate, benefits from cooler fall air temperatures are greater than those from the ground, which has been warmed to its peak by the end of summer and early fall. Two mitigating circumstances may diminish the negative effects of these phenomena. First, because the ground around the structure is not at the same temperature as natural undisturbed ground, these effects may not be as important. Second, strategies can be employed to counteract the potential negative effects of the seasonal time lag: for example, solar gain in the spring or ventilation in the fall may offset the limitations of the time lag while maintaining its benefits.

heating/cooling compromises

Although the below-grade ground environment offers potential benefits in both the heating and cooling seasons, maximizing these benefits requires insulation in the heating season but direct earth contact with no insulation in the cooling season. In some cases the necessary compromise prevents optimizing for either condition alone.

condensation

Because the surrounding earth is almost always cooler than the indoor air temperature, condensation on interior surfaces may occur, especially in summer. For condensation to occur, wall temperatures must be below the dew point temperature. This potential problem is mitigated by a number of factors. As the earth and walls adjacent to the building warm up, the temperature difference between indoor air and walls is reduced. Problems with condensation are, of course, dependent on the local climate as well as on the manner in and degree to which outside air is introduced into the building. In most nonresidential buildings, condensation can be dealt with by mechanical dehumidification as part of the HVAC system.

lack of moisture for evapotranspiration

Evapotranspiration, the process by which plant materials dissipate incoming solar radiation so that it never warms the ground or the structure, depends on the availability of moisture. In hot, dry climates, the full benefit of this effect from an earth-covered roof may be difficult or costly to realize because water may have to be supplied to the plants by irrigation.

difficulty in calculating and predicting performance

Because of the complexity of heat flow through the earth, reliable calculations of heating and cooling performance are quite difficult to obtain. Performance cannot be calculated accurately as a simple, steady-state problem because the ground temperatures change over time; similarly, the rates of heat flow change in a manner that is not instantaneously related to current outdoor conditions. In addition, the heat flow is different at different points in the structure. Performance calculations are further complicated by the fact that heat transfer is affected significantly by a number of largely uncontrollable and complex variables such as soil moisture content, soil type, vegetation, and presence of snow. Although the state of the art of calculation procedures has advanced rapidly in recent years, it is unlikely that any of the present methods—and particularly the simpler hand calculation methods—are completely reliable.

Potential for Increased Construction Costs in Cut-and-Cover Space

As stated for the cost efficiencies discussed in the previous section, generalizations about initial construction costs must be regarded with caution. Nevertheless, it is useful to identify areas of special concern that can result in increased costs. Although the basic materials and methods of construction for cut-and-cover and above-grade buildings do not differ significantly, placement of the building in the ground introduces some potential problems as well as some additional requirements that are likely to increase costs. Earth cover on the roof and lateral earth pressure against the walls require a heavier structural system than a comparable above-grade facility does. In poor soils, foundations can be expensive as well. Virtually all underground buildings require a high-quality waterproofing system regardless of the site drainage or depth of the water table.

Certain site conditions can have a significant impact on costs. If bedrock is near the surface, for example, the cost of blasting as opposed to simple excavation in soil can represent a great cost increase. Construction on very restricted sites, with adjacent buildings or streets in close proximity, may require costly temporary retaining walls. Although major underground utilities are mainly located under streets, movement of such utilities to construct any underground building can be costly. This can represent a major cost component for cut-and-cover transit systems that occur under existing streets.

One of the major construction disadvantages to large earth sheltered buildings is the uncertainty about soil and groundwater conditions that always exist during the planning and costing phase of the project. These problems tend to increase with the depth of the structure. In addition, construction work is more easily delayed by inclement weather during the excavation phase of construction than during the remainder of the project. Thus, in general, a greater uncertainty about construction progress and final cost exists for underground structures as opposed to conventional structures.

Potential for Increased Costs in Mined Space

Although the relative cost of creating mined space depends on a number of factors that are unique to specific projects such as the geology, there are a few key areas of potential cost increases in comparison to conventional structures.

Since mined space is often relatively deep—50 feet or more beneath the surface—additional costs are associated with providing access and ventilation to the space. For space near a bluff that can provide horizontal access, little or no additional costs may be incurred. When access to deep-mined space must be through vertical shafts, however, large lengthy ventilation ducts, long stairways, escalators, and elevators may be required depending on the function in the space. In addition, the construction cost of the shafts may represent a considerable component of the total cost. Some of the ventilation system costs may be reduced by the use of more efficient air purification techniques within the space and lowering of code requirements for the introduction of fresh outside air. Likewise, the number of shafts may be reduced and their spacing increased by adjustments in the building codes with regard to fire exits.

Appropriate Use of Underground Space

Determining the appropriate use of underground space is important for the successful design and long-range planning of such space. In order to do this, it is useful to examine the basic characteristics of underground space in relation to various nonresidential functions. Through this analysis, some of the more appropriate and less appropriate functions for underground space development may emerge, but more important, major design assets and liabilities for various building types will be identified. Such an analysis also serves to summarize and clarify the advantages and disadvantages of underground space discussed in the previous sections. Most benefits and limitations of underground space are not generally applicable to all building types and therefore must be examined in terms of individual functions.

In the charts that follow, twenty-four nonresidential functions are listed. Each function is rated in relation to a number of key benefits of underground space (fig. 1-15) and some key limitations of the subsurface (fig. 1-16). The benefit or limitation is rated as (1) a major requirement in most or all cases, (2) a requirement that only applies in some cases or to a moderate degree, or (3) minimum or no requirement for the function in question. Following these two charts is an indication of the occupancy patterns for each function, which correlates to both energy use and psychological considerations (fig. 1-17).

It should be noted that although the emphasis of this book is on individual nonresidential buildings, the use of underground space for various urban systems should not be overlooked. Many of the merits and characteristics of underground buildings also apply to mass transit systems, roads, service areas, pedestrian circulation, and utility systems. For this reason, three major systems—mass transit, utilities, and service areas—are included in the analysis that follows. One limitation of this analysis is that some unique nonresidential uses are not included because they are rare at the present time. Examples include the use of deep-mined spaces for agricultural purposes such as mushroom growing, starting trees, and fish farming.

Benefits of Underground Space Related to Various Functions

Many of the general advantages of underground space are not directly related to specific functions. For example, land-use efficiency, preservation of open space, protection from natural disasters, and enhancement of the environment are advantages of using the subsurface regardless of the functions placed there. Four benefits in particular, however, are more applicable to some functions than others. These benefits, shown in figure 1-15, are reduced visibility, acoustical isolation, security, and the ability to provide a precisely controlled climate more easily or efficiently.

The most notable pattern in the chart is that some benefit is associated with virtually every function at least in certain applications. Reduced visibility in particular is desirable for a wide range of systems, such as industrial and storage uses as well as recreational and entertainment functions that are often housed in massive structures that dominate but contribute little to the surface environment. Acoustical isolation, security, and precise climate control are required in a number of specialized functions.

KEY

■ MAJOR REQUIREMENT IN MOST OR ALL CASES

▨ ONLY APPLIES IN SOME CASES OR TO A MODERATE DEGREE

□ NO REQUIREMENT

BUILDING TYPES		REDUCED VISIBILITY	ACOUSTIC ISOLATION	SECURITY	PRECISE CLIMATE CONTROL
COMMERCIAL:	OFFICE	□	▨	▨	▨
	STORE, RESTAURANT	□	□	▨	▨
EDUCATIONAL:	CLASSROOM	□	■	□	▨
	LABORATORY	□	▨	▨	▨
	LIBRARY	□	■	□	▨
EXHIBITION:	MUSEUM	□	▨	■	▨
	INFORMATION CENTER	□	▨	□	□
ENTERTAINMENT:	THEATER	□	■	□	▨
	AUDITORIUM	▨	■	□	□
	SPORTS STADIUM	▨	□	□	□
RECREATIONAL:	SWIMMING POOL	□	□	□	▨
	GYM, TENNIS COURTS	▨	□	□	□
RELIGIOUS:	CHURCH	□	■	□	□
MEDICAL:	HOSPITAL ROOM	□	▨	□	▨
	EXAM, OPERATING ROOM	□	▨	▨	▨
CORRECTIONAL:	PRISON	■	□	■	□
INDUSTRIAL:	MANUFACTURING	■	■	▨	▨
STORAGE:	WAREHOUSE	■	□	□	□
	COLD STORAGE	■	□	▨	■
	ARCHIVES	■	□	■	▨
	PARKING GARAGE	■	□	▨	□
SYSTEMS:	MASS TRANSIT	■	■	▨	□
	UTILITIES	■	□	■	□
	SERVICE	■	□	▨	□

1-15: Benefits of Underground Space

Limitations of Underground Space Related to Various Functions

Unlike most of the advantages of underground space, most of the disadvantages do not apply to all functions in a general way. The key limitations shown in the adjacent chart (fig. 1-16) are only potential drawbacks for certain uses of the subsurface. These include five basic physical requirements—natural light and view, pedestrian access, vehicular access, public visibility, and large spans and heights—that are considered somewhat more difficult to provide below grade than above. The last two characteristics—high ventilation rate and high internal heat gain—are energy-related considerations. They can be considered drawbacks not in the sense that they limit the ability to construct such functions below grade but that the maximum energy-related benefits of being underground are somewhat diminished for functions with these characteristics. A few general disadvantages discussed previously are not included in the chart because they do not relate to specific functions, including potential site limitations and water problems.

BUILDING TYPES / LIMITATIONS

Legend: ■ = Major requirement in most or all cases; ▒ = Only applies in some cases or to a moderate degree; □ = No requirement

Building Type		Natural Light and View	Pedestrian Access and Circulation	Vehicular Access	Public Visibility	Large Spans and Heights in Spaces	High Ventilation Rate	High Internal Heat Gain
COMMERCIAL:	OFFICE	■	▒	▒	▒	□	▒	▒
	STORE, RESTAURANT	▒	■	▒	■	□	■	■
EDUCATIONAL:	CLASSROOM	▒	■	▒	□	□	▒	■
	LABORATORY	□	■	▒	□	□	▒	▒
	LIBRARY	▒	■	▒	□	□	▒	▒
EXHIBITION:	MUSEUM	▒	■	▒	▒	▒	▒	▒
	INFORMATION CENTER	□	■	▒	▒	□	▒	□
ENTERTAINMENT:	THEATER	□	■	▒	▒	■	■	■
	AUDITORIUM	□	■	▒	▒	■	■	■
	SPORTS STADIUM	□	■	▒	▒	■	■	■
RECREATIONAL:	SWIMMING POOL	□	▒	▒	□	■	▒	▒
	GYM, TENNIS COURTS	□	▒	▒	□	■	▒	□
RELIGIOUS:	CHURCH	▒	■	▒	▒	□	■	▒
MEDICAL:	HOSPITAL ROOM	▒	▒	□	□	□	▒	□
	EXAM, OPERATING ROOM	□	▒	□	□	□	▒	□
CORRECTIONAL:	PRISON	▒	□	▒	□	□	□	□
INDUSTRIAL:	MANUFACTURING	□	▒	■	▒	▒	▒	□
STORAGE:	WAREHOUSE	□	▒	■	□	▒	□	□
	COLD STORAGE	□	▒	■	□	□	□	□
	ARCHIVES	□	▒	▒	□	□	□	□
	PARKING GARAGE	□	▒	■	□	□	■	□
SYSTEMS:	MASS TRANSIT	□	■	□	▒	▒	■	▒
	UTILITIES	□	□	□	□	□	□	▒
	SERVICE	□	□	■	□	□	□	□

1-16: Limitations of Underground Space

KEY

■ MAJOR REQUIREMENT IN MOST OR ALL CASES

▒ ONLY APPLIES IN SOME CASES OR TO A MODERATE DEGREE

□ NO REQUIREMENT

Occupancy Levels in Various Building Types

In examining the suitability of various functions underground, it seems appropriate to consider the occupancy levels of these building types. There are two main reasons for this. First, for buildings that are used regularly but less than 100 percent of the time, energy-related benefits can occur during the time the space is unused. With the relatively constant ground temperatures and large mass surrounding relatively deep spaces, heating and cooling systems can be shut off in periods of nonuse without a significant change in temperature. Second, some of the main drawbacks of underground space relate to human habitability—the need for light and view or generally negative psychological reactions. For functions that are not used or occupied at all times, these drawbacks could be considered less significant. Figure 1-17 indicates that the vast majority of nonresidential functions are in use 50 percent of the time or less, making the potential for energy savings underground more attractive while alleviating some of the concern over the habitability of the space.

In considering the occupancy patterns of various functions, there are actually several aspects not indicated in this chart, which is limited to showing only the total time that spaces are occupied by people. For example, many functions such as museums or recreation facilities may be in operation 50 percent of the time; however, the individuals who use those spaces typically remain for relatively short spans of time (except for a limited number of employees), making habitability concerns less significant. In a similar sense, a

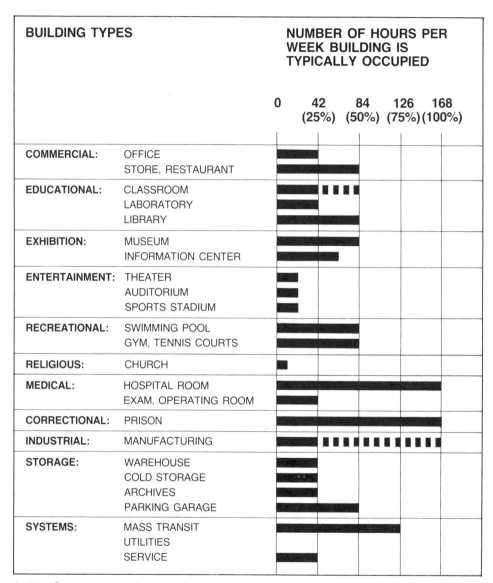

1-17: Occupancy Levels in Various Building Types

manufacturing facility may be operated continuously, but no individual spends more than eight hours per day there. Presumably, with access to natural light and psychological relief periodically during work and the remaining time away from work, a totally underground workplace would not be unacceptable. Another factor concerning occupancy not clearly reflected in this chart is that some functions such as storage and various utility and service systems do not exist for use by people. A cold storage warehouse, for example, may be occupied by a few workers from eight to twenty-four hours per day; however, it is designed to control the environment for the materials stored inside, not to create an acceptably habitable workplace. In the chart cold storage is shown as typically occupied by people eight hours a day, but a more important characteristic is that it is occupied by goods at a constant temperature twenty-four hours a day.

Conclusion

Although these basic characteristics of various building types can form a basis for assessing appropriate functions below grade, it should be recognized that there are limitations to this type of analysis. Obviously, within any individual building type, physical characteristics may vary widely. Also, for a particular building program on a particular site, one or two critical characteristics may far outweigh all of the others, making generalizations less applicable. In addition, the ratings of some critical requirements—such as the need for natural light and view—are open to interpretation, since they are based to some extent on subjective values. In spite of these drawbacks, some preliminary conclusions can be drawn concerning the appropriate use of underground space. These conclusions are open to future modification as research, design solutions, and building technology related to the subsurface continue to evolve.

Although the examination of these occupancy characteristics indicates distinct differences, problems, and advantages in locating each of the twenty-four functions underground, no building types are absolutely inappropriate below grade. A clear difference does exist, however, between what is appropriate near the surface and what is appropriate in deeper space. In deep space, functions that require relatively little vehicular and pedestrian access, no natural light and view requirements, and no public visibility, and that benefit from physical and acoustical isolation, are most suitable. These include laboratories, archives, utilities and some forms of indoor recreation. Factories, warehouses, service systems, and parking garages are also appropriate but only if horizontal vehicular access can be provided from a bluff. Although mass transit requires considerable pedestrian access and circulation at the station areas, other benefits make it uniquely suitable for location in mined space. Once major access is available to mined space for mass transit, other commercial and entertainment functions may become more feasible at this level.

For underground space near the surface, there are greater design opportunities to provide view, natural light, public visibility, direct vehicular access, and high levels of pedestrian circulation than there are in deeper space. Clearly, parking garages and manufacturing and storage facilities are suitable, since they require none of the characteristics that are difficult to provide; however, virtually all of the other nonresidential uses can also be considered appropriate below grade assuming they are properly designed. The two least appropriate functions below grade appear to be offices and hospital patient rooms, since windows often are required for a large percentage of the spaces, and this could be more difficult to achieve underground but not impossible. All of the building types on the list have been built in underground space and examples of most of them appear in chapters 3 through 8.

Although some functions are apparently better suited than others to underground space, it is often the specific site and the surrounding environment, as much as the basic physical characteristics of the building type, that suggests a building should be underground. In some cases a particular building type might seem inappropriate below grade by itself, but it may be acceptable as part of a larger underground development. Placing a particular building below the surface is a matter of choice based on many factors. Perhaps the most definite conclusion that can be drawn concerning appropriate use of underground space is that each building type has certain design problems and solutions above ground and a different set of problems that must be recognized and resolved below ground.

Walker Community Library, Minneapolis, Minnesota
Architect: BRW Architects, Inc., Minneapolis, Minnesota

Chapter 2: Design Considerations for Underground Buildings

Introduction

In the broadest sense, design considerations for underground buildings include issues as diverse as the buildings themselves. In this book the emphasis is on design concerns unique to underground buildings or at least deserving of special attention when applied to a below-grade design. Because they are so specific to particular building functions and sites, general design concepts and energy conservation strategies as well as technical site and structural design issues are discussed in the context of actual building case studies in chapters 3 through 8. Areas of particular technical concern—fire protection and life safety underground as well as waterproofing below grade—are presented in Appendices A and B.

The focus of this chapter is the design-oriented issues related to underground buildings: aesthetics and human habitability. Although these issues are also discussed in case studies in following chapters, they are particularly critical to the successful design of below-grade structures and can be appropriately discussed in a general sense as well. The chapter is divided into two major parts. In the first part, concerns related to the exterior form and character of an underground building are discussed, followed by a summary of the diverse design approaches that are typically applied. The second part of the chapter includes a summary of the potential psychological and physiological effects associated with underground or other windowless environments. Design approaches to alleviate these concerns for three critical areas—entries, openings for natural light and exterior view, and interiors—are discussed.

Exterior Form and Character

As in conventional buildings, the exterior form and character of underground structures are critical to their image and their acceptance by the public. But, unlike conventional structures, some potentially negative psychological reactions to subsurface space must be considered in exterior design. Merely compensating for such negative reactions should not, however, be the only consideration in developing an exterior form. In fact, underground structures offer unique opportunities to create exterior forms that are difficult if not impossible to attain in conventional buildings. For example, although above-grade structures can be designed to be sympathetic and reflective of natural forms, they have a physical presence on the landscape that usually creates a clear distinction between the man-made and natural environments. Placing a building partially or completely below the surface can obscure the mass and the edges of the building, enabling almost complete integration of built and natural forms. Not only can this create a more natural image, but it can provide opportunities to place relatively large structures in sensitive settings without destroying the scale, open space, or character of the area.

As evidenced by numerous underground structures presented in chapters 3 through 8, underground buildings can be designed in a wide range of forms, in which the degree of visibility and the character of the building vary greatly. Although creating an unobtrusive, even imperceptible, structure has its advantages in some cases, such an approach may be inappropriate or undesirable under other circumstances. The remainder of this section includes a discussion of design concerns related to the exterior form and character of underground buildings, along with examples of exterior forms and design elements.

Design Concerns

Although many advantages and opportunities in the exterior design of underground structures may be exploited, some pitfalls and potential problems must be overcome. First, because many basic characteristics are common to underground buildings, the exterior form and character of many subsurface structures may tend to be similar. Although this is not necessarily a problem in a general sense, it is important to consider that all buildings, above grade or below, must respond to their surroundings. An underground building surrounded by earth berms and covered with native plant materials in a rural setting may be an ideal integration of building and site. Such a design in an urban setting may be totally inappropriate, however. In the urban environment, underground buildings have significant advantages, but they must be designed to complement or reinforce the scale, materials, and forms of surrounding buildings as well as the existing patterns of circulation and open space.

Another area of concern related to the exterior form of an underground building is the need for a clear understanding of the building size, location, and entry. Most conventional buildings have very definite edges, a perceivable mass, and a clear entry so that they can be easily recognized as objects and described as specific places. An underground building may not provide these visual clues, especially if it is completely below grade with little exposure to the surface. This does not imply that an underground building must have all of the qualities of an above-grade building to be perceived correctly. It does, however, mean that the exterior form and character of a subsurface structure must take into account the problems of orientation and recognition of building and entry.

In a built-up area, a structure located under a plaza that is completely surrounded by buildings will likely be easy to describe and locate, since the adjacent buildings define the location clearly. On a more open site with fewer clear boundaries, the space above and around the underground structure must be carefully designed to reflect a sense of place and clearly indicate the entrance to the building. Exterior space around conventional buildings, when properly designed, can provide orientation, define circulation to the entrance of the building, and serve to discourage vandalism and crime. For a completely underground building, these aims are usually best accomplished by the use of grade changes, paving patterns, trees, shrubs, and variations in ground cover, along with retaining walls and other building elements.

Although many things contribute to the image that a building projects—entry, lighting, and interior design, for example—the exterior form is one of the most dominant elements. Because the exterior form of an underground building is likely to be smaller in scale than a comparably sized aboveground structure, a less visible and less monumental image will be projected. For some functions—auditoriums, libraries, museums, parking garages, and factories—this may be an advantage since a minimal presence on the site is often desirable. Other

functions, however, may require visibility to the public or may need to serve as a symbol. Although there are instances where an underground design is simply not an effective means of achieving a highly visible or monumental form, a positive image can still be created in most cases without relying on a large building mass. Partial exposure of the building, berms, and extensive landscaping can be designed to create forms on the site that will draw attention because they are attractive and provide a contrast with more conventional buildings.

A final concern related to the exterior form of an underground building is that some of the elements visible aboveground may be unattractive and may dominate the image of an otherwise unobtrusive building. For example, in most buildings loading docks, intake and exhaust vents, meters, flues, and fire exits are necessary and must appear above grade. Since these elements are usually small compared with a conventional above-grade building, they are not dominant and sometimes not even visible since they are incorporated into the building mass. On underground buildings, however, they may be the only visible elements aboveground, and they can thus have a substantially negative impact. To alleviate this, these elements may be combined into an architectural form that is integrated into an above-grade portion of the building, or they must be designed and landscaped in a very sensitive manner.

In a similar way, extensive parking areas may be acceptable when adjacent to a large above-grade building mass, but for a comparable underground structure, the parking lot may become the dominant image of the project. In certain situations it may be advantageous to use the roof of

an underground building for parking to conserve land and provide parking closer to the building entry. This can emphasize the parking area to an even greater extent. To avoid the stark, negative image of a parking lot, screening of the parking area with landscaping and building elements is essential; including parking in the below-grade structure may be necessary in some cases.

Basic Design Approaches

The exterior form and, to some extent, the character of an underground building are generally determined by the site conditions and the program requirements for the building. Two critical factors in establishing the exterior form are the relationship of the building to existing grade and the degree of building exposure. Whether a site is flat or sloping has a significant impact on both the relation to grade and the degree of exposure for the building. On flat sites the decision to place a building completely below grade, as opposed to partially below grade, may be the single most important determinant of exterior form. The degree of exposure is determined to some extent by the window requirements for certain functions as well as by the desire to combine above- and below-grade spaces and forms in the same structure. Although earth-integrated structures offer an almost limitless range of exterior images a few basic design approaches to exterior form are illustrated and discussed here in order to clarify the variety of possibilities and the special design considerations associated with each one.

Beginning with the least visible design approach, an underground building can have virtually no exterior form at all. Such a windowless chamber would be suitable only for certain functions, such as auditoriums, classrooms, laboratories, or various service and storage spaces. The nonexistent form that results from the lack of visible building mass or edges can be reinforced by not using built forms for entrances, service access, or mechanical systems. Elimination of these forms is usually possible only when the underground building is connected to the below-grade levels of an existing above-grade structure, so that access can occur through the above-grade building. No actual examples of this type of design appear in the case studies that follow, although the Law Library addition in Ann Arbor, Michigan (chapter 3) and the Mutual of Omaha Headquarters addition in Omaha, Nebraska (chapter 5) exemplify underground structures that are completely beneath the surface with no visible entrances or mechanical equipment. Both buildings are visible aboveground, however, because of large skylights.

If connecting an underground building to an existing complex of buildings is inappropriate, it is still possible to create a building with limited or minimal exposure. A structure can be placed completely below grade, with only entrances, skylights, and courtyards exposed to the surface. Although a building beneath the surface is evident, the character of a nonbuilding can still be achieved. An example of such a design is the Pusey Library at Harvard University (fig. 2-1 and chapter 3). Continuation of the existing grade and use of native plant materials can enhance the unobtrusive image. The requirements for service access and various mechanical vents and flues can present serious conflicts with this design approach. If these elements cannot be combined with those

2-1: Nathan Marsh Pusey Library, Harvard University, Cambridge, Massachusetts; Hugh Stubbins and Associates, architect; photograph by Edward Jacoby.

from an adjacent above-grade structure, they must be handled in a very subtle manner to diminish their visual impact. Otherwise, they may dominate and negatively affect the image of the project. In some cases, entry, skylights, and mechanical elements can be combined into a simple built form rather than be scattered haphazardly as they often are on conventional roofs. This can result in a small, harmonious above-grade form that does not destroy the simple, unobtrusive image that is desired.

A different approach to the exterior form of an underground structure is to place the building above grade with earth bermed

around it. Rather than being as unobtrusive as possible, the berms represent an additional object on the landscape. This can provide a distinct image and can define building edges and exterior space to some extent. Entry into a bermed building can be more easily resolved than can entry into a completely subgrade structure.

The exterior form and character of a bermed structure on a flat site can vary considerably, creating a diversity of images. The height and slope of the berms and the number of window and door openings cut into them will obviously affect the form and character of the

building. In addition to these basic factors, plant materials, retaining walls, building materials, and other landscaping elements may significantly influence the image and character of the building. The use of native plants, wood, stone, and berms that appear to be elements of the surrounding landscape can produce a natural image, as demonstrated by the Wildwood School in Aspen, Colorado (fig. 2-2 and chapter 4). On the other hand, berms can also be formed very geometrically, covered with sod, and combined with concrete and brick building forms to create a very man-made image, as illustrated by the design of the Blue Ridge Elementary School in Walla Walla, Washington (fig. 2-3 and chapter 4). The building edge can be defined even further by the use of retaining walls that form tiers of plant materials. This approach results in an underground structure with well-defined exterior spaces, which would be appropriate to an urban setting requiring much pedestrian circulation around the building. In both bermed and fully subgrade structures, earth and plant materials on the roof play important roles in blending the building with the natural landforms. A hard surface on a roof with no earth may appear to be simply a plaza, but this type of surface tends to emphasize, rather than disguise, the presence of a structure below.

Many of the inherent problems of entry, service access, and image are greatly reduced or eliminated if above-grade space

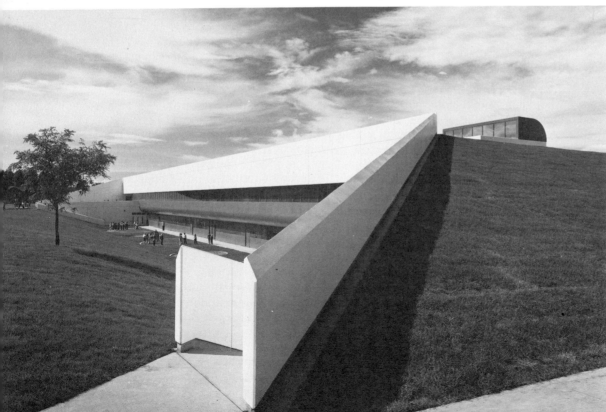

2-2 (above): Wildwood School, Aspen, Colorado; David Gibson, architect; photograph by David Marlow. 2-3 (below): Blue Ridge Elementary School, Walla Walla, Washington; Walker McGough Foltz Lyerla, architect; photograph by Photography Unlimited.

is combined with below grade in one building. Even if the amount of space above grade constitutes a small percentage of the total building, a definite built form appears above grade. In some cases the amount of above-grade space may be substantial, resulting in the more typical situation of a conventional structure with below-grade levels. The use of an above-grade portion of the structure to resolve access and image problems is certainly appropriate in many settings, although some of the benefits of underground buildings—preservation of the surface and integration with the natural environment, for example—may be compromised. It is possible, of course, to diminish the impact of a built form with proper landscaping. Several buildings presented in the case studies that follow have small above-grade forms combined with larger subsurface spaces. Examples include Williamson Hall at the University of Minnesota (chapter 5) and the Moscone Convention Center in San Francisco, California (chapter 8).

All of the design approaches discussed so far apply to underground buildings on flat sites. A site with sufficient slope provides design opportunities not available on a flat site. An underground building set into a hillside is clearly exposed on one side while completely underground on the other. This results in a definite building form on the exposed site where entry and service access can occur; on the uphill side, the site is not interrupted by any substantial grade changes or built forms. The National

Art Education Center in Reston, Virginia, exemplifies this approach (fig. 2-4 and chapter 5).

Although this discussion of exterior form and character is mainly in reference to cut-and-cover structures near the surface, some of the same concerns and approaches can be applied to deeper mined space as well. Certainly the size, shape, and form of mined space remote from the surface is not directly perceived. Some form of entry and mechanical access is necessary, however, so that portal access points along a bluff or vertical shafts from points on the surface must be included. The design of these exposed points—whether as small, separate structures or as parts of larger building complexes—requires the same considerations as near surface space

regarding exterior image, entry, and service access.

Although the exterior form and character of an underground building are central to its image and thus, to the positive psychological perception of the building, they are not the only contributing factors. The entrance design, presence of natural light and view, and interior design are also important. Moreover, the exterior form cannot be designed for image alone; certain functions must occur regardless of their desirability. Vehicular and service access are the most notable functions that will likely affect the overall design of the building. In later sections of this chapter, these critical design considerations are discussed with further implications for the exterior form and character of an underground building.

2-4 (right): National Art Education Association Headquarters, Reston, Virginia; The Benham Group, architect; photograph by Scott Dollmeyer.

Psychological and Physiological Considerations

Although the concerns discussed in this section relate primarily to underground buildings, most of the information also pertains to windowless buildings or interior zones of conventional buildings.

Underground or earth sheltered buildings cover a wide spectrum of physical characteristics and functions. In addition, the physiological and psychological response of individuals to the environment can be radically different. These factors combined make generalizations about underground buildings in relation to physiological and psychological effects potentially misleading and of only limited validity. It is possible, however, to list criteria and considerations that are potentially applicable to an earth sheltered building and to discuss how these factors have been assessed by various investigators of the psychological and physiological responses to artificial environments.

Only a few studies have directly addressed the case of below-grade spaces for working or living environments, and conflicting data has often been gathered. Assessments of the physical characteristics of an underground space are extremely difficult to separate from other general physical characteristics of the space and the interpersonal environment. In spite of the lack of definitive data, however, the major issues are fairly clear and repeatedly emerge in all studies of underground and windowless spaces. What is less clear is the extent to which architectural strategies can ameliorate the potential psychological problems associated with a relatively enclosed below-grade environment and the extent to which certain conditions pose a significant health hazard. The basic design approaches typically used to alleviate these concerns are discussed in the latter sections of this chapter.

Conditions Producing Negative Psychological Effects

lack of natural light

The lack of natural light is one of the most often mentioned negative characteristics of underground space. Access to natural light is important to users of a building even if the proportion of daylight to artificial lighting for work tasks is relatively low. The feeling produced by daylight, its variability, and the sense of contact with the outside world it provides make it desirable. It has been theorized that horizontal accessibility to daylight provides a closer reference to conventional buildings and is therefore preferable to daylighting from overhead sources [2.1]. In contrast, however, a research study conducted with groups of students viewing slides of building interiors concluded that spaces with skylights overhead were most often selected as the most desirably lit [2.2]. Another important positive psychological association of natural lighting is that sunlight connotes warmth. Direct sunlight is not always welcomed by building users, however. Sunlight can cause excessively uncomfortable conditions in a warm building interior, as well as personal discomfort to a person who must work in the full sunlight. Excessive brightness, glare, and large brightness to darkness ratios in buildings not completely illuminated by sunlight are other problems [2.3].

lack of exterior view

The lack of exterior view from an underground space is another reason for dissatisfaction with this type of building. In addition to providing natural light and sunlight, windows provide a direct view for monitoring weather conditions, creating a sense of contact with the environment, and giving visual relief from the immediate surroundings [2.4]. Different studies have indicated different relative importances for natural light and view [2.5]. People in work environments are more likely to favor a view over direct sunlight, especially if no solar shading is provided and if they are not free to relocate themselves out of the sun if desired. Occupants of high-density residential developments are more likely to cite the availability of sunlight in the home as more important than a good view [2.6]

underground location

The location of a building below grade does not preclude providing the above amenities of natural light and view to the interior of the building. There are, however, psychological barriers to the physical location of a space below grade even if it has identical physical amenities to an interior space in a conventional building. Some individuals may experience claustrophobia or fears related to safety that result in negative reactions to underground spaces. These negative reactions tend to heighten awareness of and exaggerate objections to other physical characteristics of the space that might go unnoticed in a conventional building. For example, small interior spaces, low ceilings, or entry down a narrow, dark stairway may increase these negative associations with being underground.

lack of spatial orientation

Orientation may be impaired inside a mostly windowless underground building. Visual cues normally provided by exterior views and an awareness of the overall form of the building may not be present. This disorientation can contribute to uneasiness and reinforce other negative associations with being underground.

undesirable internal conditions

Users of windowless or underground buildings frequently complain of poor temperature and humidity control and a lack of ventilation or stuffiness [2.4]. Generally, none of the problems should be any different for a below-grade or windowless building than they are for a sealed, climate-controlled conventional building. In fact, temperature and humidity should be easier to control than in an aboveground building. Thus, in addition to the actual ventilation air change rate provided, perception of ventilation by occupants is important. If awareness of the superior internal environmental control of an underground building is clearly apparent to the occupants, some offsetting positive attitudes may develop.

Individual Responses to the Environment

The physical characteristics of underground space listed above can result in a number of negative psychological reactions. These reactions will not be identical for every individual. The psychological makeup of some people will contribute to a far more negative reaction to an underground environment than others. Listed below are factors affecting individual responses to the underground environment. The first two factors—fear of the underground and claustrophobia—are conditions that some people may be predisposed to while others are not. The last two factors—sensory deprivation and interaction with the environment—are broader areas of psychological research that have some applicability to underground space use.

fear of being underground

Since information on this topic is not readily available, it is difficult to explain the negative association some people have with the concept of being underground—even when interior conditions are identical to those in an aboveground space. It is generally assumed, however, that these attitudes are related to a fear of structural collapse and consequent burial, fear of being trapped in a fire in a windowless building, or fear of flooding in a fully below-grade space. Fears for personal safety need not be related to the actual risk experienced but merely to the perceived risk. They can be affected by news of accidents such as coal mine disasters in much the same way that concern for life safety in hotels is raised by news of a major hotel fire disaster. In addition to fears related to safety concerns, there may be a generally negative association with death and burial related to underground space.

claustrophobia

Closely related to the general fear of being underground discussed above is a more specific and well-defined fear, claustrophobia. The fear of small, enclosed spaces with limited escape routes is clearly a potential problem for some users of underground buildings.

sensory deprivation

Individuals are stimulated and many bodily functions are affected by interactions with the surrounding environment. In addition to physiological effects (discussed below), psychological problems can arise from a reduction of external stimuli to an individual [2.7]. This reduction of stimuli would occur most significantly in small, enclosed spaces with little interpersonal contact and no contact with the external environment. It should be noted that a reduction of external stimuli is not always negative; it can provide a more productive work environment and reduce stress in otherwise chaotic surroundings.

interaction with the environment

It has been theorized that the three primary emotional responses to the environment are pleasure, arousal, and dominance [2.8]. Pleasure is self-explanatory. Arousal relates to the sensory information an environment provides. Dominance relates to feelings of control or influence over the environment. A lowered arousal level is to be anticipated in enclosed spaces, but the effect on feelings of dominance is not as clear. It has been suggested that, because of the practical and environmental advantages of an earth-covered building, users may feel they were "being exposed to successful attempts to cope with the demands of the environment" [2.7]. It has been found, however, that practical features of a building were not important criteria in evaluating user response to working in the space [2.9]. Nevertheless, for an individual choosing to build an earth sheltered house for energy-conserving and environmental reasons, these criteria are often very important and would be expected to create positive feelings about the house environment. A poor response to the environment of an underground building has been linked to anxiety, tension, depression, and other mental health problems, although other studies have indicated no measureable differences in achievement, health problems, or absenteeism [2.4, 2.10, 2.11].

Conditions Producing Negative Physiological Effects

Physiological effects discussed in this section are those effects caused directly by the environment of an underground or windowless structure and not indirect ailments or reactions caused by psychological stress.

lack of natural light

Lighting is probably the most important physiological criteria to be considered in designing underground or windowless structures. The human body has a direct response to certain spectra of light, including those outside the visible spectrum. For instance, ultraviolet light is known to be important in vitamin D absorption, which is necessary to prevent disease, aid suntanning, and fight bacteria. In animals the lighting level and its spectral composition have been shown to be important in reproduction, behavior, and physical disposition. Lighting also triggers a neuroendocrine function and affects the metabolic state [2.12, 2.13]. Although much research has been done on the presence or absence of light, little has been done on lighting levels and spectral composition. Alarming effects of certain light sources have been demonstrated, however, in laboratory animals [2.14]. It should be noted that effects are quite different for different animal species. Ultraviolet light is also not transmitted by normal window glass; hence, lack of ultraviolet light is common even to most buildings with windows.

lack of fresh air/indoor air pollution

Underground location of a building with only limited opportunities for window openings often precludes the use of natural ventilation. Adequate ventilation is important to prevent the buildup of indoor air pollutants and to remove excess heat from an occupied underground space. Low air change rates make ventilation particularly important in earth sheltered structures. A pollutant of particular concern is radon. Radon is a radioactive gas released in minute quantities by soil and rock materials, including such materials used in building construction as concrete and building stone. Radon is also absorbed by groundwater and then released at a free groundwater surface. Normal ventilation rates (in excess of 0.5 air changes per hour) are believed to keep radon levels to below permissible standards; this is an active area of research, and more specific data and guidelines should be produced over the next few years. In addition, it is desirable to prevent the passage of groundwater or water vapor from the surrounding ground to within the building envelope since this water is significant source of radon [2.15].

high humidity

Unless controlled, summertime humidity levels will be higher in earth sheltered structures as humid outside air is cooled by the earth covered walls of the structure.

Humid or damp conditions have not been directly linked with physiological problems, although they may exacerbate certain ailments such as rheumatism. Damp conditions may also encourage the growth of mold and thus increase the potential for allergic reactions.

excessive noise or lack of noise

Noisy building types such as factories can be placed underground to isolate them from the surface environment. Although this offers benefits to those above grade, it may create excessive noise levels within the space, which have well-known effects on hearing impairment. On the other hand, underground spaces can be totally isolated from external sources of noise, creating a totally silent environment. In some cases this total silence may be unnerving and may diminish acoustical privacy within the space.

Impact of Building Use

Before concluding which effects are most critical and suggesting design approaches to ameliorate them, it is useful to review the various factors related to building use that influence either the psychological or physiological effects. These factors, listed below, can serve to diminish the potentially negative effects and help to alleviate building user concerns.

activity within building

Internal activity within a building that can offset the lack of external stimuli will normally be beneficial in a work environment provided it is not too intrusive in terms of noise or distraction. Although internal stimuli may help to alleviate the negative psychological effects produced by no natural light and exterior view, it has no impact on the physiological effects of a windowless environment.

occupancy patterns

An individual's reaction to an underground or windowless environment may be substantially affected by the length of time he or she expects to spend in that environment. Underground facilities primarily used for short-term activities such as indoor sports facilities, restaurants, libraries, or shopping centers will thus normally raise fewer objections than an underground office. Not only are negative psychological reactions less of a concern when occupants are in underground spaces for shorter time periods, but negative physiological effects are less critical as well.

need for underground location

Employees of underground or windowless facilities appear to be more accepting of their environment if they perceive a rational basis for the location or design of the facility [2.4]. In other words, since windows are detrimental to the operation of many sports facilities, museums, restaurants, and shops, employees and visitors do not focus on the lack of windows as a drawback. Similarly, windowless laboratory and manufacturing environments provoke less criticism than windowless office buildings. Although this perception of windowless environments as being appropriate for some functions can reduce some psychological effects, it has no impact on negative physiological effects.

job satisfaction

Employees who are more involved in their work and derive considerable satisfaction from it may be more tolerant of windowless space than employees who work at repetitive tasks. The extent to which this can actually offset the various negative psychological effects is likely to vary considerably from individual to individual.

Conclusion

Although the psychological and physiological effects discussed here represent definite drawbacks to underground or windowless space, a number of modifying factors must be taken into consideration. First, these effects are influenced by the use of the space. Second, not enough information is available in some areas to draw definite conclusions. Finally, many of these effects can be alleviated or compensated for with proper design. It is clear that some earth sheltered building functions are more psychologically acceptable than others. It has been found that an earth sheltered house (with windows) was more immediately accepted as a pleasant place to be than an earth sheltered work environment [2.2]. Manufacturing, storage, and other specialized work settings are in turn more readily accepted than a general office environment. Recreational facilities, shopping centers, restaurants, and museums appear to be the most likely to be readily accepted.

As might be expected from the often conflicting factors relating to the psychological acceptance of an earth sheltered environment, no general design criteria can be followed. The difficulty for the designer is compounded because the perceived attributes of a building may not reflect the physical attributes. In a survey of the University of Minnesota employees [2.9], occupants of an interior windowless zone of a large aboveground building and occupants of a section of the basement of the same building had quite similar evaluations of their work environment as those occupants in an aboveground, exterior zone (with windows) of the same building did. Occupants of the windowless portion of a well-known earth sheltered building on campus, however, had a much lower evaluation of their work environment.

Acceptance of a building environment may involve a series of trade-offs. It is not necessarily instructive to find out how many individuals would like a window in their office (usually over 99 percent), but rather how important that amenity is in relation to other potential amenities or compensations that could be provided. For instance, the number of faculty expressing preference for a windowless office in a department at the University of Minnesota rose from close to zero to over 30 percent when an relative increase in size was offered for the interior office.

Assessing the physiological effects of being underground should be somewhat simpler than the psychological effects because there are fewer basic concerns, they do not vary as much on an individual basis, and—except for length of stay in the building—they are less affected by mitigating circumstances. But, in spite of the greater facility in clarifying physiological effects, it remains difficult to draw definite conclusions. Although the negative effects caused by complete lack of sunlight and sensory deprivation have been

documented, studies in underground buildings have not necessarily concluded such detrimental effects exist. For example, a fairly comprehensive study was made of workers in an underground factory in Sweden in the 1940s and 1950s [2.10]. Although headaches, faintness, and sickness were reported, much of this was an initial problem that occurred during an acclimatization period to the underground environment. The study concluded that no major physiological problems occurred if the proper interior climate was maintained. Blood tests on workers after eight years working underground showed no alteration in the normal blood condition. Two studies of children attending an underground school in New Mexico—the Abo Elementary School—also indicated no evidence of greater absenteeism or health problems in children attending the underground school. In fact, respiratory ailments were reduced because of better control and filtration of the air [2.16, 2.17]. In summary, although there are several issues of concern for people spending extended periods in an underground or windowless environment, a long-term detrimental effect on humans has not yet been established.

Although scientific proof of negative psychological and physiological effects related to underground buildings is not absolute and is dependent on a number of circumstances, the safest course is to alleviate the various concerns as much as possible. As demonstrated by the case studies in chapters 3 through 8, most designers intuitively respond to creating an acceptable environment underground regardless of the existing research. Based on the functional needs of the building and the opportunities available, it is advisable to provide natural light and exterior view

when possible. This addresses a variety of concerns including offering physiological and psychological benefits from sunlight and external stimuli, providing spatial orientation, and helping to overcome fears associated with the underground by providing a more conventional environment. When it is necessary to rely on artificial lighting entirely, it is most desirable to replicate the spectral composition of daylight as closely as possible. In addition, people who are in windowless environments for long periods of time can be encouraged to take breaks outdoors or in naturally lighted portions of the building.

In addition to providing natural light and view, entrances, building layout, and interior spaces should be designed with particular sensitivity to offset the negative psychological effects discussed in this section. In cases where opportunities for natural light and view are limited, these other elements of the building take on added importance. Other concerns focus on providing adequate ventilation, noise control, and proper temperature and humidity control. In contrast to the architectural areas of concern listed above, these mechanical system concerns can be handled much as they would be for any conventional building. Since some people perceive underground space to be poorly ventilated in spite of the actual conditions [2.18], the mechanical ventilation should be discernible. A system providing good local control of temperature may also improve the perception of adequate ventilation.

In the remainder of this chapter, various architectural design approaches are discussed for the key areas of concern in underground buildings—entrance design, provision of natural light and view, and interior design.

Entrance Design

The manner in which an underground structure is entered can have an important influence on the total perception of the building. The degree to which a pedestrian entry is important as a design element is, of course, related to the function of the building. In an underground warehouse, the entrance for a few workers is not as important as the functional needs of delivering and storing goods. The entrance design is of greater concern in an underground office or factory where larger numbers of people are employed. And, compared with facilities where people enter and leave once a day, a public building such as a library, museum, or auditorium with many comings and goings requires even greater attention to entry design.

Viewed from the exterior, the entrance may be the dominant image of a building that is mostly below grade. It serves as the transition from the exterior to the interior. As such, it can reinforce various fears and claustrophobia associated with underground buildings. The entry area in any building should be a key element in orienting and directing people to the spaces inside. In an underground building, this orientation function is particularly important. In addition, the entry often serves as a major area for admitting natural light and exterior view to a subsurface structure since it may be one of the few points of exposure to the surface.

In order to minimize the negative feelings associated with entering an underground building, several basic techniques are used. The most important is creating an entrance that is similar to the entrance of a conventional building. It is most desirable

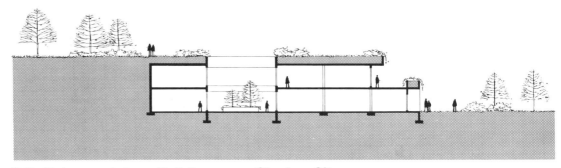

2-5: Entrance into a Building on a Sloping Site

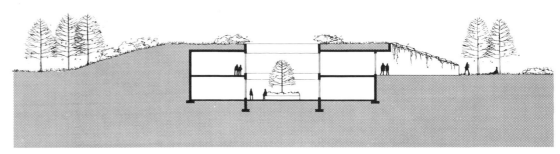

2-6: Entrance into a Bermed Structure

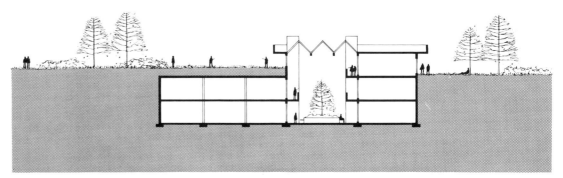

2-7: Entrance into the Above-Grade Portion of the Building

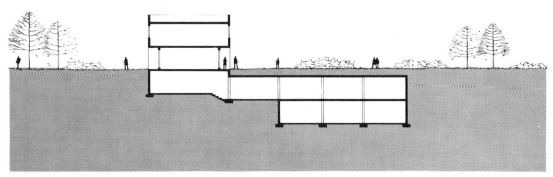

2-8: Entrance through an Existing Above-Grade Building

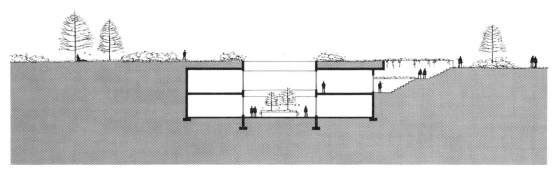

2-9: Entrance by Descending Outside the Building

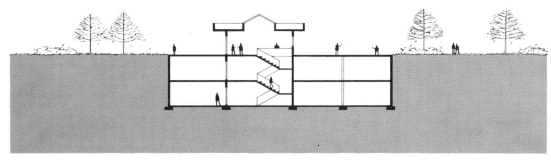

2-10: Entrance by Descending Inside the Building

to design an entrance at existing grade that does not require descending a great number of stairs either immediately outside or inside the entrance. Descending seems to have negative associations, while ascending is more positive. Historically, large public buildings were designed with a large exterior staircase leading to a main entrance on the second level of the building.

In an underground building, it is usually not possible to ascend to the main entrance. Under a number of circumstances, however, subsurface structures can be entered on grade, similar to a conventional building—for example, on a sloping site (fig. 2-5). A similar type of entry without descent is possible in a bermed structure on a flat site (fig. 2-6). When a portion of a building is exposed above grade, a conventional entrance can occur in the above-grade mass (fig. 2-7). In this case the interior spaces must be carefully designed to offset negative feelings associated with descent inside the building.

In many instances underground structures are additions to existing above-grade buildings (fig. 2-8). Thus, some of the entry design problems are overcome because the main entrance occurs through the conventional building. It is important, however, to consider the design of the connection between an above- and below-grade building. In the underground addition to the Uris Library at Cornell University, the stairway connecting the two buildings is enclosed in glass, transforming a potentially negative descent to the addition into an unusual spatial experience with a panoramic view of the valley below (fig. 2-11).

In some cases—a fully below-grade building on a flat site, for example—none of the opportunities for a conventional entry discussed above are available. To maintain the low profile of the building while creating an acceptable entrance, a sunken courtyard can be used so that one descends outside the building and enters horizontally at the upper level of the building (fig. 2-9). This approach maintains many of the features of a conventional entrance; negative associations can be reduced since the descent occurs more gradually in a spacious outdoor area. An example of this approach is the spiral-shaped courtyard leading to the main entrance of the Civil and Mineral Engineering Building at the University of Minnesota (fig. 2-12).

On particularly restrictive sites, creating exterior sunken courtyards as a means of entry may not be possible. The only option may be to enter through a small above-grade mass and descend immediately to the spaces below (fig. 2-10). This situation in particular may reinforce negative associations with entering underground buildings and requires careful attention to natural light and interior spaciousness in the stairway area.

Entering relatively deep mined space can present design problems that are difficult to resolve using any of the techniques discussed above. Although horizontal entry

2-11 (above): Uris Undergraduate Library, Cornell University, Ithaca, New York; Gunnar Birkerts and Associates, architect; photograph by Timothy Hursley, The Arkansas Office. 2-12 (below): Civil and Mineral Engineering Building, University of Minnesota; BRW Architects, Inc.; photograph by George Heinrich.

to deep spaces can occur through tunnels in bluffs, there is little opportunity to introduce natural light or offset the spatial confinement of the tunnels. Entering deep spaces through elevator or escalator shafts provides little opportunity to alleviate negative associations with descent.

Providing Natural Light and View

The lack of natural light and view is both psychologically and physiologically the single greatest concern related to underground space. With the exception of warehouses and other functions where human habitability and acceptance is a secondary concern, some natural light is desirable in virtually every type of building. The degree to which it is necessary or even desirable for each space in the building depends on specific function. In a building composed mainly of small, continuously occupied spaces, such as private offices or hospital patient rooms, the entire form of the structure may be shaped by the need for natural light and view. In buildings containing functions that are suitable in windowless spaces—classrooms, auditoriums, and exhibition spaces, for example—it may be necessary or desirable to provide natural light and exterior view only to corridors and lobby areas, thus giving the designer greater flexibility.

Although designers employ many variations and combinations of techniques, there are only a few basic approaches to providing natural light and exterior view to below-grade spaces. Aside from the functional needs of the spaces, the techniques selected for introducing natural light and view to a particular building are influenced by the site topography as well as the size

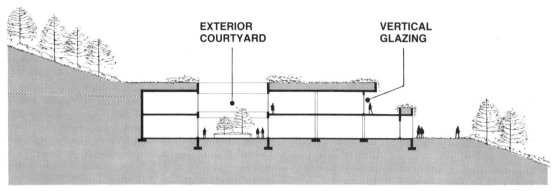

2-13: Building Set into a Sloping Site

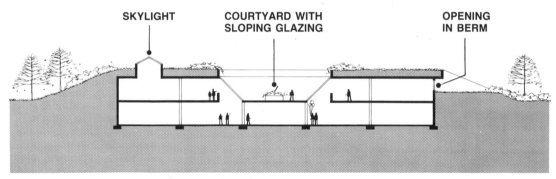

2-14: Bermed Structure on a Flat Site

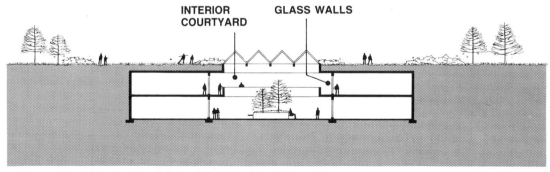

2-15: Fully Below-Grade Building on a Flat Site

and depth of the structure. On a sloping site, conventional vertical glazing can be used for the spaces on one side of the building (fig. 2-13). This approach by itself is capable of providing light and view only to the spaces on the building perimeter. If earth berms are placed around a structure on a flat site, conventional vertical glazing can be provided on the building perimeter by creating openings in the berms (fig. 2-14). For interior spaces on a sloping or flat site, natural light and view can be provided by creating courtyards (fig. 2-13). If a courtyard must be deeper to serve several floors, it must also be larger in order to permit sunlight to reach the floor of the courtyard and create the perception of looking outdoors. The view into an exterior courtyard is usually more focused and limited than a view through the building perimeter, making the landscape design of the courtyard a critical concern.

On flat sites, including skylights is a common technique for introducing natural light to at least the upper level of an underground structure (fig. 2-14). In many cases horizontally glazed skylights actually provide more natural light than a vertically glazed window, but the same opportunities for exterior views are, of course, not available. Consequently, skylights alone may not be considered an adequate substitute for conventional windows. Some designers use sloped glazing in courtyards or light wells; this glazing provides natural light from overhead while permitting exterior views from some angles (fig. 2-14). This type of glazing is used effectively in the Law Library addition at

the University of Michigan (chapter 3) and Williamson Hall at the University of Minnesota (fig. 2-16 and chapter 5).

An alternative to creating exterior courtyards is an interior courtyard with skylights overhead (fig. 2-15). In particularly large and deep buildings, an interior courtyard provides additional climate-controlled space and, like an exterior courtyard, natural light from above. The extent to which a view of an interior courtyard is a substitute for an exterior view depends a great deal on the size and design of the space. The use of glass walls between an interior courtyard and the spaces surrounding it is a common

technique for transmitting light and view to these spaces. Referred to as "borrowing light," this concept is used in many ways to provide natural light to spaces that are adjacent to spaces that have direct access to light, for example, from a skylight, perimeter window, or a courtyard.

In addition to the well-known approaches discussed above, some more novel techniques for introducing natural light and exterior view to subsurface spaces have been developed. With the increasing awareness of the advantages of underground buildings for a variety of functions, one architecture firm in particular—BRW Architects, Inc. of

2-16 (right): Williamson Hall, University of Minnesota; BRW Architects, Inc.; photograph by Phillip MacMillan James.

Minneapolis, Minnesota—has experimented with various optical techniques for providing or enhancing the effect of natural light and view in normally windowless areas. Mirrors can be used to enhance the light and view from a window by reflecting them into spaces not immediately adjacent to the window. This technique was used in the Walker Community Library (see chapter 3). Another approach is to provide exterior views using mirrors and lenses in a manner similar to a periscope. In one of the simplest applications, mirrors alone are used to provide views to below-grade offices in the Fort Snelling Visitor Center (fig. 2-17).

A more sophisticated periscope-type system using mirrors and lenses provides a clear exterior view to a lobby area 110 feet beneath the surface in the Civil and Mineral Engineering Building at the University of Minnesota (see chapter 4). In the same building, two separate systems are used to provide natural light to different areas. One system uses heliostats on the roof to collect sunlight, which mirrors and lenses then project to the offices in deep-mined space below. The other system appears to be a more conventional skylight over the main laboratory space, but reflective surfaces and lenses are used to collect,

concentrate, and project the sunlight to the space below more efficiently and accurately. These various optical techniques not only permit greater design flexibility for all underground buildings, but may enable light and view to be introduced to deep subsurface spaces or below-grade spaces on very constrained sites where more conventional approaches do not work.

Interior Design

A key element in the impression created by any building, interior design can be even more essential in an underground structure. In addition to the normal concerns of creating an attractive interior environment, special attention must be paid to offsetting the potentially negative psychological effects discussed earlier—claustrophobia, lack of view, loss of orientation, lack of stimulus, and associations with dark, damp, or cold basements. With the possible exception of alleviating some of the effects of sensory deprivation, interior design has little impact on any of the potentially negative physiological effects of underground spaces. As discussed in the previous section, introducing natural light and exterior view to below-grade spaces is probably the most effective means of alleviating many of the concerns listed above. Since opportunities to introduce natural light and view are often limited, the interior spaces must be designed to maximize the effect of what light and view there is and to compensate for the lack of light and view in other areas.

A number of techniques are used in underground buildings to create a feeling of spaciousness that helps to provide more

2-17: Periscope Section

Fort Snelling Visitor Center, St. Paul, Minnesota
Architect: BRW Architects, Inc., Minneapolis, Minnesota

visual stimulus in the absence of exterior views. Wider corridors and higher ceilings than normal, together with open plan layouts using low partitions, are simple means of creating a spacious feeling. In addition, glass partitions can be used between spaces to provide spatial relief and variety. Perhaps the most effective approach is the use of large, multilevel central spaces surrounded by smaller spaces similar to those shown in figure 2-15. Overlooking large spaces from balconies offsets the feeling of being below grade and can provide vistas nearly equivalent to some exterior views, even if the central spaces are not naturally lighted. In addition to providing variety within the building, large interior courtyard-type spaces can also help to give building users a reference point in maintaining orientation.

Although the size and arrangement of interior spaces are critical elements in the perception of an underground building, the more subtle elements of color, texture, lighting, and furnishings cannot be overlooked. In an environment that lacks outside stimuli, variation in lighting and color in particular can simulate some of the variation that would occur with natural light. Well-lighted, brightly colored surfaces, with an emphasis on warmer tones, can help to offset associations with cold, dark underground spaces. One characteristic of windowless space that can be used as an advantage is the lack of distraction, which enables manipulation of the interior design to focus the occupant's attention if desired. Dramatic lighting can effectively draw attention to artwork, for example.

In buildings with interior courtyards or central spaces, plant materials, fountains, and other landscape elements can create

2-18: Great Midwest Corporation, Kansas City, Missouri; photograph by Paul S. Kivett.

a simulated outdoor environment without natural light. Although this approach has been achieved in windowless spaces with some success, there is always the danger that imitation of conventional above-grade spaces in a superficial way—false window frames with painted exterior views, for instance—will leave a negative impression. Rather than working to create an acceptable environment within the limitations of underground space, attention is drawn to what is missing by a poor imitation.

Many of the techniques discussed above are not unconventional and can serve to create an environment that is reassuringly similar to any building. On the other hand, it is also possible and appropriate in some cases to exploit the uniqueness of being underground, creating a stimulating positive experience. An example of this approach can be found in the design of offices in deep-mined space near Kansas City, Missouri, where rock walls are exposed and often lighted in dramatic ways (see fig. 2-18 and chapter 6).

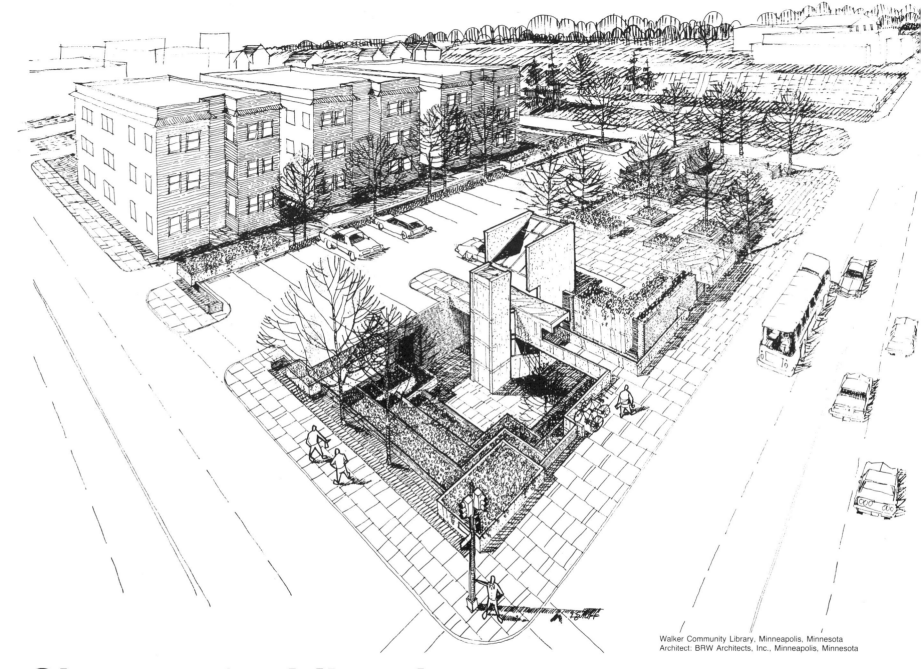

Walker Community Library, Minneapolis, Minnesota
Architect: BRW Architects, Inc., Minneapolis, Minnesota

Chapter 3: Libraries

Nathan Marsh Pusey Library

Cambridge, Massachusetts

Architect: Hugh Stubbins and Associates

Completed in 1976, the Pusey Library provides major expansion space for the Harvard University Library System and a well-controlled, secure environment for rare and special collections of books, manuscripts, and maps. With over 10 million volumes in its collection, the Harvard University Library was outgrowing the capacity of the existing older library buildings. In addition, many of the items in the collection required special provisions to ensure their preservation. The Pusey Library not only meets these requirements but, as the first phase of a long-range building program, is designed and engineered for vertical and horizontal expansion.

Any new structure inserted into the historical setting of the Harvard Yard requires great sensitivity and restraint in its design. By placing the 87,000-square foot building almost completely underground, not only is the character and open space of the Harvard Yard preserved, but the new building serves as a link between three other adjacent libraries. The subsurface design also contributes to the security of the building, with limited and well-controlled points of access. Sound reduction is another benefit of underground space that can be appropriately utilized in a library structure.

The original site of the library sloped downward from south to north and was crossed diagonally with a major path of pedestrian circulation. The design of the underground building maintained the pedestrian walkway but changed the ground level—actually the landscaped roof—to a basically flat surface. This partially exposes the northwest corner of the building, where the main entry occurs. At this point of entry, the upper floor of the library is only 3 feet below existing grade, whereas the same floor level is 12 to 14 feet below grade on the southeastern corner of the site. A secondary entry occurs on the southwestern corner of the site. In the center of the open space that is the roof of the building is a 40-foot-square sunken courtyard extending down two levels into the library.

The various functions and collections on the three levels of the Pusey Library are arranged to facilitate access and provide light and view where appropriate to the most heavily used areas. On the upper level, a major corridor directs one past displays, lounges, and the main reading rooms of the three special collections housed in the building—the Harvard University Archives, Theatre Collection, and Map Collection. The reading rooms and offices on this level all have large window areas facing the moat around the building or the central sunken courtyard. A few faculty studies as well as the stacks for the Harvard Theatre Collection and Map Collection are also located on the upper level. The larger stacks for the University Archives and manuscript stacks from the general collection occupy most of the second level. On this level, entrances to the three adjacent library buildings occur; faculty studies are located on three sides of the central courtyard. The lowest level, only about half the area of the upper two levels, contains more stacks of the general collection.

Approached from the southeast, across the rooftop landscape with lawns, shrubs, and flowering trees, the Pusey Library is not

Opposite: The main library entrance viewed from Harvard Yard, photograph by Edward Jacoby.

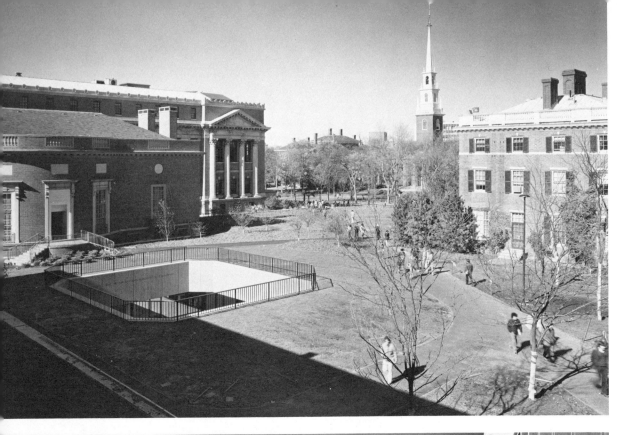

perceptible as a building mass. The edges of the building underneath are not apparent except for the relatively small sunken courtyard. Exhaust grilles and vents on the roof are carefully shielded by landscaping. From the northwest or entry side of the library, however, the building has a perceptible form—yet it remains simple and unobtrusive, appearing to be no more than earth berms, garden walls, and stairways from some angles. Although a large area of the upper-level walls are fully exposed with expansive windows, they are shielded by an earth berm surrounding the building that forms a moatlike sunken courtyard along the perimeter. The berm blocks a direct view of the upper level from most exterior angles, while diminishing the building's scale and blending it into the existing terrain. All exterior walls and stairways, including the parapet forming the roof edge, are granite, which was also used in many of the surrounding historical structures.

Special Design Concerns

Although the entire library building is restrained and unobtrusive, the main entry remains clear and direct. A wide wedge-shaped staircase is the only major interruption of the earth berm, which shields the upper-level facade. A very appealing view of a sculpture in the moatlike light well emerges as one descends a few feet to the entrance level on the exterior of the building.

Above: Landscaped roof and sunken courtyard viewed from the southeast. Below: Main corridor and the lounge area one level below grade, photographs by Steve Rosenthal.

Once inside the building, any negative associations with being in an underground space are offset by the variety of opportunities for natural light and exterior views as well as by the richly detailed interior design. On the upper level, light and view are provided to a majority of the spaces through the glass walls facing the perimeter moat and the sunken courtyard. In this respect the upper level is not remarkably different from a conventional above-grade building. The nature of the exterior views are different, however, in that they are limited, framed vistas of particular outdoor spaces, with more reflected light than direct sunlight.

Along the perimeter moat, the view is focused on the texture of the brick paving and vine-covered walls, although it is also directed upward to the older adjacent buildings and the sky. In the central sunken courtyard, the view is very controlled, dominated by the Japanese red maple tree. This courtyard view and source of light occurs along the main corridor of both upper levels. The majority of the middle level and all of the lower level are windowless and are appropriately used for stacks.

The exceptionally well-detailed and finished interiors of the Pusey Library create warmth, serenity, and visual interest that are well suited to the purpose of the building. Walls are mainly white with a few bright accent colors, carpeting is red, and oak is used extensively for furnishings and trim. Gold reflectors are used to warm the color of the artificial lighting in some places. Most of the spatial variety, as well as public displays of material from the collections, occurs along the major corridor on the upper level. Display cases are offset along the corridor, and windows with oak mullions permit views into the reading

rooms. A widening of the corridor and change of direction occur at the lounge area; the sunken courtyard can be viewed from one side of the corridor, while the other side serves as a gallery.

Building Technology and Costs

The decision to place Pusey Library underground was based on aesthetics and land-use efficiency; however, the particular site chosen presented a number of obstacles. The water table is very near the surface, and melting snow or heavy rains

can cause flooding in the site area. In addition to the water problems, the lower level of the three-story building was to be placed into the bedrock, increasing the difficulty and cost of excavation.

Since it was determined that at least one-third of the building would be located below the level of the water table, extraordinary measures were taken to ensure drainage. A grid of perforated drainpipes is laid in a bed of sand beneath the foundation slab. A similar grid of drainpipes is placed in a 3-foot-thick layer of gravel surrounding the buried walls

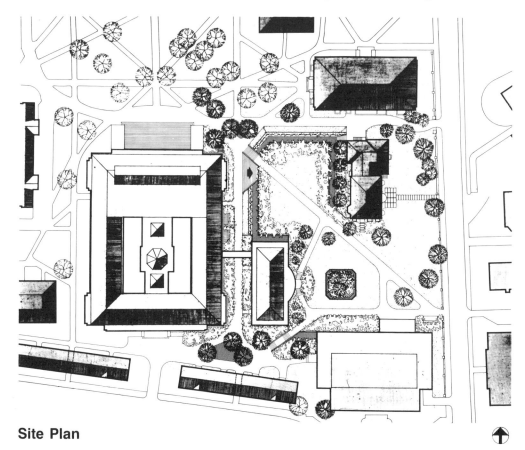

Site Plan

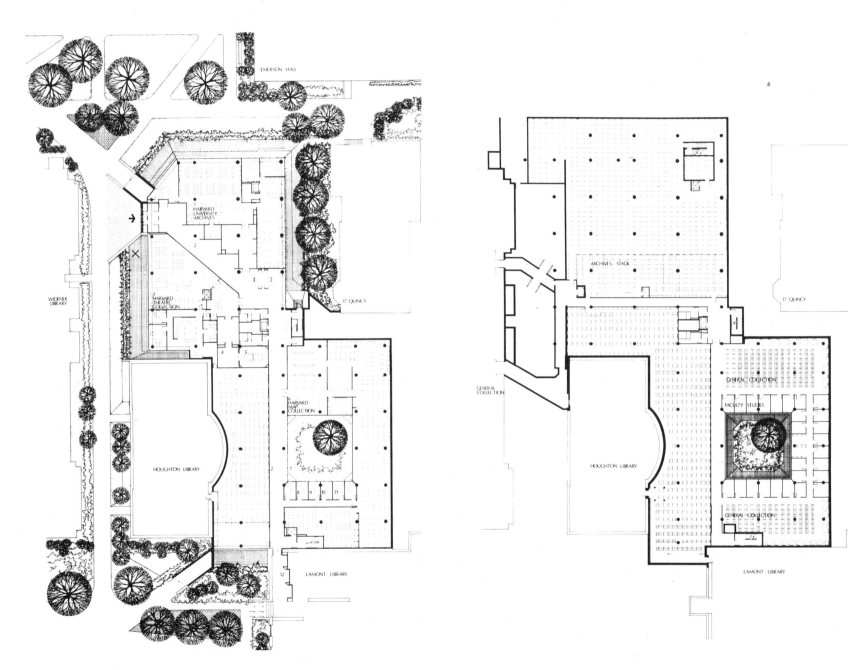

Floor Plan—One Level Below Grade

Floor Plan—Two Levels Below Grade

of the building. Any water seeping into this zone near the building is drained to two large and two small sump pumps, which operate continuously. An emergency generator is available to supply power to the sump pumps and the air-conditioning system. Ironite—metal shavings that expand when wet to seal the surface—were added to the concrete in the exterior walls. Liquid neoprene was applied to the walls as an extra precaution. The earth-covered roof, which also contains a grid of subsurface drainpipes, was waterproofed with a mastic coating applied over a neoprene sheet membrane.

Protecting the valuable collections from fire (and the water damage that accompanies fire) also required special design techniques. The entire building is protected by a system using tanks of liquid Halon stored under pressure and released as a gas. Sophisticated detection and distribution devices located in every space can deliver Halon in the precise amount needed to extinguish the fire.

In addition to water and fire protection, the need to protect the contents of the building resulted in a variety of other unusual conditions and details. For example, all fluorescent light fixtures are covered with ultraviolet shields to protect materials from deterioration. Windows are triple glazed, not for energy conservation, but to aid in the careful control of humidity required to preserve documents in the building. To maintain precise temperature and humidity conditions, the mechanical and control systems are designed to operate more accurately than required for most other buildings.

The reinforced concrete roof and wall structure of the Pusey Library is typical of many underground buildings. One aspect of the structure that is not typical is its design for future expansion. As part of a long-range plan for the library system, a large building may replace one of the older structures on the northeast corner of the site. The columns and foundations in this portion of Pusey Library are designed to support a six-story structure.

The $5.6 million construction cost ($64.37 per square foot in 1976) does not appear particularly high considering the quality of the building and some of the extraordinary techniques required. A total fund of $8.4 million was raised for the project, from which additional costs related to the building were paid. These included the unusually complicated preliminary site work—relocation of major electric lines, water lines, and storm drains—fees, furnishing, and five years of operation and maintenance.

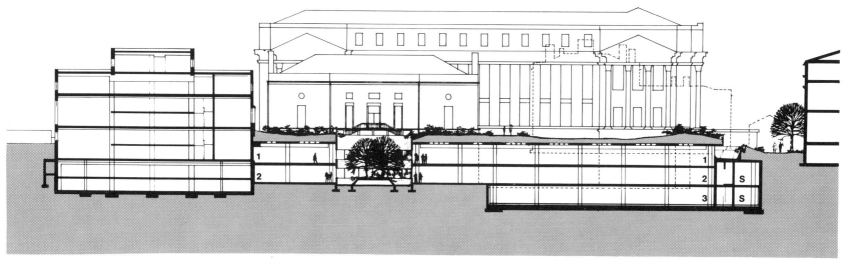

Section

Energy Use Considerations

Pusey Library was designed in the early 1970s and, according to the architects, energy conservation was not a major concern in buildings designed at that time. Nevertheless, the exterior envelope of the building has several energy-conserving characteristics. For example, most of the exterior is either in contact with the earth or shares common walls with adjacent buildings; windows are triple glazed; and the roof is adequately if not optimally insulated by today's standards.

Energy is supplied to the building in three forms—chilled water for cooling, steam for heating, and electricity for heating, lighting, and other requirements. In 1980 the combined energy use for the building was 104,000 Btu/sq ft—47 percent for chilled water, 43 percent for electricity, and 10 percent for steam. Although this level of energy consumption appears high compared with many energy-efficient buildings built more recently, the precise operating conditions very critically influence the energy consumption in Pusey Library. In large portions of the building containing rare and valuable manuscripts and other materials, interior temperature is maintained at 70°F and relative humidity at 50 percent year-round. These conditions are permitted to vary only slightly—relative humidity can vary only from 48 to 52 percent—before the mechanical system is activated. Maintaining this environment year-round obviously increases energy consumption.

Left: View from the main entrance toward Harvard Yard, photograph by Edward Jacoby.

The unusual climate control requirements of Pusey Library make energy use comparisons with conventional library buildings difficult. There is some evidence, however, to suggest that the below-grade design is contributing to energy conservation. First, the stringent temperature and humidity conditions are maintained with the air system operating only fifteen hours per day. In addition, the systems can be shut off without affecting humidity or temperature for as much as eight hours or longer. This would seem to indicate that the large mass and reduced infiltration of the underground structure are assets under these conditions. Another indication of the relative performance of the building can be found by examining the original energy use projections. When the building was first designed, electrical use was expected to be approximately twice the 1980 consumption figures and steam use was predicted to be five times as much. Some of the reduction is attributable to conservation measures taken once the building was in operation.

In 1980 Dr. Thomas Quinn studied energy consumption at Pusey Library along with several other Harvard University buildings [3.1]. Pusey Library was, in fact, consuming more energy than most of the other library buildings. For the most part, this was to be expected because the stringent environmental requirements. Dr. Quinn did suggest, however, that further energy savings could be made at Pusey Library if spaces were reorganized to consolidate rare books and desirable temperature and humidity requirements were redefined. Basically, the inherent characteristics of deep underground space—constant temperature and humidity—could be used more directly for the rare books on the lower levels of the building. Such a strategy would naturally entail some trade-offs that may not be considered acceptable in this particular building—the functional arrangement of the building would be changed, and the rare books would be in spaces that would be uncomfortably cool for people. Nevertheless, exploiting the characteristics of underground space in this manner could be useful in future designs.

Project Data

Project: Nathan Marsh Pusey Library

Location: Cambridge, Massachusetts

Owner: President and Fellows of Harvard College

Building type: Library

Completion date: 1976

Project size: 87,000 sq. ft.

Construction cost: $5,600,000 (including landscaping)

Structure: Cast-in-place reinforced concrete roof and walls; granite is used for exposed exterior walls; concrete slab-on-grade floor

Earth cover: 90 percent of exterior wall area is covered; 100 percent of total roof area is covered with 1 to 3 ft. of earth

Insulation: 2-in.-thick rigid extruded polystyrene on roof; urethane insulation on walls

Waterproofing: Mastic coating applied over neoprene sheet membrane on roof; liquid neoprene applied over concrete walls embedded with ironite

Heating system: High-pressure, single-duct, variable-volume HVAC system using centrally supplied steam with electric reheat and electric perimeter heating

Cooling system: Centrally supplied chilled water provided to cooling coils of HVAC system

Lighting: Fluorescent and incandescent

Energy Use: 104,000 Btu/sq ft/yr

Electricity	3.94×10^9Btu	(1,153,922 kWh)
Steam	$.88 \times 10^9$Btu	(884×10^6Btu)
Chilled water	4.23×10^9Btu	(14,679 ton-days)
Total	9.05×10^9Btu	

Note: Energy use figures are for 1980. Energy use in this building is heavily influenced by the strict environmental controls necessary to preserve books and manuscripts; certain zones are kept at 70°F and 50% relative humidity year-round.

Heating degree days: 5,621

Cooling degree days: 661

Credits

Architect: Hugh Stubbins and Associates, Inc., Cambridge, Massachusetts

Structural engineer: LeMessurier Associates/SCI

Mechanical engineer: van Zelm, Heywood and Shadford

Consulting soil engineers: Haley and Aldrich, Inc.

Other consultants: Bolt, Beranek and Newman, Inc.

Contractors: The Volpe Construction Company, Inc., general; Bond Brothers Inc., excavation

Photographs: Edward Jacoby/APG and Steve Rosenthal

Law Library Addition

University of Michigan
Ann Arbor, Michigan

Architect: Gunnar Birkerts and Associates

In order to harmonize with the historical character of the surrounding buildings and to preserve open space on the surface, the University of Michigan Law Library addition is placed completely below grade. The 77,000-square foot building is attached to and entered from the older Legal Research Building, one of the prominent pseudo-Gothic buildings forming the Law School Quadrangle on the Ann Arbor, Michigan, campus. In spite of limited exposure to the surface, the new addition is a remarkable example of the potential for providing natural light, view, and dramatic interior spaces in deep underground structures.

Constructed between 1924 and 1933, the buildings forming the original Law Quadrangle were designed in a Gothic style, modeled after the Inns of Court of London. The master plan for the Law School, which occupies an entire city block, was completed in its final form except for the southeastern corner of the complex. This area was designated as the site for the proposed Law Library addition. Since constructing a new addition to match the historical buildings was completely impractical, the major concern was compatibility of the new structure with the old. In addition, the architect felt that a structure placed in the open area next to the older library would shift the center of gravity of the entire complex. A completely underground design was the only solution that could achieve both compatibility with the older structures and preserve the balance and the existing open space and views on the site.

The lowest of the three levels of the library addition is at a depth of 56 feet beneath the surface. The floor plan is L shaped, with the only entrance occurring from the lower level of the adjacent older library. The central feature of the building from both the exterior and interior is a 150- by 26-foot sloping skylight facing the older building from within a V-shaped moat. A smaller, triangular-shaped skylight is located at the southeast corner of the building. Although the sloping skylights only extend down to the level of the upper floor, all levels are set back from the light well, forming balconies and permitting the light to enter the lowest level. A grand open stairway in the center of the light well area is designed as an elaborate suspended form. The busiest areas of the building—card catalogs, offices, and reading rooms—are on the top floor. The second level contains mainly stacks and individual carrels, while the lowest level has more stacks, offices, and a student lounge illuminated by the smaller triangular skylight. Each student is assigned a carrel, which is wired for anticipated computer terminals. The building is designed to accommodate approximately 500 people (246 in carrels), with 180,000 volumes in finished space and 200,000 to 300,000 volumes in unfinished space. For many of the inwardly oriented activities in a library, the underground location with its limited exposure to the outside is not considered a detriment.

Compared with other underground buildings, the exterior form of the Law Library addition is among the most subtle and understated. The site is completely flat, and no portion of the building extends above grade except for railings around the sunken skylights and two fire exits. Although the skylights indicate that a structure is present beneath the green lawn, the edges and shape of the building are not completely evident. The ability to minimize the presence of the building is aided by the fact that it is an addition

rather than an independent structure. This alleviates the problems of designing exterior masses for entrance, service, and mechanical equipment.

While the Law Library addition does not intrude on its site or neighboring buildings, it is not without character and visual interest when viewed from the exterior. The sloping, angular forms of the skylight wells are unusual and from some angles provide intriguing views of the interior and reflections of both interior and exterior elements. At night the skylights permit views of the lighted interior and, even more dramatically, emit a glow that lights the exterior of the old Law Library.

Special Design Concerns

Clearly the most notable aspect of the Law Library addition design is the manner in which natural light and exterior view are provided to the totally underground spaces. The sloping limestone wall and angled skylight above seem to direct the natural light down to all levels of the building while directing the view upward. Views of the old Gothic building, trees, and the sky are framed, and new perspectives are formed as they are seen from unique angles. Three-foot-deep mirrors are placed on the sloping supports of the glazed area, providing a variety of reflections of exterior elements. In addition, the mirrors create complex patterns of light reflected onto the large sloping limestone wall.

Since the light and view are concentrated in the light wells at the building edges, the library interior is designed essentially as one large open space to maximize the benefits from the dynamic central space. Natural light can be seen from most areas of the building, although the open plan is

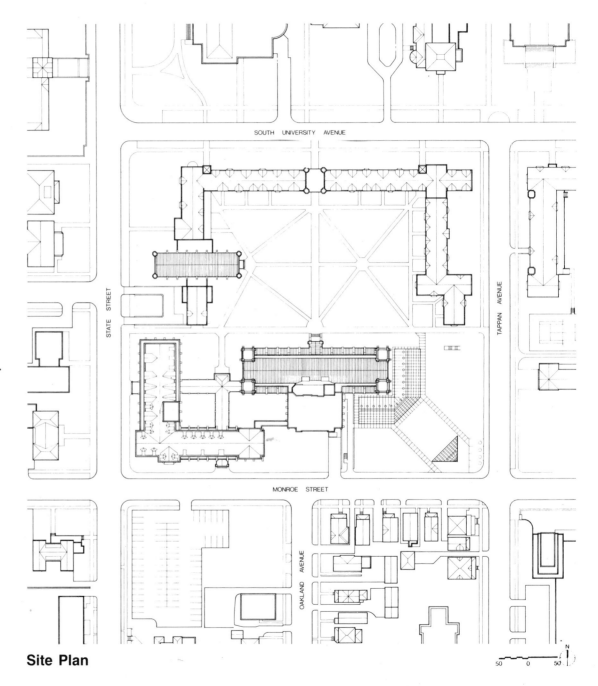

Site Plan

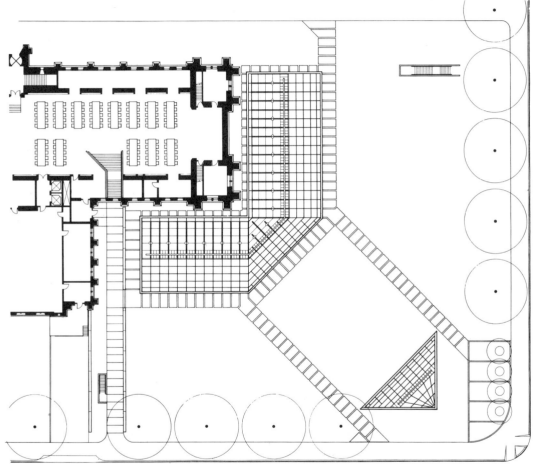

Grade Level Plan

*Above: The sloping skylight viewed from the roof of the old Legal Research Building.
Below: Light reflected onto the sloping wall three levels below grade.*

less than ideal for acoustical control. Balconies overlooking multistory spaces and the sculptural central stairway relieve any sense of enclosure from being underground. The upper portion of the sloping limestone wall on the exterior of the building helps to reflect light into the space; It may, however, eventually be covered with vines to soften the exterior appearance and bring more greenery into the building.

One area of special concern in the design of underground buildings is the entry. Because this building is attached to and entered from the older above-grade structure, many of the inherent problems are eliminated. The new addition is not intended to be perceived as a separate structure, and entry from outdoors occurs in the conventional sequence through the older building. The new building is actually entered by descending a wide stairway from the lower level of the older building. This entry leads directly to the dramatic central space along the sloping light well.

Building Technology and Costs

The roof and intermediate floors are reinforced concrete waffle-plate slabs. Interior columns and walls were minimized as much as possible in spite of the heavy loads from the earth-covered roof and book stacks on the interior. Exterior walls are cast-in-place reinforced concrete. The sloping light well is supported by vertical concrete piles. These piles are placed adjacent to each other to form a retaining wall with prestressed concrete tiebacks inserted into the earth beneath the older structure.

The roof is waterproofed with a built-up membrane of 4-ply coal tar pitch and glass

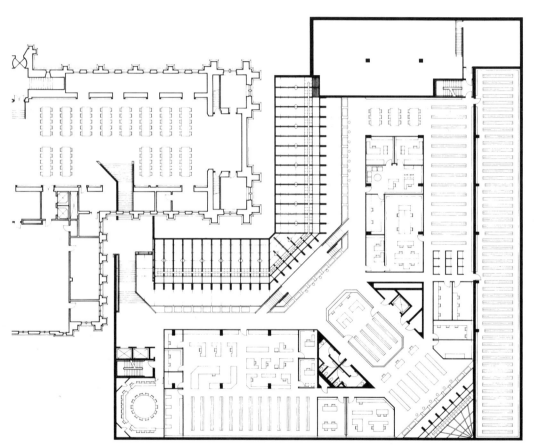

Floor Plan—One Level Below Grade

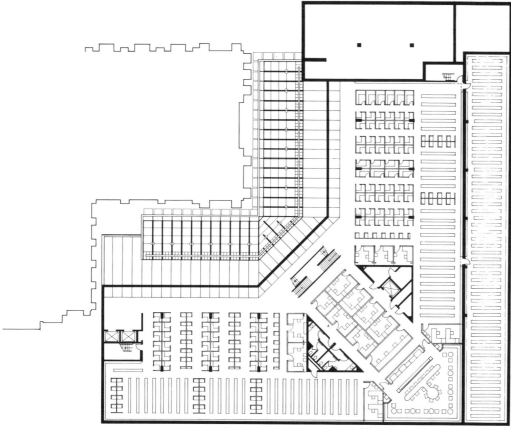

Floor Plan—Three Levels Below Grade

fabric. Placed over the waterproofing is a protection board, 1½ inches of polystyrene insulation and 1½ to 4½ feet of earth. Below-grade walls are waterproofed with a 3-ply coal tar pitch and glass fabric membrane covered with protection board. A similar 4-ply built-up membrane is placed over a mud slab beneath the concrete floor of the building. A lead membrane provides waterproofing behind the sloping limestone wall. A steam pipe is located in the base of the V-shaped trough to melt snow in winter. The $9.5 million cost of the building, contributed by law school alumni and other donors, reflects the many unique features of the building along with the relatively expensive finish materials and furnishings.

Energy Use Considerations

The two main energy conservation concepts employed in the design of the Law Library addition—maximizing contact with the earth and natural lighting—are a direct result of the aesthetic decisions made by the architect. Because of the completely below-grade placement and relatively small total glass area for a building of this size, the building envelope design is inherently energy conserving. Two problems with overhead glazing—glare and excessive heat gain—are reduced by the presence of the older building to the west. Efficient air-return parabolic luminaires are used for general lighting, and fixtures near the light wells have photocell controls so they are automatically turned off when natural light is available at an adequate level.

One significant factor in examining the energy use of the Law Library addition is the extended time it is occupied. It is open

112 hours per week, twice as long as many buildings. Based on this occupancy, it was estimated that the building would consume 64,000 Btu/sq ft/yr. If the building were operated for a more conventional 50 hours per week, the energy consumption would be reduced to 28,700 Btu/sq ft/yr according to estimates. It is important to note that steam energy used in the single absorption chiller for the building is not included in these total energy use figures. Only the electrical power to support the refrigeration has been included, because the steam is supplied as a free by-product of the university's steam turbine electric generators. The steam is at a lower pressure than is considered optimal for efficiency, but since it is an otherwise wasted source of energy, in this case it is considered a good strategy.

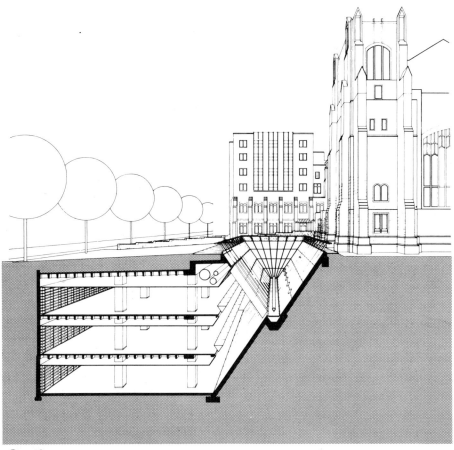

Section

Project Data

Project: University of Michigan Law Library Addition

Location: Ann Arbor, Michigan

Owner: University of Michigan

Building type: Library

Completion date: 1981

Project size: 77,000 sq. ft. (includes 14,300 sq. ft. of unfinished space)

Construction cost: $9,500,000

Structure: Cast-in-place reinforced concrete roof, walls, and intermediate floors; slab-on-grade floor at lowest level; sloping light well is supported by vertical concrete piles tied back to retain the foundation of the older adjacent structure

Earth cover: 90 percent of total roof area is covered with 1½ to 4½ ft. of earth, skylights are the only exposed area; 100 percent of exterior wall area is in contact with earth (assuming glazed areas are included in roof area)

Insulation: 1½-inch-thick extruded polystyrene on the roof; 2-inch-thick extruded polystyrene on below-grade walls in some locations only wall insulation below grade

Waterproofing: 4-ply coal tar pitch and glass fabric membrane on roof and beneath floor; 3-ply coal tar pitch and glass fabric membrane on walls; lead behind limestone wall in light well

Heating system: Centrally supplied hot water delivered to reheat coils in variable-air-volume distribution boxes

Cooling system: Low-pressure steam, a by-product from the central University steam turbine electric generators, is used in a single absorption unit to supply chilled water to the coils in the air-distribution system

Lighting: 1- by 4-ft. two-lamp, air-return parabolic luminaires

Energy use: 64,000 Btu/sq ft/yr projected based on 112 operating hours per week

Heating degree days: 6,228 (Detroit)

Cooling degree days: 743 (Detroit)

Number of occupants: Approximately 500 capacity

Occupancy schedule: 16 hours per day, 7 days per week

Credits

Architect: Gunnar Birkerts and Associates, Birmingham, Michigan

Structural engineer: Robert M. Darvas and Associates

Mechanical and electrical engineer: Joseph R. Loring and Associates

Cost consultants: Wolf and Company

Waterproofing consultants: Construction Consultants, Inc.

Contractor: J. A. Fredman, Inc., general

Photographs: Timothy Hursley, The Arkansas Office

Walker Community Library

Minneapolis, Minnesota

Architect: BRW Architects

Located at a busy intersection in a south Minneapolis commercial center, the Walker Community Library is a satellite facility serving the immediate neighborhood. The 18,500-square foot structure contains a large reading room with a moderate size book collection and a public meeting room for a variety of community functions. The almost completely subsurface design resulted from a combination of site-related factors and the desire to take advantage of the sound reduction and energy-conserving benefits of underground space. In a general sense, a library and community meeting room are functions that are well suited to a subsurface location. The more limited exposure to the surface is not a major drawback for these inwardly oriented activities, and except for the library staff, most of the users are in the facility for limited amounts of time.

One important factor in placement of the library below grade was the desire to create a community amenity on the site. A small urban plaza was thus created that provides space for neighborhood activities, such as a well-established annual art fair, and also serves as a gateway to the adjacent boulevard leading to the city's extensive lake and park system. An even more significant site influence is the very limited size of the site and the requirement for parking. In this case the underground design makes it possible to place an 18,500-square foot building on a 20,000-square foot site and provide the necessary parking on the roof. This alternative costs less than acquiring additional land and building a conventional above-grade building with on-grade parking adjacent to it. Another alternative, elevating the building with parking beneath it, was determined to be less cost-effective and less desirable for other reasons related to the building, program, and site. Thus, the

underground design made it possible to utilize a very convenient site in the most desirable of available locations in spite of the site's physical limitations.

The very high level of activity and noise created by traffic on the adjacent streets represented a third major site force that was resolved by the underground design. Not only does the large reading room benefit from its quiet, isolated location, but the exterior sunken courtyard is buffered from street noise as well.

The exterior form and character of the building is designed in response to its urban site. The concrete and brick forms visible on the surface are appropriate extensions of the hard surfaces and brick buildings surrounding the site, although they are softened by extensive planters. On rural sites, underground structures are often designed to blend the building form with the natural landscape, sometimes making the edges almost indistinguishable. In this case however, planters, walls, and other above-grade elements were necessary to define the edges of the building and to direct people along sidewalks and to the entrance of the building. The street-level entrance, mechanical equipment, and elevator shaft are designed as a small grouping of above-grade concrete forms, giving the building an identifiable form and easily recognizable entrance.

Special Design Concerns

The means of entry in underground buildings is an important design concern; entryways should be designed to alleviate any negative feelings associated with going downward. In most cases architect David Bennett prefers to enter a building horizontally at a lower level through exterior

ramps and courtyards, just as one would enter any conventional building. The very restrictive Walker Library site, however, presented too many constraints. Thus, the entry occurs in a small building mass at grade enclosing a large open staircase and elevator leading to the meeting and library spaces below. Any potentially negative feelings are offset by natural light from skylights and windows in the entry area, open space around the stairwell, and views into the courtyard at all levels.

Since the main occupied spaces in this building are completely underground, with only the relatively small sunken courtyard available as a connection to the outside environment, interior design and maximizing opportunities for natural light and view become important. Aside from the small employee lounge and eating area located adjacent to the courtyard, the main reading room space is the major concern, since meeting rooms, library storage, and work rooms do not typically require natural light. The interior space of the reading room is relatively high (approximately 20 feet) with an open grid suspended from the ceiling that contains light fixtures. This feeling of openness is effective and also increases the impact of the available natural light.

In addition to the high interior space of the reading room, the unique use of a large mirror adjacent to a single large window facing the courtyard greatly enhances the available view and natural light. Although the window is located at one end of the large space, the mirror set at 45 degrees to the wall reflects light into the majority of the room and creates the illusion of looking out a large window from nearly any point in the room.

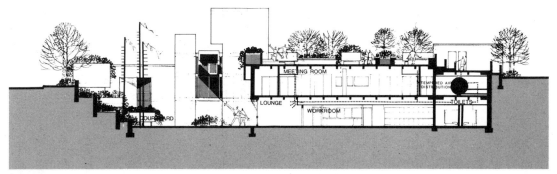

Section

Building Technology and Costs

The structural system of the Walker Library consists of conventional reinforced concrete roof and walls. The roof structure, which spans the entire reading room area, is more heavily designed than normal to support the earth and parking area above. The incremental cost of improving the roof (parking and landscaping) compared with a conventional structure was $3.78 per square foot. This additional expense was more than offset by the smaller site that could then be used. A net savings to the client of $125,000 resulted from not having to purchase additional land.

Because the building occupies the entire site and is bounded on three sides by streets and the fourth by existing buildings, the surrounding earth had to be retained by sheet piling during construction. This represents an expense that is required only on restrictive, infill sites and is not necessary for all underground construction. Even with these additional costs, savings in exterior finishing materials resulted in a total cost of approximately $75 per square foot, comparable to above-grade library buildings of this general quality.

Energy Use Considerations

Although actual energy-use figures are not yet available, the designer's original estimates for the building are that demand for heating and cooling will be reduced by 40 percent compared with a conventional above-grade building with similar characteristics. This saving results primarily from placing the building almost completely below grade with little exposure to the surface environment. Because of the decreased energy demand, only two

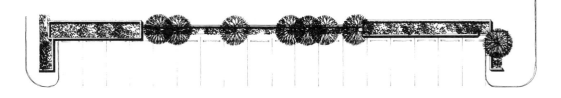

PARKING 32 AUTOS

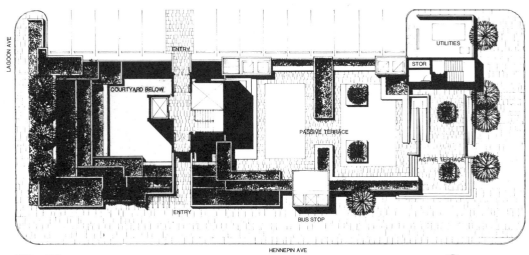

Site Plan

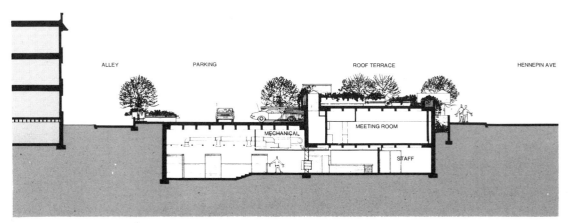

Section

79

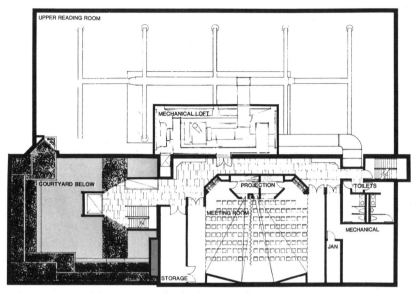

Floor Plan—One Level Below Grade

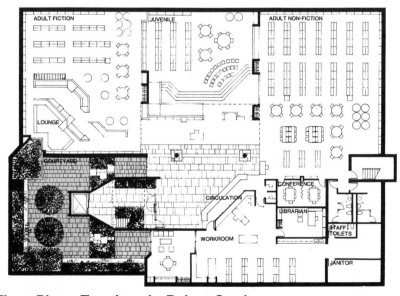

Floor Plan—Two Levels Below Grade

residential-sized gas-fired furnaces and condenser units are required for heating and cooling.

Several other devices and techniques are also used in this building to enhance energy savings. A heat recovery system reduces the energy used to heat and cool outside air for ventilation, and insulating shutters arc rolled down over the windows at night. In addition, the hard surfaces on the roof are shaded by plant materials and vines hanging from trellis structures supported by light fixtures over the parking area.

Project Data

Project: Walker Community Library

Location: Minneapolis, Minnesota

Owner: City of Minneapolis

Building type: Public library

Completion date: 1980

Project size: 18,500 sq.ft.

Construction cost:

General	$1,131,500
Mechanical	173,500
Electrical	132,000
Total	$1,437,000

Structure: Cast-in place reinforced concrete roof and walls; slab-on-grade floor

Earth cover: 95 percent of total wall and roof area is earth covered; roof is covered with a 4-in.- to 2-ft.-thick layer of earth

Insulation: Extruded polystyrene, 2 to 4 in. on roof, 2 in. on walls to a depth of 6 ft.

Waterproofing: 60-mil. rubberized asphalt and polyethylene film

Windows: 210 sq. ft. total area

Heating system: Gas-fired forced air

Cooling system: Two zone condensing units with forced-air delivery

Lighting: Quick-connect fluorescent and metal halide

Energy use: Information not available

Heating degree days: 8,159

Cooling degree days: 585

Occupancy schedule: 40 to 60 hours per week

Credits

Architect: BRW Architects, Inc., Minneapolis, Minnesota (formerly Myers and Bennett/BRW)

Structural engineer: Meyer, Borgman, and Johnson, Inc.

Mechanical engineer: Oftedal, Locke, Broadston and Associates, Inc.

Interior design: Kalbac and Associates, Inc.

Contractors: George F. Cook Construction Co., general; A.C.G. Mechanical Inc., mechanical; and Sterling Electrical Construction, electrical

Photographs: Pat Siegrist

Above: Aerial view of sunken courtyard.
Below: Interior of main reading room with mirror reflecting outside light and view.

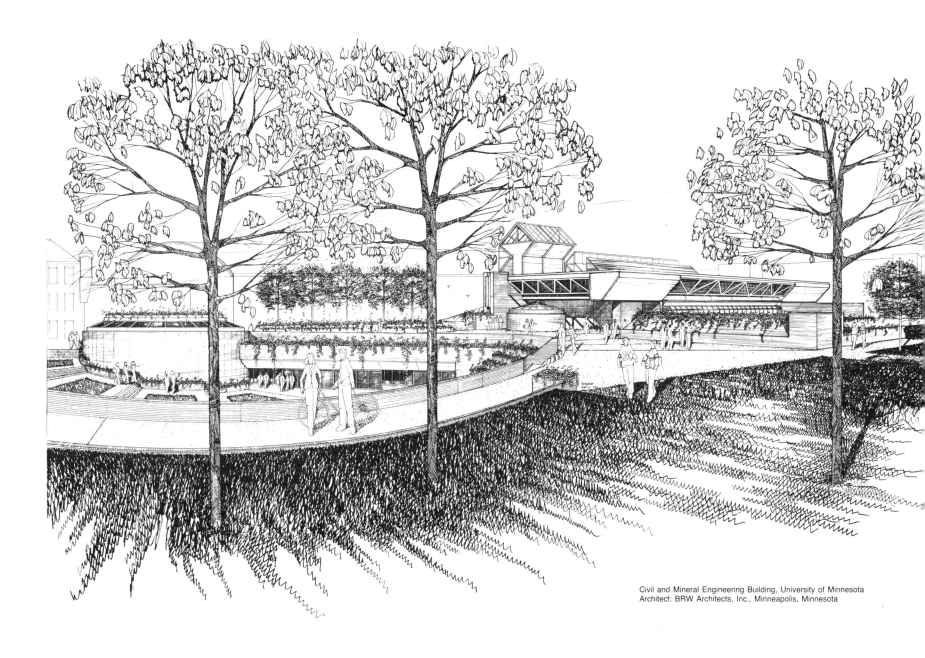

Civil and Mineral Engineering Building, University of Minnesota
Architect: BRW Architects, Inc., Minneapolis, Minnesota

Chapter 4: Educational Institutions

Civil and Mineral Engineering Building

University of Minnesota
Minneapolis, Minnesota

Architect: BRW Architects

The Civil and Mineral Engineering Building on the Minneapolis campus of the University of Minnesota represents one of the most innovative underground structures in the United States. Named the Outstanding Civil Engineering Achievement of 1983 by the American Society of Civil Engineers, the 150,000-square foot structure includes classrooms and laboratories as well as department and faculty offices. The complex building is shaped by diverse program requirements and numerous site forces, as well as the desire to demonstrate energy-conservation techniques and the use of underground space. Placing the building 95 percent below grade is not only an energy-conservation strategy, but also provides open space on the densely built campus and significantly reduces the mass of the structure.

Because of the unique geology of the Minneapolis-St. Paul area, this building includes two distinct types of underground space—the more conventional cut-and-cover space near the surface and the deep mined space in the bedrock. Approximately 50 feet of soil lie above the bedrock, in which up to three floor levels of cut-and-cover space occur. The soil is underlain by a 30-foot-thick layer of limestone, which acts as a natural roof over the space mined out of the softer sandstone below. The mined space is connected to the building above by two shafts through the limestone. The resulting space, used mainly for laboratories with some offices, is on two levels with the lowest floor level 110 feet beneath the surface. At this depth there is a virtually constant moderate temperature and complete isolation from surface noise and vibration.

The organization of the site plan and the resulting form of the building are determined mainly by a few key features of the site combined with special program requirements. In particular, the site was designed to serve as a major bus terminal for the campus and as the northern gateway to the Institute of Technology portion of the campus. In addition, the building is connected to adjacent structures underground to permit indoor pedestrian circulation. Finally, in spite of the presence of a tall building directly to the south of the site, good exposure to the sun is required for the various solar energy systems.

The site and program issues are resolved by dividing the building into distinct portions with differing functions. On the western half of the site near the adjacent buildings, classrooms with connections to the adjacent structures are placed completely underground. On the surface is a spiral-shaped courtyard that provides open space, serves as the major building entry, and formally symbolizes the gateway to the Institute of Technology. On the eastern half of the site, out of the shadow of the tall existing building, are the laboratory and office spaces requiring solar exposure.

A central feature of this portion of the building is the four-story-high main structures laboratory where testing on large structural assemblages can take place. The roof of the main structures lab projects above grade, although the floor of the laboratory is three levels below grade. This above-grade mass allows for the at-grade delivery of large structural components and supports the various solar systems and devices. To the south of the laboratories are the faculty offices clustered around a

sunken courtyard. The bus terminal is placed along the northern edge of the site, where it will have the least impact on the environment visually as well as in terms of noise and air pollution.

The exterior form and character of the visible building elements reflect the diversity of the major components of the design. The spiral-shaped plaza on the western half of the site has the character of a heavily landscaped urban open space. The curved form directs pedestrians to the major entry of the building as well as around the site. Although this is an active, urban space with brick-enclosed planters and extensive hard surfaces, it maintains the character of a nonbuilding. It is not necessarily evident that a major building lies beneath this area—or at least the extent and edges of the building are not apparent.

In contrast to the courtyard area, the above-grade mass on the eastern half of the site serves many of the same functions that a conventional building does. Although the one-level mass that projects above grade is quite a small portion of the 150,000-square foot structure, it is large enough to serve as a symbol for the engineering department. The large, exposed trusses, the solar elements on the roof and south face of the mass, and the brightly colored metal elements in all of the exposed portions of the building contribute to the high-tech appearance of the structure. These elements, however, are combined with brick surfaces and extensive use of plant materials to merge the building with the site and create an appearance harmonious with the surrounding brick buildings. The above-grade building mass also serves to define the edges of the site more clearly, screens the pedestrian areas of the site from the

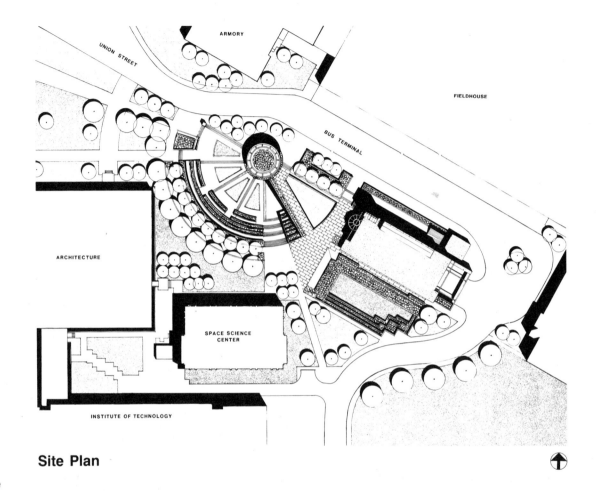

Site Plan

road, and provides the loading dock for the building on the east end, which is also screened from the courtyard.

Special Design Concerns

Similar to most public buildings that are predominantly underground, special attention is warranted in certain key areas of design. These areas—the entry, interior design, and provision of natural light and

exterior views—are those that differ most from conventional buildings and thus have the potential to reinforce any negative reactions to underground space.

The main entry to the Civil and Mineral Engineering Building is approached by descending through the spiral-shaped courtyard. This entrance does not emphasize the feeling of going downward but offsets it by providing a large open area with a relatively gradual decline. One

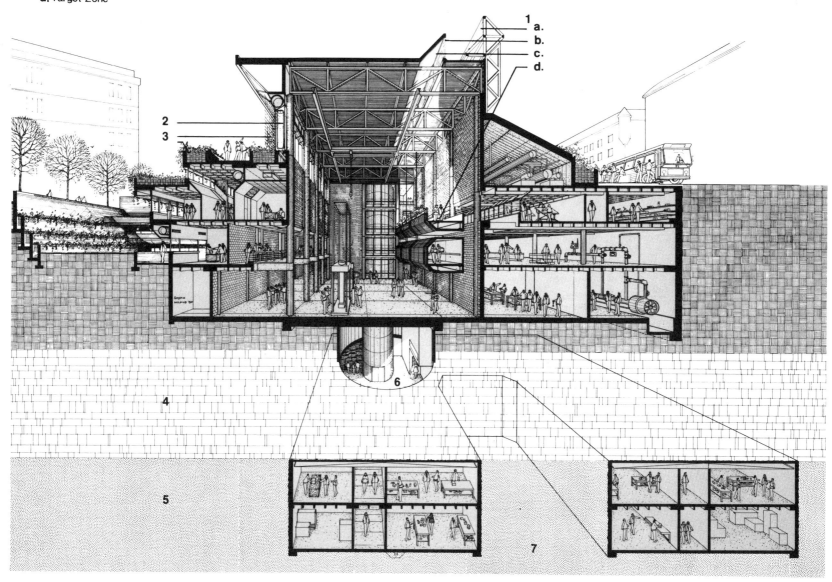

1 Passive Solar Optic System
  a. Fresnel Reflector
  b. North Skymonitor
  c. Fresnel Mirror
  d. Target Zone

2 Trombe Wall Passive/Active Solar Collector

3 Deciduous Solar Shading

4 Earth Sheltering

5 Mined Space 110 Ft. Below Grade

6 Active Solar Optic System Beamed Sunlight

7 Active Ground Water Cooling System

then enters the building horizontally and finds naturally lighted public area similar to a conventional building. Entry can also occur from the lower levels of adjacent buildings. In this case the entrance corridor terminates in a high, naturally lighted public space also. The bright red metal which appears on the building exterior is used on certain interior surfaces as well providing warmth and visual interest. While the metal-covered elements and red carpeting serve as accent colors, most of the interior surfaces are light in color to maximize the natural light that does enter the building.

In this large underground building with limited window area, variety in the size and arrangement of interior spaces and

the maximum use of the available natural light are essential for orientation and for habitability of the spaces. The actual allocation of windows is closely related to the functions in the building. For example, most of the faculty offices have exterior windows with views into the sunken courtyard. Offices that are not located on exterior walls have clerestory windows that provide natural light from the corridors or public spaces with exterior windows. Natural light in most of the classroom and laboratory spaces in the building is considered not only unnecessary but undesirable in many cases.

The main design strategy in these areas is to provide orientation to the surface and spatial variety with high, naturally lighted

public spaces and circulation areas. This is accomplished with the two-story rotunda from which the classrooms are entered, the multilevel space near the building entry, and most prominently, with the four-story-high structures lab that can be viewed from several below-grade levels in the building. The main structures lab serves as a central atrium for the surrounding spaces and receives natural light from above by two means—through the translucent Trombe wall on the upper level and by means of a passive solar optical system that projects light downward through a roof monitor onto a major walkway suspended in the lab space.

Many of the design techniques evident in the cut-and-cover space—skylights,

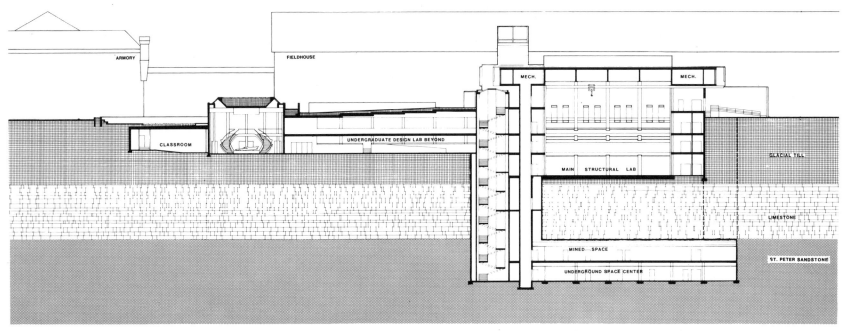

Section

courtyards, borrowed light, and high spaces—are commonly used in underground buildings near the surface. The mined space in the Civil and Mineral Engineering Building presents unusual constraints, however. The only connection to the surface is through two shafts containing stairs and elevators, and the height of the space is limited to two levels. For this reason most of the mined space has been designed as mining and environmental engineering laboratories. Exposure to the surface is not desired for these functions, and in fact, they can benefit from the isolation from climate, noise, and vibration.

In spite of the predominant use of mined space for laboratories in this building, windowless, isolated spaces should not automatically be assumed to be suitable for only a very limited range of functions with as few inhabitants as possible. In fact, many massive above-grade structures include extensive areas on the interior with no direct access to outside light and view. As a means of exploring the design possibilities and requirements for human habitation in these isolated spaces, offices for the faculty, researchers, and staff of the Underground Space Center are located in a portion of the mined space of the CME Building. The interior design of the office area employs glass partitions between the private offices and the general open plan office area, as well as between the corridor and the office complex, to give a greater sense of space and openness. Of particular interest is the use of a solar optical system to provide natural light to the circulation area 110 feet beneath the surface. Two heliostats on the roof capture sunlight and direct it through lenses in a vertical shaft so that it can emerge through openings in the

ceiling similar to a conventional skylight. In addition, an experimental remote view optical system (Ectascope) provides an exterior view of the campus to the same circulation area. This system functions much like a periscope, using mirrors and lenses.

In most underground buildings with occupied spaces no more than three levels below grade, it is not difficult to comply with conventional building codes in terms of fire safety. Enclosed stairways can provide paths of escape and the buildings often include sprinkler systems over the entire floor area. In mined space with occupied areas 110 feet below the surface, however, more unusual conditions exist requiring special considerations. The two shafts containing elevators and stairways to the surface are placed so that they are within safe distances specified by the codes and provide two paths of escape from all areas. The major concern is that a person may not be able to climb ten flights of stairs. The difficulty of such a climb for many people is much greater than descending the same number of stairs from a high-rise structure. For this reason, there is a room halfway up each stairwell that will have its own pressurized outside air supply thus enabling occupants to take a safe refuge if they are unable to continue out of the building.

Building Technology and Costs

In the major portion of the building above the bedrock, the structural system consists

Above: Elements of the passive and active solar optical systems on the building roof. Below: Walkway through the main structures lab illuminated by the passive solar system.

of cast-in-place concrete walls, columns, and waffle-slab floors. Over the large structures laboratory, a steel truss roof supports a 15-ton capacity traveling crane. In the mined space, the maximum span of the limestone roof is approximately 50 feet. The space is created in a room-and-pillar configuration that can be replicated or expanded wherever the same geological conditions are present and could be connected to entrances at the nearby river bluffs. The self-supporting limestone roof is rock-bolted to ensure its structural integrity. The relatively soft sandstone walls are curved and lined with concrete to enhance their effective strength.

A perched water table, which is drained to a storm sewer below, exists above the limestone. Water that seeps through the rock is collected on a lightweight galvanized metal roof suspended from the rock above and is drained away to the existing deep sewer tunnels in the sandstone. A second water table exists at roughly the floor level of the mined space but is drawn down in the vicinity of the building by wellpoint drains.

In spite of the complexity of this building, as well as the innovative technologies and methods of construction, the total cost—$86 per square foot—is within the range of conventional large campus laboratory and classroom buildings. Part of the reason for the cost similarity is that the portion of the costs for mechanical and electrical systems in a laboratory building is a significant percentage of the total—29 percent in this case—but does not differ much when installed below rather than above grade. Sitework on an underground building is likely to be higher than on a conventional building, but in this case the sitework does not seem unreasonably high since it includes atypical features such as extensive landscaping to provide a gateway to the entire Institute of Technology.

The cost of creating mined space is lower than creating unfinished space in the cut-and-cover or above-grade portions of the building. In fact, additional mined space was included in the project when construction bids for the mined space were below estimates. The most expensive

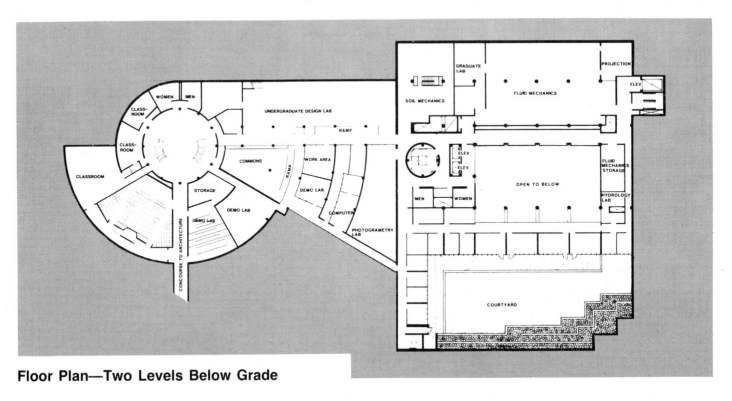

Floor Plan—Two Levels Below Grade

aspect of creating mined space is blasting the shafts through the limestone layer. The incremental cost of creating more space at this level would be favorable as long as the existing shafts can be used for fire exits, access, and ventilation. Extensive expansion will be most cost-effective if shafts can be minimized and horizontal access from the nearby river bluffs can be utilized.

Energy Use Considerations

The Civil and Mineral Engineering Building is unique in that the Minnesota State Legislature mandated that the building serve as a demonstration of earth sheltering and energy-conservation

techniques. As a result, the building includes a variety of systems and devices ranging from accepted, proven technology to experimental systems that serve educational and research purposes.

One of the major energy-related design strategies is the placement of the building 95 percent below grade. Unlike most underground buildings that are generally within 30 feet of the surface, nearly one-third of this building is significantly deeper—80 to 110 feet—which presents a far more isolated, constant thermal environment. The degree to which this environment represents savings in heating and cooling depends on the ventilation requirements of these spaces. For this reason, heat recovery devices reduce the

energy expended to heat and cool incoming fresh air. In addition, the mechanical system was redesigned to take advantage of the supply of cold groundwater from the drainage network to augment cooling in parts of the building.

Most of the windows in the faculty office area are oriented to the south and southwest to benefit from solar gain in the winter. To offset the heat gain in summer, deciduous vines hang over some of the windows to provide shade while still permitting the sunlight to penetrate in winter. Most of the shading, however, is provided by permanent overhangs above the office windows. Another use of landscaping to enhance energy conservation in the building is the placement of deciduous overstory trees around the hard surface plaza areas that form the roof of the classroom spaces. Such trees reduce summer heat gain while allowing the sun to penetrate and warm the surfaces in winter.

To augment the space heating in the building, a water-filled Trombe wall is located along the south face of the above-grade mass of the building. Because of the extreme variations in the Minnesota climate, the system will operate in a different mode each season. During the spring and fall when the temperature difference between the interior and exterior is not too great, the Trombe wall will collect solar heat during the day and provide it to the building at night. During the winter, however, the great temperature difference between the building interior and exterior would result in losing any heat gained during the day through reradiation and conduction before it could be used to heat the building at night. Therefore, return air is forced through the Trombe chamber

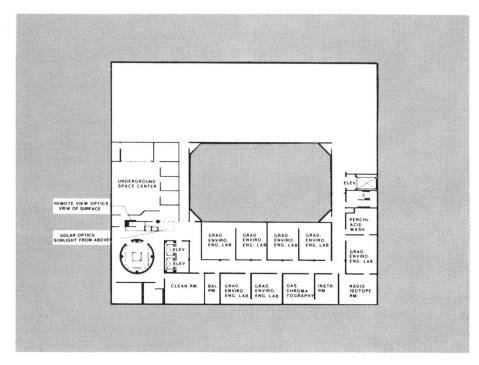

Floor Plan—Mined Space

during the day, making it an instantaneous solar collector. During the summer the Trombe wall system will be shaded from solar impact by vines and an automatic Mylar roll-down shade.

It is not expected that the heat provided by the Trombe wall system will supply the majority of the total heat required for such a large laboratory building. It is anticipated, however, that it can provide a cost-effective portion of the heating while serving as a highly visible demonstration of a hybrid passive/active solar heating system.

The most innovative energy-related systems in the building are the active and passive solar optical systems and the remote-view optical system. A solar optical system is a means of collecting sunlight, concentrating it, and directing it through the interior of a building by an assembly of lenses and mirrors to provide natural light. Such a system can affect energy consumption in three ways. First, it can reduce the amount of artificial lighting required. Second, by replacing artificial light with a light source that generates less internal heat, the cooling load can be decreased. Finally, some solar optical systems can provide natural light to deep underground or interior building spaces. Thus, the habitability of windowless spaces that have inherent energy-conserving characteristics can be enhanced, making such spaces acceptable for a wider range of functions.

According to the architect, solar optical systems promise to be among the most cost-effective of all solar energy systems. Beginning with a light source that provides about 8,000 footcandles of light at the surface, the system optically compresses the sunlight into narrow light streams, passes it through smaller apertures and corridors, and then spreads it out over the target space using no additional transmission energy. Furthermore, the light does not have to be converted into another form of energy. When combined with conventional artificial lighting under controlled conditions, the system has the potential to substantially reduce energy consumption for lighting interior spaces.

In this building the active and passive solar optical systems represent a limited installation mainly for demonstration purposes. The active system provides sunlight to one area of the mined space 110 feet beneath the surface, and the passive system provides light to a pedestrian walkway one level below grade in the main structures lab.

The Ectascope is a remote optics system based on the principal of the periscope. Being a purely optical system, it has the immediacy and three-dimensional quality of looking through a window. Although it is not directly related to reducing energy consumption, it contributes to enhancing the habitability of deep underground and other remote interior spaces. The demonstration application in this building provides a view of the campus to the reception area of the offices in the mined space.

Project Data

Project: Civil and Mineral Engineering Building

Location: Minneapolis, Minnesota

Owner: University of Minnesota

Building type: Classroom, laboratory, and office building

Completion date: 1982

Project size: 150,000 sq. ft. (including 48,000 sq. ft. in mined space)

Construction cost:

General	$7,446,000
Sitework	1,760,000
Mechanical	2,314,000
Electrical	1,380,000
Total	$12,900,000

Structure: Cast-in-place reinforced concrete roof, walls, and floor in most of the building; steel trusses spanning structures laboratory; self-supporting limestone roof and sandstone walls in mined space

Earth cover: In portion of the building above bedrock, 90 percent of total wall area is earth covered; 37 percent of the roof is covered with 12 to 48 in. of earth (remainder of the roof is 48 percent plaza and 15 percent conventional roof); entire envelope of mined space is in contact with the bedrock

Insulation: Extruded polystyrene, 2 in. on earth-covered roof and plazas, 3 to 6 in. on conventional roof, 2 in. on walls to a depth of 6 ft.

Waterproofing: 60-mil. rubberized asphalt and polyethylene film below grade and under plazas; built-up roof on exposed roof area

Heating system: Heating provided by coal-fired steam delivered from central plant with forced hot water to forced-air distribution system; heating augmented by solar Trombe wall system and passive solar direct gain

Cooling system: Steam-fired absorption water chiller with an outdoor cooling tower; chilled water is piped to variable-air-volume boxes for cool-air distribution; cooling augmented by the use of groundwater

Lighting system: Metal halide, H.P. sodium, and fluorescent; total connected load of 225,700 watts; lighting levels: 100 fc in laboratories, 30-60 fc in corridors, offices, and classrooms; lighting augmented by passive and active solar optical systems

Energy use: 50,000 to 65,000 Btu/sq ft/yr projected, excluding process energy

Heating degree days: 8,159

Cooling degree days: 585

Occupancy schedule: 40 to 60 hours per week in most areas, 70 to 80 hours per week in classrooms

Credits

Architect: BRW Architects, Inc., Minneapolis, Minnesota (formerly Myers and Bennett/BRW)

Structural engineer: Meyer, Borgman, and Johnson, Inc.

Mechanical engineer: Oftedal, Locke, Broadston and Associates, Inc.

Consulting engineer on mined space: Charles Nelson and Associates

Optical consultant: Dr. Michael Duguay, Bell Labs

Contractors: M.A. Mortenson Company, general; New Mech Companies, mechanical; Premier Electric Company, electrical

Photographs: George Heinrich

Wildwood School

Aspen, Colorado

Architect: David F. Gibson

Located in White River National Forest near Aspen, Colorado, Wildwood School is unique in its function and philosophy as well as its architecture. Built in 1974, the 3,600-square foot structure serves as a center for preschool education with an emphasis on the realms of nature and art. Based on the philosophy of the school's founder, Robert Lewis, the purpose of the school is to foster the creation of an environmental ethic in our society—something that can best be accomplished in the formative, creative, preschool years.

Nestled into a clearing between towering pines at an elevation of 8,000 feet, the building is almost entirely earth covered,

blending into the surrounding landscape. Rather than placing the building below existing grade, the earth is bermed around the domed and vaulted structure, making it a new landform on the site. Generally, the inwardly oriented activities of school classrooms are well suited to the controlled environment that is possible in underground space. In the case of the Wildwood School, the decision to build an earth-integrated structure was made for three primary reasons. The first is to blend with the natural setting to reinforce the environmental aesthetics that are part of the school's philosophy. Second, the uniqueness of a free-form, earth-covered structure serves to

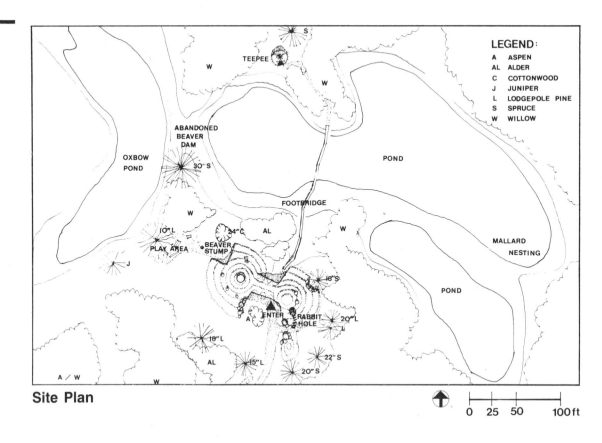

Site Plan

LEGEND:
A — ASPEN
AL — ALDER
C — COTTONWOOD
J — JUNIPER
L — LODGEPOLE PINE
S — SPRUCE
W — WILLOW

0 25 50 100 ft

introduce preschoolers to art and nature in a very special environment. Finally, the massive earth-covered structure is energy conserving.

The form and interior layout of the school reflect its philosophy that creative capacities are awakened in early childhood and that nature and art are intertwined in these early discoveries. Two large dome-shaped rooms are placed at the ends of the structure connected by a barrel-vault housing support services. School activities for the fifty preschoolers alternate between these two poles of activity called the "Nature Room" and the "Arts Room." Both rooms are constructed with a central space

for group activities and small spaces on the periphery for individual activities. All of the interior spaces are shaped in domed or vaulted forms with details reflecting nature—such as a tree-trunk fireplace—as well as many child-scale elements, such as small doorways, lofts, and a "rabbit-hole" entry at the top with a slide leading to the main floor. According to the architect, these intimate rooms and openings create a place where the child feels comfortable and confident, making it more conducive to self-expression and exploration.

The exterior image of the Wildwood School is unlike most conventional as well as

other underground buildings. The design concept goes beyond simply making most of the building invisible by placing it below grade. The organic curving forms of the structure itself and the arched openings create a distinct image of the building while giving it a quality that is more natural than man-made.

Even though the building is really an artificial landform, in this mountainous setting it is not clear where the building extends. This integration of building and site is reinforced by the planting of native grasses on the berms and rooftop and the lack of man-made, hard surface elements around the building. Such a naturalistic

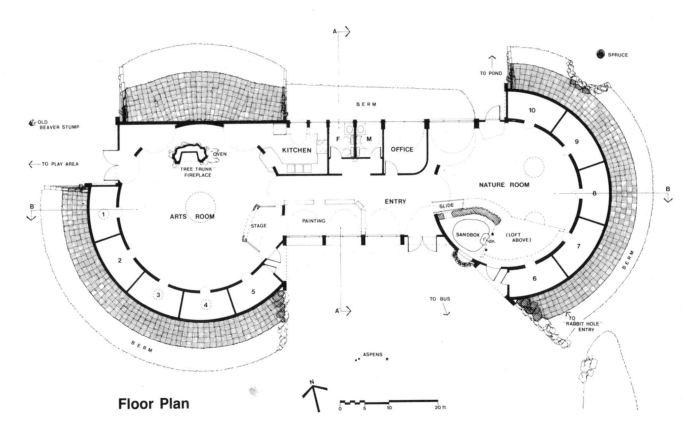

Floor Plan

design concept would be difficult, if not impossible, to achieve to this degree without an earth sheltered structure.

Special Design Concerns

In most underground buildings, the special design concerns focus on offsetting potentially negative aspects of underground or windowless space by attempting to create environments that are similar to conventional above-grade buildings. In the case of the Wildwood School, however, a very special and unique environment is desired. Entries and window openings almost appear to be holes burrowed into the earth, and interior spaces are designed to emphasize and exploit their unconventional shape. Natural light is provided through skylights over the large spaces; the lack of windows is desirable in the small activity areas where different ecological systems are modeled and distinct sensory experiences are created.

Building Technology

The domed and vaulted structure of the Wildwood School is intriguing not only for the exterior form and interior spaces created, but also for the efficiency demonstrated by the structural system.

Shell structures represent a far more efficient means of supporting heavy earth loads than flat roofs. In this case the ferro-concrete structure was formed by spraying concrete onto metal lath attached to reinforcing steel until the desired thickness was attained—5 inches at the top and 7 inches at the base. Concrete lips are formed above the door and window openings to retain the earth on the roof. Since standard rigid insulation products are unfeasible for a shell structure, polyurethane insulation is sprayed over the concrete to a thickness of 3 inches; the insulation is then covered by a liquid-applied waterproofing membrane.

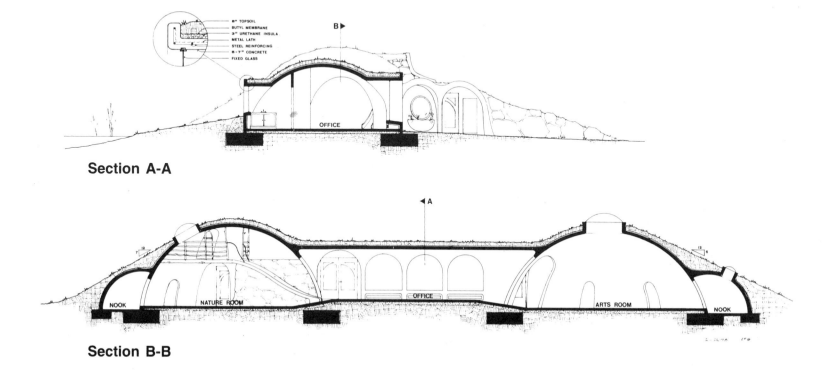

Section A-A

Section B-B

Energy Use Considerations

Wildwood School was built in 1974 when energy costs were lower and energy construction techniques were not as developed as they are today. Nevertheless, the total energy use—47,170 Btu/sq ft/yr—is quite reasonable considering the severe winter climate—8,948 heating degree days. The users report that in winter, covered by a three-foot blanket of snow, the indoor temperature is quite stable; and on the hottest summer days, the building remains cool all day.

Energy use is less than was originally expected. Unfortunately, it is not clear what portion of the total energy use can be attributed to space heating since the total includes electrical energy used to heat the Clivus Multrum treatment box, which is outside and must be kept at a 50°F minimum temperature year-around. It is assumed that this use of energy is significant, making the energy required for space heating somewhat less than 47,170 Btu/sq ft/yr.

Although the structure has a reasonably low energy use, is mostly earth covered, and is fairly well insulated, the architect suggests that a few minor changes would undoubtedly increase the building's performance. The provision of thermal breaks would prevent high conductive losses where the concrete shell is exposed around door and window openings. Also, single glazing, originally chosen in 1973, is now being replaced with double glazing. Insulated shades or shutters, particularly over the skylights, would also be beneficial.

Above: Entrance to the Arts Room. Below: Interior view of the Arts Room.

Project Data

Project: Wildwood School

Location: Pitkin County, Colorado (near Aspen)

Owner: Wildwood Board of Directors

Building type: Preschool education

Completion date: 1974

Project size: 3,600 sq. ft.

Construction cost: Information not available

Structure: Ferro-concrete shell forms roof and walls—4,000 psi concrete shell is 5 in. thick at the top and 7 in. at the base; concrete slab-on-grade floor

Earth cover: 98 percent of roof is earth covered; 60 percent of exterior walls is earth covered

Insulation: Urethane foam, 3 in. on roof and walls

Waterproofing: Butyl rubber membrane, liquid application

Heating system: Electric baseboard

Cooling system: No mechanical cooling

Lighting system: Incandescent supplemented by daylight

Waste disposal: Clivus Multrum sanitary system

Energy use: 47,170 Btu/sq ft/yr

Electricity: 169.8×10^6 Btu (49,800 kWh)

Note: Energy use figures are for 1981. A major use of electric heat is for the Clivus Multrum treatment box, which is outside and must be kept at a 50°F minimum temperature year-round.

Heating degree days: 8,948

Cooling degree days: 22

Occupancy schedule: 40 hours per week; 11 months per year

Credits

Architect: David F. Gibson, AIA, Aspen, Colorado

Structural engineer: John Morgan and Associates

Design consultant: William N. Gardner

Environmental and educational planning: Robert Lewis

Contractor: J. Veteto and Son

Perspective rendering: GeorgeAnn Waggaman

Photographs: David Gibson and David Marlow

Blue Ridge Elementary School

Walla Walla, Washington

Architect: Walker McGough Foltz Lyerla

The Blue Ridge Elementary School in Walla Walla, Washington, illustrates underground building design for both energy- and site-related reasons. In addition, it represents a simple and direct aesthetic expression of earth-integrated architecture. The 13-acre site for the school was formerly a portion of the Veterans Administration reservation property. The rich history of the land and buildings has qualified the entire reservation adjacent to the school for listing on the National Register of Historic Places. The site for the school was deeded with the conditions that the new building have a restrained visual appearance to blend with the character of the area, and that the character and effect of the tree-lined entry road south of the school site be maintained.

The plan of the 70,135-square foot school is long and narrow, extending along a northeast-southwest axis on the site. Since the school is only partially below grade, with berms rising from the flat site, the building and earth forms effectively divide the site into two portions. The southeastern portion of the site is open recreation area, and the northwestern portion is devoted to vehicular access, parking, and the main entrance to the school.

Most of the southeastern facade of the building is exposed, with 95 percent of the windows facing in this direction. This maximizes passive solar heating and provides a view of the main amenity on the site—the mature locust trees along the road to the south. Setting the school back from the road and diminishing its scale with earth integration helps achieve the goal of preserving the formal entry drive to the reservation. The siting of the school also ensures solar access in the future.

The remaining three sides of the building are almost completely covered with earth. The entry court on the northwest side is the only major interruption of the earth berms. This arrangement serves to buffer or separate the school from the noise and less desirable view of the parking area and warehouse district to the north of the site. The lower level of the two-story structure is below existing grade, with rooms opening into a sunken courtyard on the southeast side of the building. The upper level is above existing grade, with the earth berms rising to cover the walls. The roof is completely earth covered except for a series of forms containing skylights and mechanical equipment.

The interior plan arrangement divides the school into two basic parts—the classrooms, which comprise the majority of the building, and the gym and cafeteria located at one end. Classrooms and other heavily used spaces are placed on the southeast wall, while service functions and the circulation corridor extend along the northwest wall. To permit a variety of spaces suitable to different teaching methods, the classrooms for grades one through six are arranged in three clusters of six rooms, all on the upper level, that can be combined or separated.

Although one purpose of integrating the Blue Ridge school with the earth is to diminish its visual impact, the building has a distinct presence on its site. This is attributable partially to the bermed rather than fully below-grade design; however, the use of materials and the clean, geometric lines of the building also contribute to its simple, bold forms. The exposed structure of the building and retaining walls are white concrete, in stark contrast to the green berms and dark bands of windows. The large retaining walls reflect the

massive structure inside while defining the edges and form of the earth berms. The sod and the geometric form of the berms are parts of the architecture of the building with clearly distinguished edges, rather than less-defined transition areas between building and site. Blue-painted metal is used in the southeastern window wall and on the light scoops that occur on the roof. The blue metal provides a colorful but subdued accent to the white concrete. Approaching the building from the north entry drive, these blue light scoops are the major visible forms emerging from the large green earth berms.

Special Design Concerns

The areas of special concern in designing completely underground buildings—the sense of entry, natural light and view, and interior design of windowless areas—are not great problems in the partially below-grade Blue Ridge Elementary School. The main entry on the upper floor of the school is at the level of existing grade so no negative association with moving downward must be overcome. The sunken courtyard along the southeastern facade of the building may be entered from several places, much like the exterior of any conventional structure.

Because of the extended geometry of the building and its one completely exposed facade, natural light and view are provided to the majority of the classroom spaces in a conventional manner. Although some special program classrooms are

Above: Entrance courtyard cut into the earth berm on the north side of the school. Below: All classroom windows face south to maximize solar gain.

windowless, this is not necessarily a detrimental compromise. Lecture and demonstration spaces in schools represent functions that work well in windowless environments because activities therein are inwardly focused; moreover, the windowless spaces offer fewer sources of distraction. The gymnasium and cafeteria, which double as the school auditorium in this design, are also acceptable functions to place in windowless spaces.

Although the majority of the northwestern facade of the building is covered by earth berms, natural light may enter through the windows of the entry court and three large light monitors penetrating the roof. The curved form of the light monitors with vertical south-facing glass maximizes the natural light brought into these areas. These three light wells occur over open stairways along the main corridor on the north wall. This permits the light to reach the lower level and also creates spatial and lighting variety as one proceeds through the long corridors. In addition to providing natural light and higher spaces at the light wells, the architect has chosen to use color to enhance the lighting and create more variety. The walls of the main corridors are white; other pastel colors around the stairwells also reflect light. A progression of brighter colors is used in the secondary corridors and classroom spaces.

Building Technology and Costs

As with most nonresidential underground buildings, the exterior walls and retaining walls extending outside the school are cast-in-place reinforced concrete. In this building, precast concrete "single tees" are used to support the earth load on the roof,

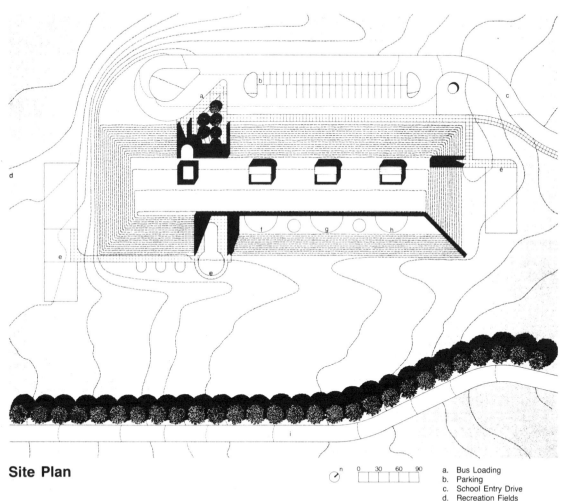

Site Plan

n   0   30   60   90

a. Bus Loading
b. Parking
c. School Entry Drive
d. Recreation Fields
e. Play Area
f. Kindergarten Play Area
g. Special Education Play Area
h. Outside Court
i. Wainwright Drive

and precast concrete "double tees" form the intermediate floor between the two levels. Waterproofing is applied to the outside of the concrete structure, and rigid insulation is placed over the membrane. Unlike many buildings in which wall insulation extends down only 4 to 8 feet from grade, the entire earth-covered two-story wall is insulated. The architects determined this to be cost-effective; it may well be more advisable in bermed buildings like this where the lower portion of the wall is not as isolated from the surface as in a completely below-grade building.

The construction cost of the Blue Ridge Elementary School is $72.15 per square foot. Although this figure is in the general range of school construction costs, the cost breakdown shown on the following page permits a more accurate comparison with a conventional above-grade building. Nearly 40 percent of the total costs occur in one category, the structure and exterior building envelope. This includes not only the concrete structure but the insulation, waterproofing, glass curtain wall, and other components of the exterior envelope. Although the costs of the concrete structure and waterproofing systems are higher than those for an above-grade building, costs for exterior finishing materials are almost eliminated.

Energy Use Considerations

In the design of the Blue Ridge Elementary School, the architects employed a number of interrelated strategies to reduce energy consumed for heating, cooling, and lighting. The extended plan arrangement, with 95 percent of the windows on the southeast facade, is designed to maximize passive solar heating and natural lighting to most of the spaces in the building. It was determined that a southeast orientation permitted the sun to warm the building in the morning, when temperatures are cooler; the contribution from internal heat sources such as lights and people would increase indoor temperature in the later part of the day. In the summer, heat gain through the glass curtain wall is reduced by the careful placement of overhangs on both levels. The architects estimated that extending the roof over the upper level and the upper

Section

a. Electrical
b. Mechanical
c. Reception
d. Principal's Office
e. Conference Room
f. Health Room
g. Nurse's Room
h. Staff Lunch Room
i. Conference Room
j. First Grade
k. Second Grade
l. Third Grade
m. Fourth Grade
n. Fifth Grade
o. Sixth Grade

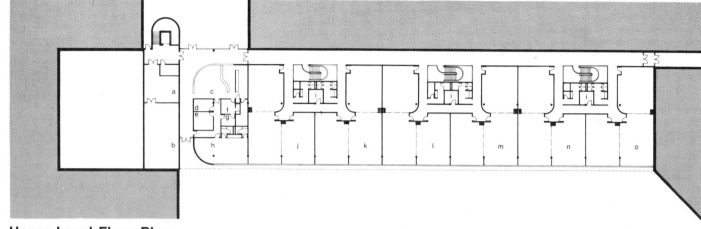

Upper Level Floor Plan

a. Gymnasium
b. Cafeteria
c. Food Service
d. Physical Education Office
e. Band Room
f. Choral Room
g. Special Program Classroom
h. Conference
i. Laundry
j. Deaf Education
k. Kindergarten
l. Orthopedic Classroom
m. Special Education Classroom
n. Observation Room
o. Toilet Room
p. Tub Room
q. Resource Room
r. TMR Classroom
s. Library Media Center
t. Storytelling Area

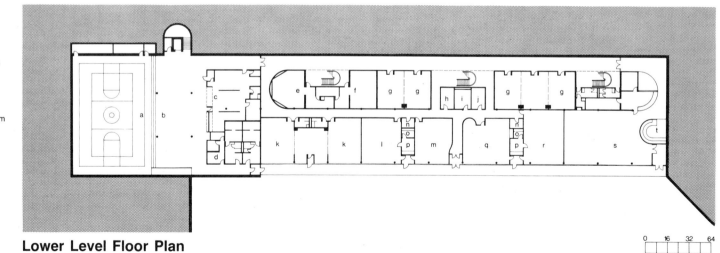

Lower Level Floor Plan

0   16   32   64

level over the lower for shading reduces the total cooling load by 30 percent.

A major design strategy to reduce energy consumption in the school involves placing a majority of the exterior building envelope in contact with the earth. The earth protects the building from infiltration and provides it with a more moderate temperature environment. In addition, the mass of the earth and the concrete structure permit the mechanical system to be operated at a lower capacity and for shorter periods of time. Finally, heat gain

in summer is reduced through the sod- and earth-covered roof and walls.

In addition to the strategies reflected in the design of the building envelope, several energy-efficient devices and techniques are included in the operating systems and building equipment. A multiple variable-air-volume distribution system permits various areas of the building to be operated independently. Thus, unoccupied areas do not have to be heated and cooled to the same extent as occupied ones. An economizer cycle is used to provide

outside air for cooling when the outside temperature falls below 60°F. Efficient lighting fixtures use 1.9 Watts/square foot in the classrooms and 1.7 Watts/square foot in the gymnasium.

The projected total energy use of 44,000 Btu/sq ft/yr is considered to be 30 to 40 percent lower than that for similar conventional buildings in this region. A majority of the energy use (55 percent) is for heating and cooling; 35 percent is for lighting, and the remaining 10 percent is for water heating and other uses.

Project Data

Project: Blue Ridge Elementary School

Location: Walla Walla, Washington

Owner: Walla Walla Public Schools

Building type: Elementary school

Completion date: 1982

Project size: 70,135 sq. ft.

Construction cost:

General requirements	$142,456
Site improvements	203,097
Earth work	292,124
Structure and exterior building envelope	1,839,216
Interior finishes	557,635
Misc. specialties	318,574
Vertical transportation	41,163
Food service work	97,501
Mechanical	903,837
Electrical	407,550
Contract sum	$4,803,153
Sales tax 5.3%	254,567
Total construction cost	$5,057,720

Structure: Precast concrete "single tees" at roof; precast concrete "double tees" with concrete topping at upper level floor; 10 in. cast-in-place reinforced concrete exterior walls; cast-in-place reinforced concrete columns, interior bearing walls, and exterior retaining walls; slab-on-grade floor.

Earth cover: 60 percent of total wall area is covered; 90 percent of total roof area is covered with 14 in. of earth

Insulation: Extruded polystyrene, 4 in. on roof, 2 in. on walls

Waterproofing: Rubberized asphalt sheet membrane on roof and walls in contact with earth; liquid-applied modified polyurethane membrane for dampproofing earth side of retaining walls

Heating sytem: Gas-fired boiler provides water to heating coils in the ventilation system; each space contains an independently controlled variable-air-volume unit

Cooling system: Electrically driven reciprocating water chiller provides water to cooling coils in the ventilation system

Lighting: Recessed deep cell parabolic fluorescent lighting in classrooms; recessed luminaries with asymmetric lenses over chalkboards; recessed incandescent lights in lobby and other areas; high bay industrial luminaries with metal halide lamps in gymnasium

Energy use: 44,000 Btu/sq ft/yr projected

Heating degree days: 4,835

Cooling degree days: 862

Credits

Architect: Walker McGough Foltz Lyerla, P.S., Spokane, Washington

Structural engineer: Walker McGough Foltz Lyerla, P.S.

Mechanical and electrical engineer: Riley Engineering, Inc.

Acoustical consultants: Towne, Richards and Chaudiere, Inc.

Contractor: Sceva Construction Company, Inc., general

Photographs: Photography Unlimited

Terraset and Terra Centre Elementary Schools

Fairfax County, Virginia

Architect: Douglas N. Carter

Located in Fairfax County, Virginia, the Terraset and Terra Centre Elementary Schools demonstrate many benefits of underground buildings and provide unusual insight into energy conservation in building design. Completed in 1977, Terraset Elementary School, in Reston, Virginia, represented a major innovation in school design and was one of the first buildings to be placed underground primarily for energy conservation. Terra Centre Elementary School, in Burke, Virginia, was completed in 1980 and appears to be nearly identical to the first school. In fact, Terra Centre was designed with a number of modifications—mainly in the mechanical systems—that represent an improvement over the Terraset design. The architect and client have been afforded the opportunity to test a number of innovative concepts, monitor the results, and apply the information to a second-generation design of a similar building.

Although energy conservation is cited as a primary reason for placing these buildings underground, preserving the character of the rolling, heavily wooded Virginia countryside was a contributing factor as well. On the site of the first school, the top of a knoll was cut off, the structural shell was built, and then the earth cover was placed over the structure to create a landform similar to the original hill. The earth berms are sloped at 30 degrees to blend into the landscape and provide access to the grass-covered roof. The second school was adapted to a similar site in a similar manner. These sites are not particularly restrictive in area, making the rooftop play areas an amenity but not an absolute necessity. On a slightly smaller site, however, the concept of using the roof as a playground could have significant land-saving and cost benefits.

The one-level schools are completely earth covered on the roof except for skylights and penetrations for ducts and vents. Over the majority of the spaces, the roof is flat, with 2 to 3 feet of earth increasing to as much as 9 feet as the grade rises to cover the higher roof of the gymnasium.

The plan arrangement of the two schools is based on fulfilling the requirements of the educational philosophy, as well as on achieving the most efficient layout to reduce wasted floor area. The architect determined that a circular floor plan created the greatest amount of enclosed space with the least perimeter wall area. Based on this analysis, the classrooms are placed into four circular bays. The 100-foot-diameter bays each open to an exterior courtyard and have a single supporting column in the center. The media center is in the middle of the four bays and serves as a focus of activity. The architect estimates that 11 percent less hallway space is required with this plan compared with a more conventional rectilinear arrangement. One difference between the two schools is that Terraset has a completely open plan, whereas walls are placed around the classroom bays in the Terra Centre School, reflecting the different teaching philosophies. In both cases the gymnasium, multipurpose space, and offices are located near the main entrance of the building. This permits direct access for community use of these spaces and reduces energy consumption since they can be operated separately from the remainder of the school.

Opposite: Exterior view of Terra Centre Elementary School, photograph by Stephen Fridge.

In discussing the exterior form and character of underground buildings, they are often categorized into those that have a minimal presence, becoming a part of the site, or those that have a definite presence and character in a manner similar to conventional buildings. The exterior images of the Terraset and Terra Centre Elementary Schools reflect both a minimal presence and a visual architectural statement. Viewed from some angles, the buildings virtually merge with the rolling countryside. On flatter sites, bermed buildings such as these might not blend into the surroundings so easily.

Although the earth berms and earth-covered roof are dominant features, the buildings actually have extensive exposed concrete and glass facades, large solar collectors above the building, and concrete forms on the roof. The low, extended form of a one-story school seems to diminish the impact of these features when viewed from a distance, but they become more imposing at closer range. The architect has chosen to treat potentially negative visual elements such as the mechanical equipment and roof penetrations in positive

ways. The main exhaust and intake air vents, as well as the skylights, are enclosed in sculptural concrete forms on the rooftop play area. In the Terraset design, the solar collectors are placed on a space frame spanning the entry courtyard. The effect on the lighting and spatial feeling of the courtyard is dramatic: the collector system thus becomes part of the major image of the school. The solar collector system at Terra Centre is placed over the center of the roof to provide easier access to the equipment.

Special Design Concerns

Although the two Fairfax County schools are predominantly underground, the main entrances to the schools and access to the outside from the classrooms are quite similar to conventional buildings. The floor levels of the classrooms are basically at the level of existing grade, with the earth berms rising to cover the roof. The driveways at the entrances of the two schools are depressed to the floor level of the buildings so that one can enter the courtyard and then the school without

descending further. The entry courtyard also serves as a transition space from the bus loading and drop-off area to the interior of the school.

Natural light and views of the wooded surroundings are provided through large window walls in each of the circular classroom bays. The effect of these window areas is enhanced by the open floor-plan. In Terraset no walls divide the classrooms, making it possible to see through two or more windows from almost anywhere in the interior of the school. Although the classrooms in the Terra Centre design do have walls, a similar effect is achieved by using glass in the walls, permitting light and view outside to extend through the classrooms to interior areas. In both schools the entry courtyard provides an additional source of light and view to the classroom areas as well as to the office and multipurpose spaces.

The most dramatic interior space in the Terraset Elementary School is the media center. The ceiling extends upward in a pyramidal form, creating a high space in contrast to the 8- and 10-foot ceilings in

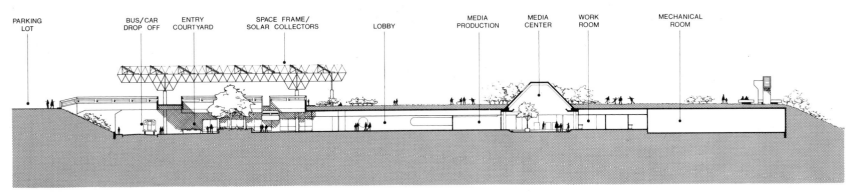

Section

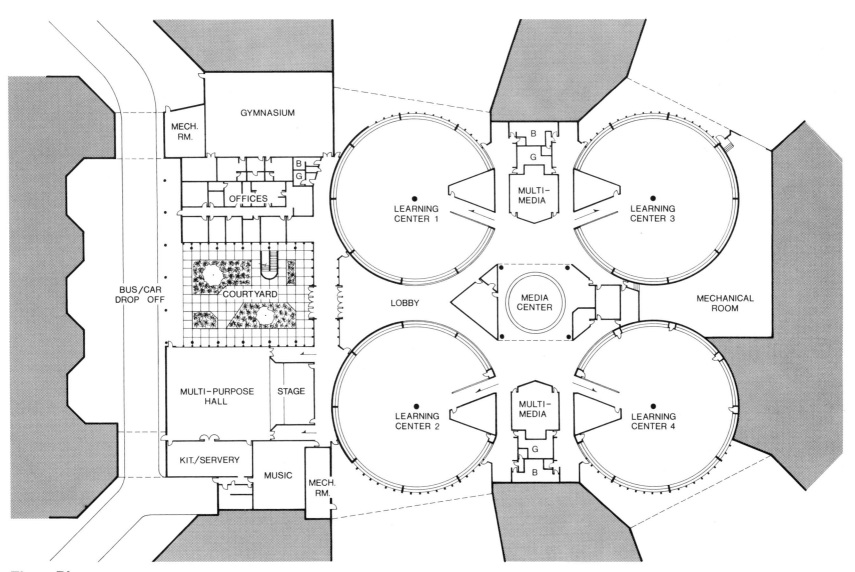

Floor Plan

GYMNASIUM

MECH. RM.

OFFICES

B
G

COURTYARD

BUS/CAR DROP OFF

MULTI-PURPOSE HALL

STAGE

KIT./SERVERY

MUSIC

MECH. RM.

LOBBY

LEARNING CENTER 1

MULTI-MEDIA

B
G

LEARNING CENTER 3

MEDIA CENTER

MECHANICAL ROOM

LEARNING CENTER 2

MULTI-MEDIA

G

B

LEARNING CENTER 4

111

the rest of the building. At the top of the space is a large skylight that provides a direct source of natural light to this interior area. In spite of the amenities of the skylight and higher interior space over the media center at Terraset, the same features were not repeated in the Terra Centre design. Apparently the skylight was not considered essential in Terra Centre since other sources of natural light were available and a major roof penetration represents additional construction and energy costs. Also, elimination of the skylight form on the roof permits the solar collector system to be placed over this area.

Building Technology and Costs

In each of the schools, the relatively large loads imposed by the earth are supported by a 10-inch-thick reinforced concrete roof slab and 12-inch-thick reinforced concrete walls. The rubberized asphalt membrane on the roof was flood-tested over a period of days to locate and repair any leaks before the building was covered with earth. A 1½-inch layer of rigid insulation, which also serves as protection board for the waterproofing, and a gravel drainage layer were placed on the roof before backfilling.

The construction costs for Terraset and Terra Centre provide a comparison of earth-covered and conventional schools as well as a comparison between the two nearly identical schools. When Terraset was first designed, the school board required that it not exceed the cost of a conventional school. The construction cost was held to the $2.86 million limit set by the client, although it was estimated that the building cost actually was 5 to 7 percent higher than for a similar

conventional school. As with many underground buildings, the additional structural costs were somewhat offset by reduced costs for exterior finishing materials. The costs of the schools (not including the solar collector systems) increased from $38.69 per square feet for Terraset in 1977 to $43.11 per square feet for Terra Centre in 1980. The increase is more attributable to inflation during this period than any changes in the buildings. In both cases the costs appear to be quite comparable to conventional school structures.

Energy Use Considerations

In 1977, in response to the energy crisis, Terraset Elementary School was designed to explore a variety of energy-conserving concepts in building design. Many of the concepts were generally accepted as being effective strategies, but previous experience in their use was limited. Fortunately, a nonprofit organization, the Terraset Foundation, in cooperation with Virginia State University, was established to monitor and study the school's performance. These studies provided much useful information about the building's design and operation. Recommendations were developed for further improvements in the operation of Terraset as well as the design of future buildings. Many of these modifications were incorporated into the Terra Centre design.

The energy-conserving concepts employed in the original design of Terraset fall into two categories: strategies related to the form of the building and strategies related to the mechanical system. In the first group, the use of earth cover is the most significant. The earth-covered roof and

walls are intended to place the building into a more moderate environment in summer and winter; to provide storage mass around the building, reducing the amount and duration of mechanical heating and cooling; and to reduce heat gain in summer. The large overhangs (at least 5 feet) also protect from excessive summer heat gain through the windows. In addition, the unique building layout was designed in part to reduce wasted floor area, and ceiling heights were reduced in corridors to reduce building volume.

The relatively sophisticated HVAC system at Terraset combines heat reclamation and solar energy for both heating and cooling. Conventional electric heating and cooling is provided when the renewable energy sources are not available. The basic mechanical system is a variable-air-volume system including a double-bundle heat exchanger and three 10,000-gallon water storage tanks. An economizer cycle provides free cooling when outside air temperatures permit. This system permits excess heat from lights and people in the center of the building to be stored and provided both at the building periphery, where heat is needed, and at night, when internal sources of heat are not available. The 6,000 gross square feet of evacuated tube solar collectors provide high-temperature water that can be used both to provide heating directly and to provide cooling through absorption chillers. Two 2,500-gallon storage tanks are required for the high-temperature water, and two 25-ton absorption chiller units are used in the cooling system. The entire system is monitored by microprocessors and operated by manual pneumatic controls.

The energy performance of the building was monitored for three years from 1977 to 1980. During the 1978-79 school year, the building required 46,257 Btu/sq ft (24,010 Btu/sq ft during the heating season and 22,246 Btu/sq ft during the cooling season). This figure compared favorably with two conventional schools also being monitored; Terraset used approximately 50 percent less total energy. The solar collector contributed an estimated 14 percent in winter and 10 percent in summer of the total energy needed. During 1978-79 approximately 25 percent of the total energy use was for lighting (11,299 Btu/sq ft) [4.1].

One important lesson learned from the monitoring of the Terraset School is that the operation of the systems by knowledgeable people makes a significant difference in energy efficiency. The energy use figures discussed above for 1978-79 apply to a period when the school was operated by engineers from the Terraset Foundation who were attempting to optimize performance. During 1977-78 and 1979-80 when the building was operated in the conventional manner, total energy use was 40 to 50 percent more than during 1978-79 [4.1]. This still represented a 20 percent reduction in energy use compared with the conventional schools but fell short of the predicted performance and the potential of Terraset as originally designed.

Even though the study of the Terraset building indicated quite good energy performance, particularly when operated properly, certain problems were observed that led to modifications in the design of

Above: Entrance courtyard of Terraset Elementary School covered by a space frame supporting the solar collector system. Below: Media center in Terraset Elementary School, photographs by John Russell.

Terra Centre. For example, the massive earth-covered concrete roof provides a dampening of outdoor temperatures. The use of the space between the acoustical ceiling and roof slab as a return air plenum does, however, have some negative side effects. Losses through the roof slab are accelerated by circulating the return air adjacent to it, and significant losses appear to occur through concrete overhangs and other structural elements that extend from the interior zones to the exposed exterior of the building. An estimated 50 to 60 percent of the total heat loss in the building occurred through the roof slab.

To alleviate the problems discussed above and improve on the performance of Terraset, the Terra Centre design included a number of changes. Although additional insulation over the entire roof would reduce heat loss, modifying the air-distribution system was determined to be more cost-effective. Rather than using the plenum, a ducted return air system is employed, and thermal breaks are provided in the concrete structure to reduce conductance from the slab directly to the outside air. In addition, the operation of the overall mechanical system was simplified. A variable-air-volume system was not included in Terra Centre because it was not considered necessary for a relatively open-plan building. Most important, the mechanical system is monitored and operated by microprocessors, requiring little intervention by the maintenance personnel.

Project Data

Project: Terraset Elementary School

Location: Reston, Virginia

Owner: Fairfax County Public Schools

Building type: Elementary school

Completion date: 1977

Project size: 69,000 sq. ft.

Construction Cost:

General	$2,470,000
Mechanical	393,000
Total	$2,863,000

Note: The total construction cost above does not include the solar system. The $551,500 cost of the system was provided by a grant.

Structure: Cast-in-place reinforced concrete roof slab, 10 in. thick; cast-in-place reinforced concrete walls, 12 in. thick; slab-on-grade floor

Earth cover: 60 percent of total wall area is covered; 100 percent of roof area is covered with 2 to 9 ft. of earth (average depth is 3½ ft.)

Insulation: Expanded polystyrene, 1 in. on roof and walls

Waterproofing: Rubberized asphalt sheet membrane

Heating system: Heat reclaim system assisted by evacuated tube solar collectors; conventional electric boiler is standby heat source

Cooling system: Evacuated tube solar collectors provide heat for absorption chiller used with conventional condensor unit

Lighting: 2 × 4 fluorescent fixtures

Energy use: 46,257 Btu/sq ft/yr (1978-79)

Heating season: 24,010 Btu/sq ft
Cooling season: 22,246 Btu/sq ft

Note: Energy use figures are for the 1978 through 1979 school year. The annual energy consumption per square foot for a conventional school in the same system during 1978-79 was approximately twice as much as for Terraset. Annual energy use for Terraset in 1978-79 was considerably better than the previous or following year because of improved operation of the system. During 1978-79 approximately 25 percent of the total energy use was for lighting (11,299 Btu/sq ft) [4.1].

Heating degree days: 4,211 (Washington, DC)

Cooling degree days: 1,415 (Washington, DC)

Number of occupants: 990 students plus 50 teachers and staff

Occupancy schedule: 70 hours per week, 48 weeks per year (only occupied 5 days per week)

Credits

Architect: Douglas N. Carter, AIA, Davis and Carter, McLean, Virginia

Structural engineer: Tibor Szegezdy and Associates

Mechanical engineering: Vinzant and Associates

Solar systems engineer: Smith, Hinchman and Grylis

Contractors: E. H. Glover Inc., general; James A. Federline Inc., mechanical and solar

Photographs: John Russell

Project Data

Project: Terra Centre Elementary School

Location: Burke, Virginia

Owner: Fairfax County Public Schools

Building type: Elementary school

Completion date: 1980

Project size: 74,000 sq. ft.

Construction cost:

General conditions	$159,951
Site preparation	361,761
Excavation and foundation	253,892
Structural and exterior walls	409,783
Roof and floor deck	655,916
Masonry	100,050
Glazing	89,051
Building insulation	5,000
Waterproofing	124,985
Mechanical	508,000
Electrical	225,000
Interior finishes	172,000
Flooring and carpeting	75,000
Acoustical ceilings	50,000
Total	$3,190,389

Note: The total construction cost above does not include the solar system which cost approximately $350,000.

Structure: Cast-in-place reinforced concrete roof slab, 10 in. thick; cast-in-place reinforced concrete walls, 12 in. thick; slab-on-grade floor

Earth cover: 60 percent of total wall area is covered; 100 percent of roof area is covered with 2 to 3 ft. of earth

Insulation: Expanded polystyrene, 1½ in. on roof and walls

Waterproofing: Rubberized asphalt sheet membrane

Learning center in Terra Centre Elementary School, photograph by Stephen Fridge.

Heating system: Heat reclaim system assisted by solar collectors, conventional electric boiler is stand-by heat source

Cooling system: Solar collectors provide heat for absorption chiller used with conventional condensor unit

Lighting: Fluorescent

Energy use: Information not available

Heating degree days: 4,211 (Washington, DC)

Cooling degree days: 1,415 (Washington, DC)

Number of occupants: 990 students plus 50 teachers and staff

Occupancy schedule: 70 hours per week, 48 weeks per year (only occupied 5 days per week)

Credits

Architect: Douglas N. Carter, AIA, Davis and Carter, McLean, Virginia

Structural engineer: Tibor Szegezdy and Associates

Mechanical engineer: Davis, Smith, Carter and Rider

Contractor: Kimmel and Kimmel, Inc.

Photographs: Stephen Fridge

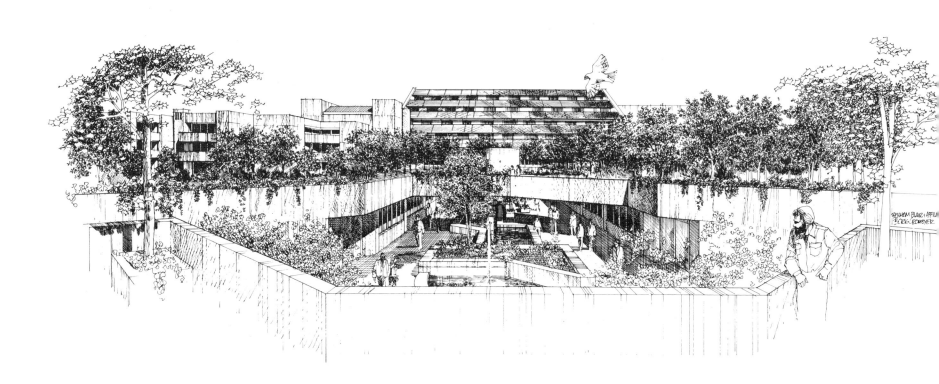

California State Office Building, Sacramento, California
Architect: The Benham Group, Oklahoma City, Oklahoma

Chapter 5: Office and Commercial Buildings

Williamson Hall

University of Minnesota
Minneapolis, Minnesota

Architect: BRW Architects

Williamson Hall, located on the University of Minnesota campus in Minneapolis, serves as the student bookstore and contains the admissions and records offices for the university. The building is 95 percent below grade; the majority of the space is on two subsurface levels with only a small lounge and entry area above ground surface on one edge of the flat site. Included in the total area of 86,500 square feet is the original building completed in 1977 and a 7,000-square foot storage area on two below-grade levels that was added to the south side of the structure in 1982. Williamson Hall is an excellent illustration of an underground design resulting from a diversity of site-related, programmatic, and energy-related concerns.

One predominant feature of the site is the presence of several historic buildings clustered around it. On this particularly crowded area of the campus, it was desirable to preserve views of these attractive structures as well as provide as much open space as possible. By placing the new building almost completely underground, these objectives were met while the character of the area was preserved by avoiding any aesthetic conflict arising from placing older and more recent structures in close proximity. In addition, it became possible to place a relatively large building on a very constrained site, resulting in efficient land use.

Another important site constraint was the desire to preserve cross-site circulation. The site is basically square with a considerable amount of pedestrian traffic moving diagonally across it. This movement results from the location of the site between a campus commercial area

with major mass transit stops and the remainder of the campus. Not only was it preferable not to interrupt this pedestrian traffic, but it was, in fact, desirable to encourage it to pass by and through the bookstore. The underground design provides an advantage over an above-ground structure by permitting the circulation to continue uninterrupted over the building. In fact, the diagonal cross-site circulation is one of the major form determinants of the design, serving to bisect the building with major pedestrian walkways both on the surface and inside on the lower levels as well.

The pedestrian walkways through the center of the building essentially separate its two distinct functions—bookstore and office space. The differing requirements of the two functions are reflected in the design. The bookstore is mainly covered by grass and plaza areas on the surface except for a single row of clerestory windows providing light and view into the store for passing pedestrians. The half of the building containing the office areas, on the other hand, is designed with extensive windows surrounding a sunken courtyard, which provide light and view out for the office workers. Clearly, an inwardly oriented function such as a bookstore, where most users spend little time, is well suited to underground space, even with no exposure to the outside. The major concern for the client in this case was not so much the interior space, but the lack of visibility inherent in an underground commercial structure. This is alleviated by the design, which includes clerestory windows at the plaza level and an interior walkway, both of which provide dynamic views overlooking the store. Offices in completely underground space must be

more carefully considered, but this design demonstrates that potential problems can be resolved.

Although the underground design of Williamson Hall diminishes its impact on the historical character of the area, the building still maintains a distinct form and character of its own. Unlike some underground buildings beneath open spaces that can almost go unnoticed, this structure is quite apparent and can be clearly perceived as a definite place. The exposed concrete walls on the skylights, sunken courtyards, and above-grade portions of the building give the entire site an urban character. The extensive concrete surfaces, however, are softened considerably by the fluted board-form texture on the concrete and tiers of planters that contribute to a very natural appearance in the courtyard.

The limited but very apparent above-grade forms of this building serve a number of purposes that help to organize the site and create a very active urban space. The largest above-grade form defines the most open edge of the site, serves as one main entry, supports the solar collector system, and provides on-grade service access to the building that is screened from the pedestrian areas. Other smaller above-grade elements serve to permit light and view for the spaces below and clearly define circulation around and through the site.

Special Design Concerns

Since Williamson Hall was one of the first almost completely underground buildings on the University of Minnesota campus and the future users of the space initially

had reservations about such a design, the architects placed particular emphasis on three critical aspects of the design—the entry, the interior design, and exposure to natural light and view.

It was determined by the architects that moving downward on ramps or stairs outside the building and then entering was preferable to entering and then proceeding down an interior stairwell. It was assumed that less of a negative feeling of going downward would occur if it were done more gradually outside the building. In addition, since large volumes of people move through the building, ramps and wide exterior stairs are more convenient than more constrained interior stairwells. The building is actually designed with three major entrances. Two of them are located at either end of the site with ramps or stairs on the exterior leading to the major pedestrian walkway through the building. The third entrance is located in the small above-grade portion of the building leading to an interior staircase and elevator. Once inside the building at the first level below grade, escalators provide convenient access to the second level down, where the bookstore and most public offices are entered.

The interior design of Williamson Hall is intended to create a feeling of openness and maximize the available light and view. Consequently, the bookstore is basically one large open space, two stories high with clerestory windows providing light to the whole space. Even more effective is the light and view that penetrate the bookstore area from the sunken courtyard through the glass enclosed walkway. Although lacking windows to the outside, offices on upper levels around the perimeter of the bookstore receive light through their glass walls and overlook the larger space.

In a similar manner, much of the office space in the other half of the building is open, with lower partitions not only providing flexibility, but permitting light, view, and a general feeling of spaciousness to be maximized. Although the concrete walls and structural elements are exposed, any associations with typical basement spaces are reduced because of the complex geometric patterns of the structure, the fluted texture of the concrete, and the extensive use of color in furnishings and elements of the mechanical system.

This building has no horizontal skylights overhead. Most of the glazing is sloped at a 45-degree angle to permit greater light penetration to the lower level while still maintaining horizontal views out of the building into the courtyard. Considering the relatively small area of glazing in the building—3 percent of the total floor area—it is remarkable that the great majority of the building feels very light and open with exterior views available in most spaces.

Building Technology and Costs

The structural system of Williamson Hall consists of reinforced concrete walls, roof, and floors. Where the walls are exposed both inside and outside the building, they are formed with a random pattern of vertical protrusions. The roof structure is a two-way waffle-slab system that is also exposed on the interior. Only in one limited area—7 percent of the total roof area—does the roof structure support the additional load of earth covering. Most of

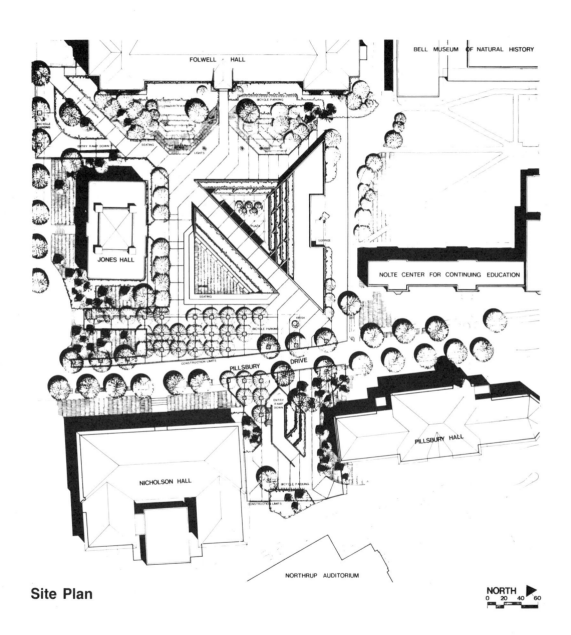

Site Plan

NORTH ▶
0   20   40   60

the roof is covered with removable precast concrete pavers that provide convenient access for maintenance of the waterproofing.

Generally, the initial construction costs of Williamson Hall—$3.47 million—are considered to be quite reasonable. In fact, at the time of construction, they were slightly less than a comparable conventional campus building of similar function and quality. As with many underground buildings on constrained sites, sheet piling on two sides represented an additional cost, but the lack of expensive exterior finishing materials was one of the major reasons for keeping costs comparable to above-grade buildings. The cost of the 7,000-square foot addition completed in 1982 was $265,000. Although this appears to be within a reasonable range, it is higher than if it had been built with the original building. Construction of the addition involved removing a plaza area and re-excavating on the south side of the building.

The solar collector system and the additional structure to support it were not included in the original construction cost total of $3.5 million. The collector structure was actually completed in 1980 and the entire cost (approximately $600,000) was borne by the U.S. Department of Energy as an experimental facility. It has been estimated that the system would have cost considerably less had it been designed and constructed with the original building.

Energy Use Considerations

Although the Minnesota winter is far more severe than the summer, cooling is a greater concern than heating in a public

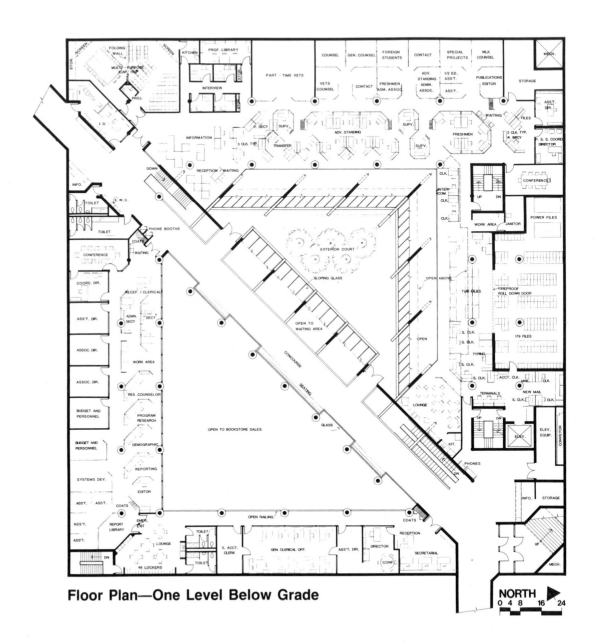

Floor Plan—One Level Below Grade

NORTH ▶
0 4 8 16 24

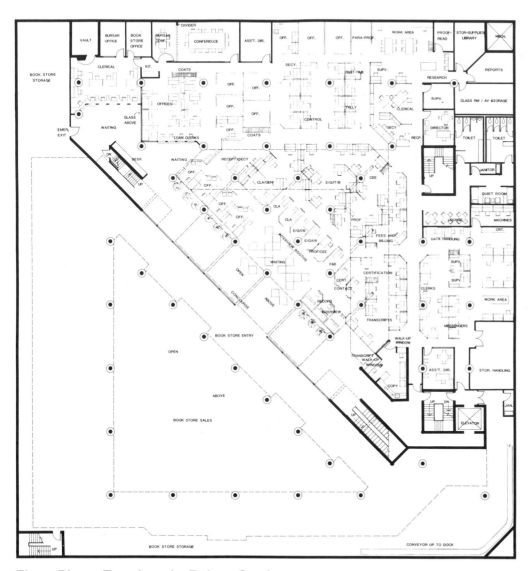

Floor Plan—Two Levels Below Grade

Labels visible in plan: VAULT, BURSAR OFFICE, BOOK STORE OFFICE, BURSAR CONF., DIVIDER, CONFERENCE, ASS'T. DIR., OFF., PARA-PROF., WORK AREA, PROOF READ, STOR-SUPPLIES LIBRARY, MECH., BOOK STORE STORAGE, CLERICAL, KIT., COATS, OFF., SECY., PART-TIME, SUPV., RESEARCH, REPORTS, OFFICES, OFF., SUPV., CLASS RM / AV & STORAGE, GLASS ABOVE, OFF., OFF., CONTROL, TALLY, CLERICAL, EMER. EXIT, WAITING, LOAN CLERKS, COATS, OFF., SECY., DIRECTOR, RECP., TOILET, TOILET, DESK, ON, UP, WAITING, RECEPT/SECY, OFF., CLA/GEN, E/G/IT/B, CEE, UP, JANITOR, QUIET ROOM, WAITING, OFF., OFF., CLA, E/G/A/B, PROF, LOUNGE, MACHINES, CRT., OPEN, CLA, FEES AND BILLING, DATA HANDLING, INTERVIEW BOOTHS, E/G/A/B, PROF/CEE, F&B, CERTIFICATION, CONCOURSE, ABOVE, WAITING, CERT CONTACT, SUPV., SUPV., CLERKS, WORK AREA, RECORD, INTERVIEW, TRANSCRIPTS, MESSENGERS, BOOK STORE ENTRY, OPEN, WALK-UP WINDOW, TRANSCRIPT WALK-UP WINDOW, COPY, ASS'T. DIR., STOR. HANDLING, ABOVE, BOOK STORE SALES, UP, ON, JAN., ELEVATOR, BOOK STORE STORAGE, UP, CONVEYOR UP TO DOCK

Above: Lounge area one level below grade with sloping glazing overhead. Below: Main concourse two levels below grade.

building like Williamson Hall that requires substantial ventilation with outside air and has significant internal heat gain. Predominant features of the design that contribute to energy conservation in both summer and winter are its underground location and the limited amount of glazing compared with most office buildings. Most of the glazing in Williamson Hall is oriented to the south and west, providing passive solar heat gain that can be readily absorbed by the massive concrete structure. Because of the potential for overheating in summer, however, tiers of planters are placed over the major areas of south-facing glass. The Engleman ivy that hangs from these planters provides shade in the summer but drops its leaves in winter to permit greater solar heat gain. According to measurements taken by the architects, vines with normal growth reduce solar radiation entering the space by 50 percent, and vines with heavy growth by 75 percent.

Not only does the glazing provide some solar heat and view for the occupants, but the overhead position of the sloping glazing provides natural light that contributes to reducing the general lighting load. Another efficient lighting concept is employed in the office area. Above the suspended ceilings, a system of bus ducts is installed with standard three-prong receptacles at 4-foot intervals. This is integrated with a system of interchangeable acoustic tiles and fluorescent fixtures on a 2-foot-square grid. Thus, fixtures can be moved to provide task lighting without the services of an electrician. This flexibility permits the use of approximately 20 percent fewer fixtures, since the light is not wasted on areas not requiring higher lighting levels.

One of the important effects of placing Williamson Hall underground is the smaller-size HVAC system that is required in such a massive structure. The air-conditioning tonnage per unit area is about half that used in standard practice. Other energy-conserving features include a heat recovery system for the outside ventilation air, full economizer capability (the ability to use 100 percent outside air for cooling when appropriate instead of air-conditioning), and a low-pressure variable-air-volume distribution system.

The solar collector system on Williamson Hall is a linear concentrating system employing movable mirrors with a total area of 6,600 square feet. The system is designed to provide not only heating in winter, but also cooling in summer, since it serves as a preheater for a 150-ton absorption chiller. In spite of the relatively small collector area, the system was originally designed to meet 50 to 80 percent of the building's heating and cooling needs. In fact, one advantage of underground buildings with limited heat loss and gain is the reduced collector area required to provide benefits equal to those of a larger system for an above-grade building. Preliminary indications are that the collector system is only providing for less than 5 percent of the building's heating and cooling load. This is apparently not because of lack of collector area or available solar energy but is

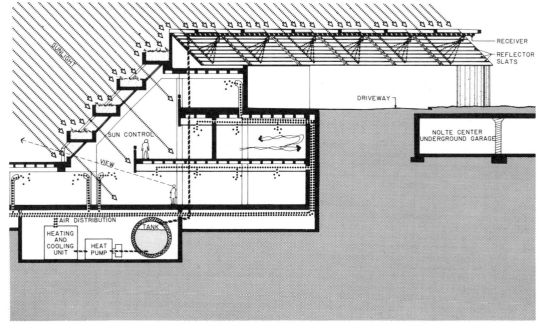

Section

caused by inefficiencies in the storage, control, and delivery of the heat [5.1]. Nevertheless, the relatively small contribution of the solar system is an indication that the building itself is performing quite well with respect to heating and cooling energy use.

In 1981, the actual energy use for Williamson Hall was 49,346 Btu/sq ft/yr which was further reduced in 1982 to 41,872 Btu/sq ft/yr. One factor accounting for the difference in energy consumption during the two years is the 7,000-square foot addition included in the calculations of the energy use for 1982, but not for 1981. This produces an improvement in energy use because the total building area is larger but the addition requires very little additional energy—it is a windowless area used for storage and is not heated or cooled to the same extent as other areas of the building. Using underground space for storage can be particularly effective in conserving energy because adequate interior temperatures can be maintained with no auxiliary heating or cooling.

The addition of the storage space is not the only factor creating a difference in energy use between 1981 and 1982. Originally, automatic sliding doors were installed in the main entrances to the building to facilitate the flow of pedestrian traffic. The constant opening and closing of these doors accounted for considerable heat loss resulting in a large amount of electricity consumed by heaters near the doorways. In 1982, the sliding doors were replaced with two sets of conventional doors forming vestibules at the main entrances. This one change is considered the major reason that total electrical consumption in the building was reduced by over 30 percent in 1982. It is less clear why steam consumption increased in 1982. Two possible explanations are the very severe winter in 1982 and differences in operating procedures. Nevertheless, Williamson Hall can be considered a very energy-efficient design—one that performs considerably better than originally predicted even with little contribution from the solar collector system.

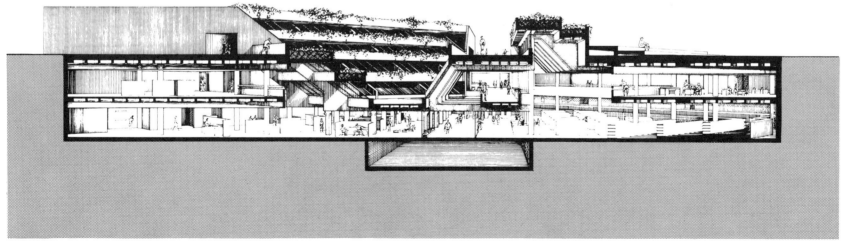

Section

Project Data

Project: Williamson Hall

Location: Minneapolis, Minnesota

Owner: University of Minnesota

Building type: Office building and campus bookstore

Completion date: 1977 for original building, 1982 for addition

Project size: 86,500 sq. ft. (including 1982 addition)

Construction cost:

General	$2,207,000
Mechanical	601,285
Electrical	406,000
Transport	126,471
Site work and utilities	127,702
Total	$3,468,458

Note: Figures do not include solar collector system installed in 1980 or the cost of the 7,000 sq. ft. addition built in 1982 which was $265,000

Structure: Cast-in-place reinforced concrete waffle-slab roof and intermediate floors supported on cast-in-place reinforced concrete columns and exterior walls; slab-on grade floor

Earth cover: 98 percent of exterior walls are earth covered; 7 percent of roof area is covered with 30 in. of earth (remaining areas of roof are 18 percent conventional roof and 75 percent precast concrete pavers)

Above: Sunken courtyard with overhanging vines shading the windows. Below: Entrance to the main concourse at the south end of the building.

Insulation: Extruded polystyrene, 1-½ in. on roof and 1-½ in. on walls to a depth of 6 ft

Waterproofing: Rubber membrane waterproofing on roof, 1/16 in. thick; silastic rubber waterproofing applied to below-grade walls; conventional built-up roof on above-grade portions

Windows: 2,500 sq.ft. total area, all double glazed

Heating system: Heating provided by coal-fired central campus steam system in parallel with solar system

Cooling system: Cooling provided by one nominal 150-ton (derated to 97 tons) absorption chiller driven with solar preheated, steam-boosted hot water.

Solar system: 6,000-sq. ft. linear concentrating system (fixed receiver, movable mirrors) and 8,000-gal. thermal storage tank

Lighting system: Ceiling and wall-mounted metal halide lamps for general lighting, movable ceiling-mounted fluorescent fixtures in bus-duct distribution system for task lighting; total load of 163,500 watts; lighting levels: 70 fc for task lighting, 35 fc for general lighting

Energy use:

49,346 Btu/sq ft/yr in 1981

41,872 Btu/sq ft/yr in 1982

See energy use chart for complete data.

Heating degree days: 8,159

Cooling degree days: 585

Number of occupants: Original design was based on 180 full-time staff in office area, 220 actually occupy the space; bookstore occupancy varies

Energy Use for Williamson Hall

Month	1981 Electricity (kWh x 10³)	1981 Steam (lbs x 10³)	1982 Electricity (kWh x 10³)	1982 Steam (lbs x 10³)
January	77.2	112.3	47.0*	160.4
February	69.1	60.0*	45.8*	142.9
March	74.9	46.1	58.0	121.0
April	63.4	25.4	39.0	48.7
May	62.8	37.3	47.0	148.9
June	78.3	173.9	48.2	184.9
July	31.7	210.0	56.7	377.4
August	72.6	194.0	53.7	308.8
September	74.9	65.7	50.6	132.3
October	71.0	20.0	32.9	67.4
November	63.0	44.3	41.5	114.7
December	92.0	98.3	50.0	100.0
Total	830.9	1,087.3	570.4	1,675.1

*estimated

1981 Energy Use Totals:

Electricity	$2,836 \times 10^6$ Btu
Steam	$1,087 \times 10^6$ Btu
Total	$3,923 \times 10^6$ Btu

49,346 Btu/sq ft/yr

1982 Energy Use Totals:

Electricity	$1,947 \times 10^6$ Btu
Steam	$1,675 \times 10^6$ Btu
Total	$3,622 \times 10^6$ Btu

41,872 Btu/sq ft/yr

Note: Energy use for 1981 is based on a total building area of 79,500 sq. ft. Energy use for 1982 is based on a total building area of 86,500 sq. ft. since a 7,000-square foot addition was completed in early 1982. The estimated contribution of the solar collector in both years is less than 5 percent of the total heating and cooling load. For additional information on Williamson Hall, see references 5.1 and 5.2.

Source: University of Minnesota Physical Plant Operations

Occupancy schedule: 60 hours per week

Credits

Architect: BRW Architects, Inc., Minneapolis, Minnesota (formerly Myers and Bennett/BRW)

Structural engineer: Meyer, Borgman, and Johnson, Inc.

Mechanical engineer: Oftedal, Locke, Broadston and Associates, Inc.

Energy consultant: Dr. Thomas Bligh, M.I.T.

Contractors: Lovering Associates, general; Anderson-Cerney, mechanical; Langford Electric Corporation, electrical

Photographs: Phillip MacMillan James

California State Office Building

Sacramento, California

Architect: The Benham Group

With energy conservation as a primary requirement, the California State Architect's Office held a national competition for the design of a government office building. Completed in 1982, the winning design by The Benham Group demonstrates a wide range of energy-related concepts and systems. In addition, the combination of both underground and above-grade building forms results in a diversity of spaces both on the site and within the building complex.

Covering approximately 1½ city blocks, the site forms part of the Sacramento Capitol Area Plan. The site is bounded by streets on the south, east, and west. Another east-west street separates the site into a full city block on the south side and a half-block to the north. Major neighboring structures include a sixteen-story office tower to the south that shades a portion of the site and a six-story building to the north to which the new office space must be connected. In general, a mixture of low- and medium-scale buildings surround the site.

In order to resolve many of the constraints of the site and maximize opportunities for energy conservation, the design consists of two distinct parts—a one-story underground building covering the city block on the south side of the project, and a six-story building rising along the northern edge of the site. Approximately 75,000 square feet of the 264,000-square foot complex is underground. With this arrangement, access to sunlight for the solar collectors mounted on the six-story building is maximized and shadows from the tall building to the south fall only on the below-grade areas of the structure. A long, narrow sunken courtyard forms an outdoor circulation spine through the underground

building, extends under the street, and ties together the two parts of the site divided by the street.

In addition to reducing energy use, several urban planning advantages result from placing a portion of the complex below grade. On the rooftop of the underground structure is a public park with an outdoor amphitheater. A portion of the earth-covered roof area is intended for medium-density housing development in the future. Using the roof of the underground building in this manner provides an open space amenity for the community, uses land more efficiently and thus saves land acquisition costs, and creates a desirable mixture of office, residential, and recreational functions. Future residential development on the southwestern portion of the site is in harmony with the scale of adjacent structures to the west.

The six-story structure on the northern edge of the building supports 25,000 square feet of concentrating solar collectors. The form of the structure extends along an east-west access to maximize collection area and minimize exposure directly to the east or west. By stepping the floors back at a 45-degree angle to form a sloping southern facade, solar collection is more efficient; the collectors and overhangs are also designed to shade all south-facing windows. Using a multilevel bridge, the six-story building is connected to the six-story Employment Development Department building to the north. A tall, narrow courtyard is created between the two buildings that provides some natural light to the offices but is completely shaded from any direct heat gain. This space on the north edge of the site also provides service access to the complex and is at one end of the

underground pedestrian circulation spine extending along a north-south axis through the site.

On the southern edge of the site, pedestrians enter the below-grade portion of the complex through two diagonal ramps leading to the central outdoor walkway. A 150-seat auditorium is located at the south end of the mall, and underground office areas are entered from the central spine. The underground office area is divided into two separate buildings, each with windows that face the central walkway permitting views of plants and fountains. Offices also have windows facing into four sunken courtyards located on the perimeter of the site. Continuing along the central circulation spine, one passes under the street and arrives in an entrance gallery within the six-story structure. Vertical circulation to various levels of the above-grade structure occurs

via elevators or stairs contained in three cylindrical forms along the north wall of the building.

Viewed from the exterior, the dominant image of the complex is the six-story structure. Not only does an above-grade mass naturally tend to dominate a below-grade one, but the unique sloping form and facade covered with collectors create a visual attraction and an identifiable symbol of solar technology. Over the below-grade portion of the complex, concrete balconies, retaining walls, paving, small areas of sod, and trees in planters contribute to the character of an urban park appropriate to its surroundings. Although sunken courtyards clearly indicate the presence of a building below, with its edges well defined by retaining walls, the true mass of the structure is diminished, and the main impression is that of an open space within the city. This image will

be modified somewhat by the introduction of above-grade housing masses on the western half of the park area. One asset of combining above- and below-grade masses in one complex is that unsightly mechanical equipment can be placed on the roof of the above-grade structure without disturbing the landscape design on the underground portion.

Separating the project into above-grade and below-grade components that are divided on the surface by a street creates some concern that the entire project may be perceived as two distinct and unrelated structures. The architects have resolved the issue in an interesting manner. Clearly, the two components of the building are fundamentally different in many respects and appear so from the exterior. They are also related, however, by two strong forms on the site—the central circulation spine and the sloping form of the above-grade

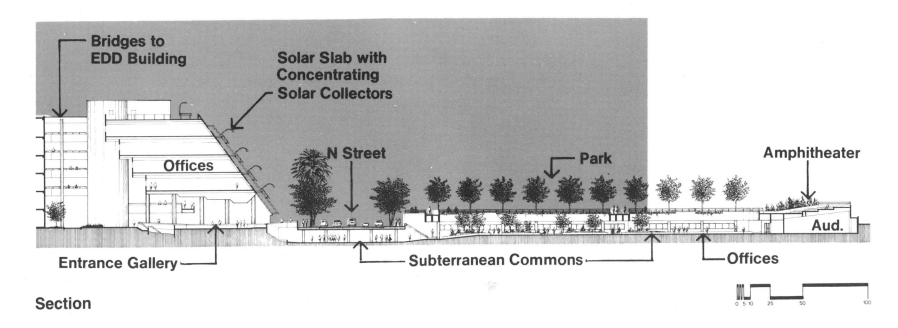

Section

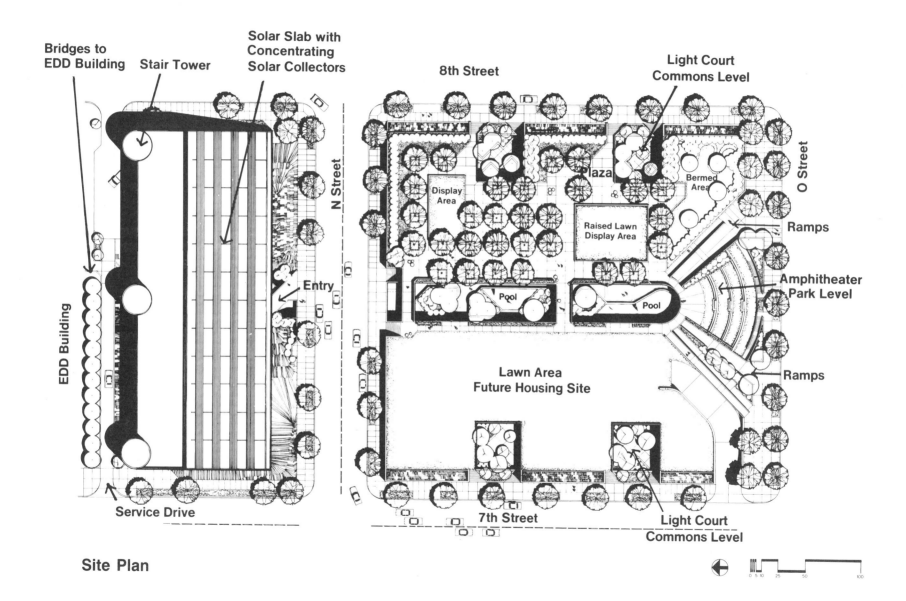

Bridges to
EDD Building

Stair Tower

Solar Slab with
Concentrating
Solar Collectors

8th Street

Light Court
Commons Level

O Street

N Street

EDD Building

Entry

Plaza

Display
Area

Bermed
Area

Ramps

Raised Lawn
Display Area

Amphitheater
Park Level

Pool

Pool

Lawn Area
Future Housing Site

Ramps

Service Drive

7th Street

Light Court
Commons Level

Site Plan

0 5 10   25   50   100

building. Because the facade of the six-story structure slopes down to the ground, it appears to be more integrated with the open space in front of it than a vertical building would be. More importantly the long sunken walkway that is the central form created in the underground building area directs the eye to the entry of the above-grade building.

Special Design Concerns

Underground buildings typically require particular attention in certain key areas of design, such as providing clear entry and circulation, acceptable transitions from grade to below grade, and adequate natural light and view in interior spaces when appropriate. These concerns are considered particularly important in office space, where people often spend the entire day and require elements of stimulation and psychological relief in their environment.

In the below-grade portions of the California State Office Building, each of the concerns listed above—entry, orientation, light and view—is addressed by the designers. Since the rooftop plaza is actually raised one-half level above grade, the only below-grade floor is just a few feet lower than the level of the sidewalks, thus easing the problem of entry and transition. Sloping ramps on the south side of the site provide access to the long central sunken courtyard, which serves as the main entrance to the offices and provides the major sense of orientation from both the exterior and interior of the below-grade spaces. Secondary entrances occur via exterior staircases leading to the central spine and to the four smaller courtyards. Circulation through exterior

courtyards, which is possible year-round in warmer climates, provides greater design freedom and facilitates below-grade entry and orientation.

Sunken courtyards with plants and fountains not only create a transition area to the below-grade space, but provide natural light and exterior views as well. The layout of the office space and the location of the courtyards in this building are designed to place the majority of the office area within view of the windows.

Glass partitions are used to permit light and view to penetrate to areas not immediately adjacent to the windows. In order to maximize the amount of natural light, highly reflective surfaces are used in the courtyards—white stucco walls and light-colored concrete paving.

Building Technology and Costs

The six-story steel-frame structural system of the above-grade building is typical of

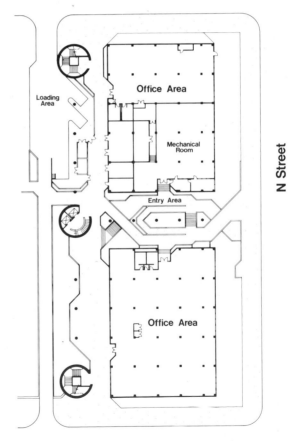

Floor Plan—First Level Above Grade

conventional buildings. Likewise, the structural system of the underground portion of the building is similar to most below-grade structures. The roof, which supports a 9-inch to 3-foot layer of earth as well as loads from the plaza above, is a cast-in-place reinforced concrete waffle slab. In addition to loads from the earth and from people on the plaza, the structure is designed to support future housing development on part of the site. Exterior walls in contact with the earth are reinforced concrete, and a rubberized

asphalt membrane is used to waterproof the structure.

The $18.5 million total cost of the project ($78 per square foot) appears to be quite reasonable considering the numerous unique features of the project. Calculations by the engineers indicate that the costs for the special mechanical systems and equipment in the building, such as the solar collectors, will be recovered in four to six years by reduced operating costs. Focusing on the underground portion of

the project, extra costs attributed to this type of construction must be compared with the value of two assets created by the below-grade design—the landscaped public park and the future housing development on the roof.

Energy Use Considerations

Unlike most buildings in which energy use is one of many competing concerns in design, conserving energy was a primary

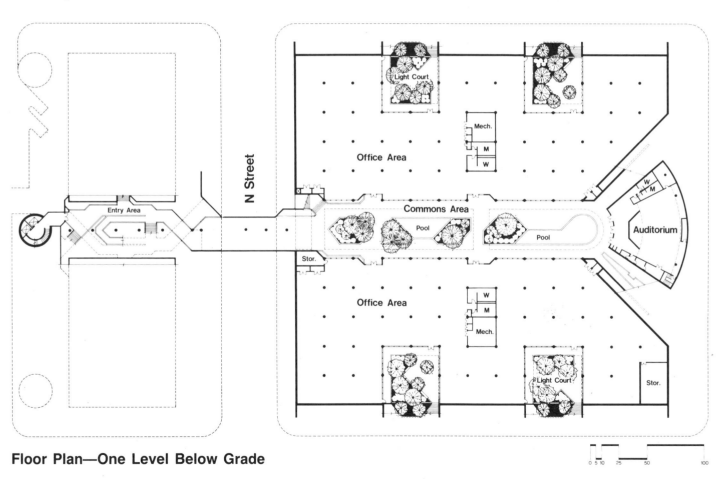

Floor Plan—One Level Below Grade

determinant of the form, the operating systems, and many of the details in the California State Office Building. The form and location of the above-grade portion of the building are based on maximizing solar exposure for the collector system. The remaining portion of the building is placed underground to conserve energy in a number of ways. The increased mass surrounding the underground spaces enables interior comfort conditions to be maintained for several hours with no heating or cooling. In addition, the grass-covered surfaces contribute to reduced heat gain on the roof and walls.

The projected energy use of the building is 19,800 Btu/sq ft/yr—a substantial reduction from conventional buildings even in the mild climate of Sacramento. An important characteristic of the local climate is the potentially great variations between daytime and nighttime temperatures. A major goal in the design was to utilize natural sources of energy as much as feasible before turning to conventional supplies. It is estimated that 10,500 Btu/sq ft/yr are provided by natural sources—6,000 by using an economizer cycle to cool the building with nighttime air; 4,200 from the solar collector system; and 300 by using diurnal temperature changes to chill water directly at night for use the next day.

Heating and cooling are provided from a variety of sources. The entire HVAC system and central plant is monitored and controlled by a computer that can select the most efficient means available at a given time. In the winter, the major heat

Above: Grade level view of the complex from the landscaped roof of the underground offices. Below: Central sunken courtyard at the level of the underground offices.

sources are hot water from the concentrating solar collectors and reclaimed heat from various building functions, with backup heat provided by a central steam plant. Heat pumps supply heat through baseboard fin tubes and a variable-air-volume ventilation system.

In the summer, hot water from the concentrating solar collectors drives an absorption machine to produce chilled water, and backup chilled water can be supplied from a central plant. The cooling cycle is supplemented by flushing the building with cooler nighttime air using an economizer cycle. Nighttime air is also used to chill water stored for daytime use directly. In addition, a rotary screw compressor and brine chiller are used to make and store ice during the night for daytime cooling. Converting chilled water into ice requires less storage volume. This system is designed to take advantage of lower electric rates available during the night. Hot water for uses other than space heating or cooling is provided from the solar collectors or rejected condenser heat when available.

Providing natural lighting in this building required special attention in the underground areas to offset any negative associations with being below grade. In order to explore the potential of substituting natural light for artificial lighting, the designers used scale models to simulate and predict lighting levels [5.3]. After examining numerous alternatives, a 3- by 3-foot fixture with two pairs of crisscrossed fluorescent lamps was selected. These fixtures are set into a 5-by 5-foot ceiling grid and are supplemented by task lighting. In order to efficiently use natural lighting, photoelectric cells detect light levels and shut off part or all of the artificial lights when they are unnecessary.

Project Data

Project: State Office Building

Location: Sacramento, California

Owner: State of California

Building type: Office building

Completion date: 1982

Project size: 264,000 sq. ft. (includes 75,000 sq. ft. in below-grade office space and auditorium)

Construction cost: $18,500,000

Structure: In below-grade structure: cast-in-place reinforced concrete waffle-slab roof, cast-in-place reinforced concrete walls, slab-on-grade floor; in 6-story above-grade structure: structural steel frame

Earth cover: 100 percent of exterior walls on first level are covered (not including courtyards); 100 percent of exposed roof on first level is covered with 9 in. to 3 ft. of earth

Insulation: Extruded polystyrene, 3 in. on earth-covered roof, 1 in. on below-grade walls; 6 in. of fiberglass insulation inside all above- and below-grade walls

Waterproofing: Rubberized asphalt membrane on earth-covered roof and below-grade walls

Heating system: Using a heat pump, hot water from concentrating solar collectors and reclaimed heat from various building functions is supplied to baseboard fin tubes and variable-air-volume ventilation system; backup heat provided by central district steam plant

Cooling system: Hot water from concentrating solar collectors drives an absorption machine to produce chilled water; cooling cycle is supplemented by nighttime cooling of building with economizer cycle, chilling of water with nighttime air, and rotary screw compressor and brine chiller that make and store ice during the night for peak daytime use; backup chilled water provided by central plant

Lighting: 3-ft. by 3-ft. fixture with two pairs of criss-crossed fluorescent lamps set into 5-ft. by 5-ft. ceiling module; supplemented by daylighting and task lighting

Energy use: 19,800 Btu/sq ft/yr projected

Heating degree days: 2,843

Cooling degree days: 1,159

Occupancy schedule: 40 hours per week, 52 weeks per year

Credits

Architect: The Benham Group, Oklahoma City, Oklahoma

Landscape architect: The Benham Group

Structural, mechanical and electrical engineers: The Benham Group

Geotechnical consultants: J. H. Kleinfelder and Associates

Lighting consultant: Dr. Lester L. Boyer, P.E.

Contractor: The Swinerton and Walberg Co., general; Ray O. Cook Co., mechanical

Photographs: Scott Dollmeyer of The Benham Group

National Art Education Association Headquarters

Reston, Virginia

Architect: The Benham Group

Located in a campuslike setting for several education association buildings in Reston, Virginia, the National Art Education Association Headquarters is a relatively small but distinctive earth-covered office building. The National Art Education Association (NAEA) is an organization devoted to the advancement of the professional interests and competence of those teaching art at all educational levels. The design of the 4,000-square foot building was intended to project a strong public image for the NAEA; however, since it is one of the smaller organizations with headquarters on the site, achieving this with a dominant architectural form was not possible. Placing the building into the sloping hillside created a positive, unique image independent of size. In addition, the earth-integrated design is a natural response to the contours of the land, provides usable open space on the roof, and contributes to energy conservation.

Completed in 1976, the one-level structure is set into a south-facing slope. The earth-covered roof is an extension of the landscaped grounds to the north of the building. The low profile of the NAEA building contrasts sharply with its immediate neighbor to the north, the six-story headquarters for the Council for Exceptional Children. Approached from the east end of the site, one arrives at a parking area on the south (or downhill) side of the building. Separated from the parking area by a small earth berm, the south, east, and west facades are all exposed—only the north wall of the structure is earth covered. Elongated on an east-west axis to maximize window exposure to the south, the building may be entered from either the east or west end.

Within the building, functions are arranged so that those requiring windows—mainly private offices—are placed along the south wall. In addition, a large conference room and library are located adjacent to the south wall. Other functions with a lower priority for windows—the reception area, a work area, and storage—are located on the building interior. The two entrances lead to a corridor along the north wall that serves as an art gallery.

Because it is set into a hillside, the NAEA Headquarters actually projects two different images when perceived from the exterior. Viewed from the north, one sees no entry; the entire building appears to be below grade, covered with grass. Although it could be described as a nonbuilding, certain elements do indicate the presence of a structure underneath the surface. Two cylindrical concrete forms that enclose skylights project several feet above the rooftop. Another cylindrical form covered with cedar encloses mechanical equipment and vents. Rather than permitting these potentially unsightly elements to conflict with the landscaped character, the architect has chosen to emphasize them as sculptural forms. The rooftop is defined on three sides by a concrete parapet that serves as a balcony.

In contrast to this almost nonexistent northern appearance, the building has a very strong image when approached and viewed from the south. Much as any conventional building, the facades are completely exposed. The scale of the building is actually made more imposing by the use of a large, overhanging parapet around the roof, bold concrete forms on the roof, and large retaining walls flanking the building. In spite of the massive forms, the large parapet and retaining walls give the building a long, low profile. The inherently cold, hard character of the concrete is softened by large glass areas,

cedar on the exterior walls, and landscaping.

Special Design Concerns

Placing office space below grade in large buildings with limited potential for exposure to the outside can create some difficult design problems and trade-offs. In a small structure like the NAEA Headquarters, however, these problems are far more easily resolved, particularly because the sloping site permits exposure on three sides of the building. For the majority of the spaces located on outside walls, natural light and exterior view are more than adequate. In the remaining spaces in the building, the architect has provided natural light and views very effectively in spite of the earth-covered north wall.

The entrance to the building is quite conventional: it occurs at grade, with no need for descent. Inside, however, the space is surprisingly light. Natural light floods the reception and gallery area from two large light wells. The cylindrical concrete forms seen on the roof extend through the structure, forming recessed areas in the north wall. Light bounces off the curving walls into the interior spaces; large plants fill the area beneath the skylights. Natural light as well as some exterior view is also provided to the building interior by the use of glass partitions in the office and conference rooms. Low partitions surrounding the central work area permit natural light to

Above: Glass partition wall divides the conference room from the reception area. Below: Earth-covered roof viewed from the north.

penetrate and minimize feelings of enclosure within the building.

On the interior the exposed concrete north wall is sandblasted and the concrete waffle-slab roof structure is exposed. Interior partitions are covered with cedar to contrast with the concrete and establish similar materials both inside and outside the building. Neutral furnishings allow the artwork and large interior plants to serve as the main visual focuses.

Building Technology and Costs

The cast-in-place concrete waffle-slab roof structure is supported on reinforced concrete columns. The north wall of the building and the retaining walls extending beyond the east and west walls of the building are also reinforced concrete. Placed over the roof structure is a rubberized asphalt waterproof membrane, 3 inches of polystyrene insulation and 18 inches of earth, covered with sod. Construction costs for the building in 1976 were $258,818 ($64.70 per square foot).

Energy Use Considerations

The design of the NAEA Headquarters is a natural response to the contours of the site and the desire for a positive, unique image. Without sacrificing function or aesthetics, the building design encompasses a number of basic strategies to reduce energy consumption. The building is elongated to create a larger south facade; the majority of the window area is on the south side of the building to maximize passive solar heat gain. This configuration minimizes the exterior surfaces exposed to excessive heat gain from the east and west in the summer. Overhangs are sized to shade windows in summer but permit the sun to enter in winter. The cylindrical forms enclosing the skylights on the roof actually shade them from direct sunlight a majority of the time, helping to reduce unwanted heat gain while still providing natural light.

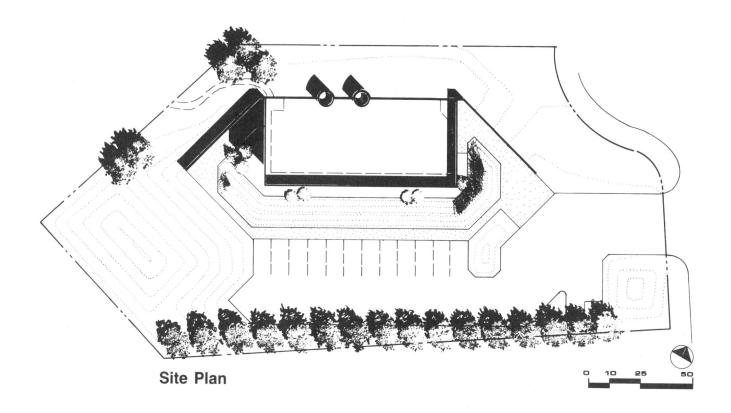

Site Plan

0 10 25 50

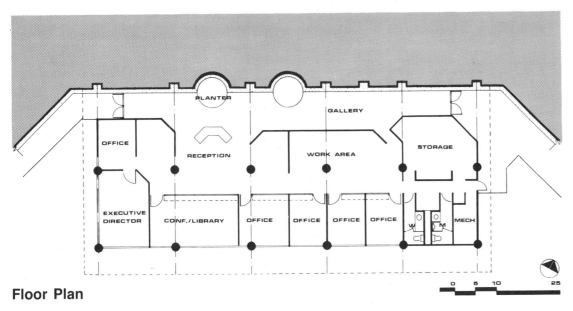

Floor Plan

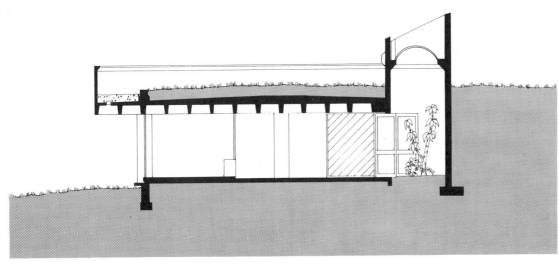

Section

Project Data

Project: National Art Education Association Headquarters

Location: Reston, Virginia

Owner: National Art Education Association

Building type: Office building

Completion date: 1976

Project size: 4,000 sq. ft.

Construction cost:

General	$106,741
Concrete	102,700
Roofing, sheet metal, and waterproofing	10,940
HVAC	10,750
Plumbing	9,353
Electrical	18,334
Total	$258,818

Structure: Cast-in-place reinforced concrete waffle-slab roof supported by concrete columns; cast-in-place reinforced concrete walls retaining earth; slab-on-grade concrete floor

Earth cover: 35 percent of exterior wall area is covered; 100 percent of roof is covered with 18 in. of earth

Insulation: Extruded polystyrene, 3 in. on roof, 1 in. on below-grade walls

Waterproofing: Rubberized asphalt membrane on roof and below-grade walls

Heating system: Electric resistance coils in forced-air distribution system

Cooling system: Conventional closed-loop refrigerant air conditioning system

Lighting: Incandescent supplemented by task lighting and daylight

Energy use: Information not available

Heating degree days: 4,211 (Washington, DC)

Cooling degree days: 1,415 (Washington, DC)

Occupancy schedule: 40 to 50 hours per week, 52 weeks per year

Credits

Architect: The Benham Group, Oklahoma City, Oklahoma (formerly Benham-Blair-Winesett-Duke)

Structural engineer: The Benham Group

Mechanical engineer: The Benham Group

Site engineer: John A. Brady, P.E.

Contractor: E. H. Glover, Inc.

Photographs: Scott Dollmeyer and NAEA

Right: Reception area with recessed light wells along the north wall.

Mutual of Omaha Headquarters Addition

Omaha, Nebraska

Architect: Leo A. Daly Company

A major addition to an existing building, particularly one with a very definite character and image, can be a difficult architectural problem. Conflicts may arise from connecting buildings of different styles, and the form of the older structure and spaces around it may be significantly altered. In the case of the 184,000-square foot addition to the Mutual of Omaha International Headquarters, these potential problems were resolved by placing the building completely underground. The familiar image of the Omaha, Nebraska, insurance company building was important to preserve, and the style of the older building is difficult and expensive to duplicate. In addition, creating a landscaped plaza on the flat site—formerly an unsightly parking lot—rather than another massive building enhanced the company's image with the surrounding residential community.

Along with the visual and image-related benefits of the underground design, several very practical advantages emerged as well. First, the company was able to use existing property, saving land acquisition costs for the new facility. The underground design also increases land-use efficiency: the building mass exceeds normal setbacks, but below grade, its exterior walls can extend to nearly the edge of the property. Second, the new structure, housing employee services as well as record storage, could be located in close proximity to the existing office building complex that it serves. Also, the underground design contributes to energy conservation and is considered to be less expensive to build than an above-grade structure in the style of the existing headquarters building.

Entered from the lowest level of the existing high-rise building, the addition consists of three levels completely below grade. The central feature of the addition viewed from both the exterior and interior is a 90-foot-diameter glass dome rising 15 feet above the rooftop plaza level. The largest dome of its kind in the United States, it covers a garden court with a fountain and trees in the center of the upper level. Surrounding the garden court is a 1,000-seat employee cafeteria, library, lounge, kitchen, and a conference and training center. These facilities serve 5,000 workers from the entire headquarters complex. The second and third levels of the addition are large, open-plan office spaces with no direct connection to the surface. Machine repair, files, and some offices are on the middle level, and record storage covers the lower level. Continuous transfer of files can occur between this area and the older building using a conveyor system. Because ceilings are higher and the structure is stronger in the new addition, files occupy about half the floor space they did in the older structure.

The basically flat site is dominated by the symmetrical, monumental form of the older headquarters building. In response to this, the design of the rooftop plaza is also quite geometric and symmetrical. Because the addition is completely underground and is entered only through the below-grade level of another building, awareness of the size and boundaries of the structure is diminished. Many elements of the formal circular garden are similar to those of a plaza that might occur in front of any large office building. The glass dome rising from the plaza, however, not only indicates the presence of a structure below, but is the central focus of the entire landscape design. At night the light from inside glowing through the dome creates an attractive effect. Other elements related to

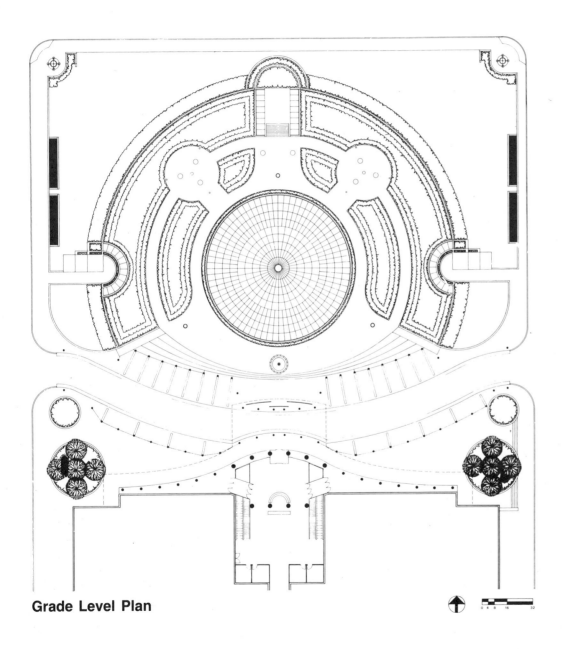

Grade Level Plan

the structure below, notably the three fire-exit stairways that emerge on the plaza level, are carefully incorporated Into the landscape design to diminish their scale.

Special Design Concerns

The underground addition to the Mutual of Omaha Headquarters Building houses several functions. Some are treated quite differently than others with respect to natural light, view, and interior design. For one group of functions— employee cafeteria, library, and lounge—the goal was not only to offset negative associations with being underground but to create a very attractive environment that would provide a pleasant break from the typical office spaces. This is achieved in a spectacular way by placing these functions around the glass-covered garden court, which is large enough to provide amenities for the entire upper floor. In addition to natural light, views of the sky and building above, and plant materials in the central court, this placement offers a great sense of a high, open space, as it is roofed only by the intricate structure supporting the dome. Granite and Kasota stone, the basic materials used in the older buildings, are also used in the garden court. The library is separated from the court by a glass partition wall that provides an acoustical barrier without diminishing natural light from and view of the courtyard. A conference and training center on the upper floor is appropriately enclosed in windowless space on the upper level. Its proximity to the central space creates a positive image and environment for those attending conferences and for other visitors to the complex as well.

On the two lower floors of the addition, functions such as record storage, offices, and machine repair are placed in completely windowless space. Although lacking the amenities of the upper level, these are appropriate functions in this type of space, which differs little from storage and office space found in the interior zones of large above-grade buildings. Access to these levels occurs through elevators and stairs from the courtyard level above.

Entering a completely underground building is usually a special design concern, the goal being to avoid the negative associations of going down while maintaining the conventional recognition and orientation an entry provides. These concerns are resolved more easily when the underground building is an addition to an above-grade structure that provides the major entrance. Within the existing structure, entry to the new addition is facilitated by large escalators running from the main floor lobby to the first level below grade. From the lower lobby, one proceeds through a short, wide corridor to the attractive, naturally lighted central courtyard, which provides orientation to the surface and gives the new addition an identity of its own.

Building Technology and Costs

The most significant problem in constructing an underground addition to the Mutual of Omaha Headquarters was excavating and building next to the foundation of the older building without disturbing it. Great care was required since the footings of the existing 14-story structure were only 14 feet below grade, while the lowest level of the new structure was to be about 45 feet beneath the surface. To permit the load from the older building to be distributed to the soil, the

three levels of the addition are terraced away from the shallow footings. Excavation took place in two stages—an open cut was made away from the building to the lowest level, and then, with shoring in place, the area closest to the building was excavated. During excavation, movement in the older foundations was carefully monitored and contingency plans were made to move the addition further from the old building if too much movement occurred. Approximately 150,000 cubic yards of earth were removed from the site.

In addition to special problems with the excavation, the water table on the site is actually above the lower floor level. The primary strategy employed to minimize water problems is a drainage system with pumps and sumps that effectively lower the water table around the building. A liquid-applied rubber-base waterproof membrane is applied to the exterior concrete walls and concrete roof deck. The waterproof membrane on the roof is covered by a protection board, 3 inches of crushed rock, 3 inches of high-density polystyrene insulation, and another 1½ inches of crushed rock. Over this is laid a permeable membrane to prevent soil from clogging the drainage layers, and 18 to 24 inches of soil—enough to support sod and small ground cover.

The structure of the addition consists of steel columns, girders, and beams supporting metal deck and concrete fill floors. The exterior walls and roof deck are cast-in-place reinforced concrete. Exterior walls act as shear walls to resist any lateral forces from the foundation of the existing building. Floors on all three levels carry electrical power supply and telephone lines in the cells of the metal deck. The 90-foot-diameter glass dome is made of two layers of tempered glass

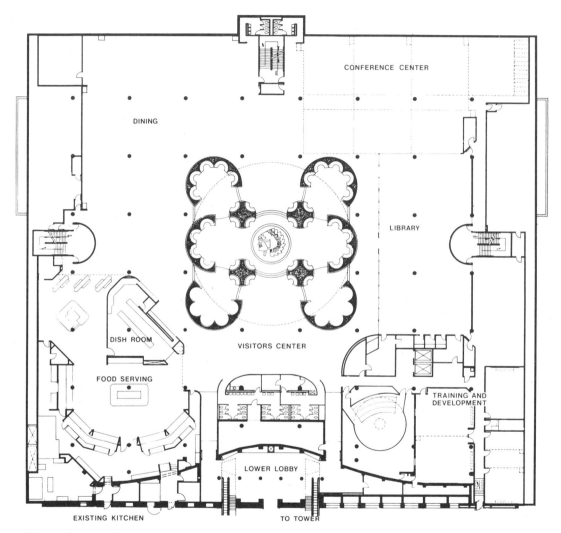

Floor Plan—One Level Below Grade

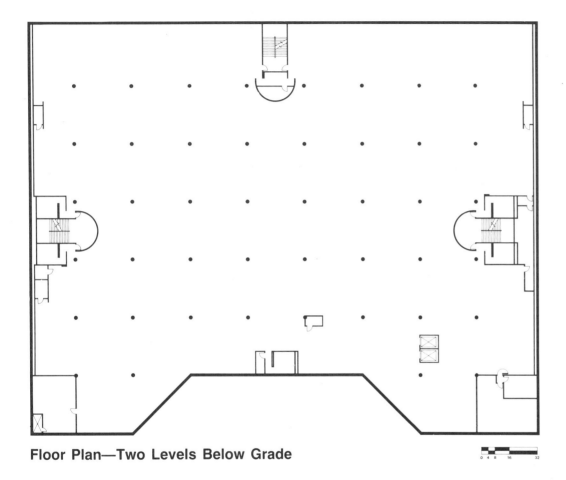

Floor Plan—Two Levels Below Grade

0 4 8   16   32

designed to resist 30 pounds per square foot snow loads and 20 pounds per square foot wind loads. Consisting of 505 glass panels, the outside layer is solar bronze glass and the inside layer is clear glass; ½ inch of air space separates the two layers.

In some cases underground construction is regarded as more expensive than comparable buildings above grade—particularly if there are special water and retaining problems. The owner and architects of the Mutual of Omaha addition, however, consider the underground design to be significantly less expensive than the above-grade alternative. Costing $12.3 million ($67 per square foot), the addition is in the range of high-quality office construction. It is considered less expensive in this case because it is assumed an above-grade addition would be done with Kasota stone and granite to match the existing buildings.

Energy Use Considerations

The primary energy-conserving feature of the new addition is its completely underground location. Lights, people, and machines should supply the majority of the heat needed in winter, with little loss occurring through the building envelope. Auxiliary heating and cooling are supplied from a central steam and chilled water plant serving the entire complex. Although made of insulated glass to reduce heat loss and using bronze-colored glass to reduce summer heat gain, the dome will constitute a significant portion of the heating and cooling load. In spite of this, the architect estimates that the addition will consume 30 to 50 percent less energy than a comparable facility above grade.

Construction Costs for Mutual of Omaha Headquarters Addition

Architect/Engineer, contractor fees, and general conditions	$1,174,650
Site preparation	119,700
Excavations, foundations, shoring	891,100
Structural, exterior walls, roof deck, and metal floor deck	3,592,900
Dome structure, glazing, and all other glass and glazing	512,050
Waterproofing, caulking, and building insulation	358,150
Fireproofing	90,250
Stone, Kasota and granite	979,450
Elevators and escalators	190,950
Fire protection	134,900
Mechanical	1,731,050
Electrical	803,650
Kitchen/cafeteria	513,570
Lawns, landscaping, and lawn sprinklers	134,900
Operable walls	131,100
Interior finishes, wall covering, carpet, and tile flooring	171,610
Interior carpentry and millwork, lath, plaster, drywall, ceramic, and quarry tile	531,050
Acoustical and integrated ceilings	259,350
Miscellaneous operating equipment	10,450
Total	$12,330,830

Above: The underground addition viewed from the roof of the original Headquarters Building. Below: Library interior with glass partition wall permitting a view of the garden court.

Project Data

Project: Mutual of Omaha Headquarters Addition

Location: Omaha, Nebraska

Owner: United of Omaha

Building type: Office building including employee cafeteria and lounges

Completion date: 1979

Project size: 184,000 sq. ft.

Construction cost: $12,330,830
See construction cost table for detailed breakdown.

Structure: Steel columns, beams, and girders support metal deck and concrete fill floors; cast-in-place reinforced concrete walls and roof deck; concrete slab-on-grade floor

Earth cover: 100 percent of exterior walls are covered; 90 percent of roof is covered with 12 to 18 inches of earth

Insulation: 3-in.-thick high-density extruded polystyrene on the roof; no insulation on below-grade walls

Waterproofing: Liquid-applied rubber-base waterproof membrane on roof and below-grade walls

Heating system: Connected to central steam plant in remote aboveground facility; variable-air-volume induction bypass boxes and box light troffers

Cooling system: Connected to central chilled water plant in remote above ground facility

Lighting: Two-lamp fluorescent, parabolic louvers

Energy use: Information not available

Heating degree days: 6,049

Cooling degree days: 1,173

Occupancy schedule: 50 to 60 hours per week

Credits

Architect and engineer: Leo A. Daly Company, Omaha, Nebraska

Foundation consultant: Woodward-Clyde Consultants

Audiovisual consultant: Jamieson and Associates

Contractor: Peter Kiewit Sons' Company

Photographs: Leo A. Daly Company

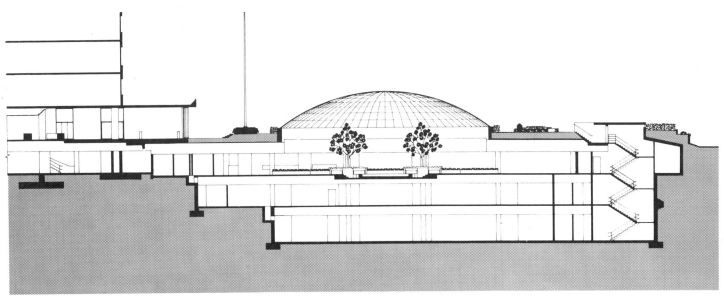

Section

Terratech Center

St. Paul, Minnesota

Architect: Criteria Architects

Unique in its form and concept, the Terratech Center in St. Paul, Minnesota, was built to demonstrate a number of energy-efficient techniques and advantages of underground buildings. Completed in 1979, most of the 14,750-square foot structure serves as office space for the Control Data Corporation; the building also includes a large garden court and a single residential unit. Initially, Criteria Architects chose the site for the Terratech Center because it had so many negative characteristics. Located in an inner-city redevelopment area with a mixture of industrial, institutional, and residential structures, the site is bounded on the north by a busy freeway. The site slopes to the north, providing the least desirable terrain for maximizing solar collection. The philosophy behind this site selection and the subsequent building design is that a building can and should be a positive force in restoring and enhancing the natural environment, not a negative or destructive influence.

Cutting into the north-facing slope and berming and covering most of the structure with earth resulted in a number of benefits. The most obvious advantages are the reduction in noise from the adjacent freeway and the contribution of the surrounding earth mass to energy conservation. In addition, the building presents an unobtrusive image to the neighborhood and serves to enhance the environment visually and ecologically. Key concerns of the designers, often overlooked in conventional building design, were maintaining plant materials over as much of the site as possible and using natural rather than energy-intensive mechanical systems whenever feasible. For example, rainwater from the site is collected and used to water plants within the central garden court.

Underlying many of the typical advantages of underground buildings demonstrated by the Terratech Center are benefits related to land use, energy efficiency, and environmental preservation that go beyond the influence of a single building. Basically, earth-integrated design enables marginal land within the existing city to be used and restored in ways not possible with conventional structures. Not only does this provide aesthetic and environmental benefits, but city tax bases can be increased, formerly incompatible functions can be placed in closer proximity, and more concentrated development patterns can reduce energy for transportation and the costs of extending the existing infrastructure of roads and utilities.

Based on the decision to place the building almost entirely underground, a thin shell structural system was selected that has the ability to support much larger earth loads than is typically considered economical with conventional structures. The system consists of corrugated, curved steel plates that are typically bolted together to form vaults used to support large earth loads over culverts or tunnels. In the Terratech Center, the basic structure of the building consists of two 30-foot-diameter, 100-foot-long steel vaults. Each vault encloses two levels of space and is open along one side, permitting windows to face a large glass-enclosed atrium in the center.

The building can be entered through the two-story courtyard or through the main entrance penetrating the berm on the north side. Of the 14,750 square feet of enclosed space, 11,070 square feet are

Opposite: Main entrance on the north side of the building, photograph by Richard Cottrell.

open-plan office space on two levels within the steel vaults. The central garden court comprises an area of 1,725 square feet. The remaining floor area is devoted to circulation, mechanical space, and a 600-square foot residential unit. Similar to many features of this building, the residential unit is intended as an experiment to determine both social and energy-related benefits of mixing commercial and residential functions within the same structure.

Although the Terratech Center is largely shielded by earth berms when viewed from the freeway, it is not invisible—it presents a definite form and a distinct character compared with more conventional structures. Because the site slopes downward to the freeway, the earth berm covering the north side of the building rises steeply; a series of wooden retaining walls creates a terraced effect and forms a walkway to the main entrance. The intriguing curved form of the main entrance penetrating the berm on the north side echoes the vaulted structure within. In contrast to the urban character of many underground buildings dominated by hard surfaces and closely manicured landscaping, the Terratech Center illustrates a more natural approach to earth-integrated design. Not only are unusual curving forms used in the structure, but native plant materials provide a more varied, informal character and require less maintenance than sod.

Proceeding around the building, the exterior image changes as the large

Above: South-facing office windows and solar collectors viewed from the southeast, photograph by Gerald Allan. Below: Office space on the upper level, photograph by Gerald Allan.

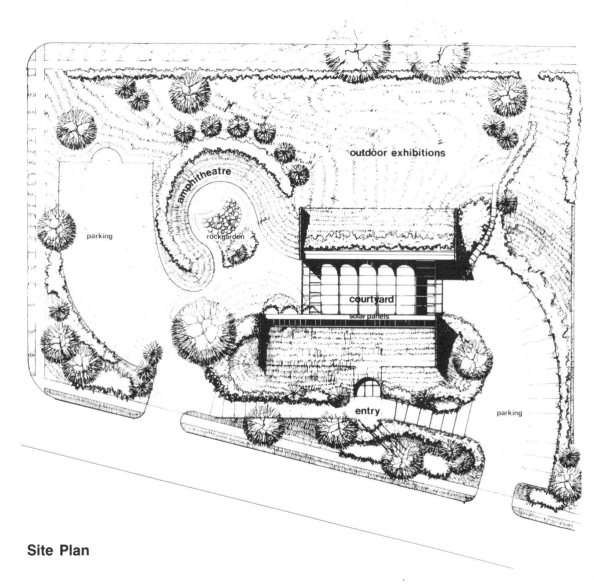

Site Plan

concrete retaining walls and glass-enclosed atrium become visible. Viewed from the east and west ends, the banks of windows and glimpses of the plant-filled atrium inside create an unexpectedly light feeling compared to the large earth berm on the north side. Since the highest ground level is on the southern portion of the site, the building appears to be completely below grade when viewed from that side. This creates a very unobtrusive image in relation to the residential neighborhood to the south and results in views and a sense of open space extending across the freeway corridor.

Special Design Concerns

Entering an underground building is always considered a special concern because of potentially negative associations with descending—particularly in a dark or confined space. These concerns are completely alleviated by the design of the entrances to the Terratech Center. From the east or west ends, the building is approached on grade and a conventional entry sequence occurs through an outdoor courtyard and then into the glass-enclosed atrium. This type of entrance creates a very positive image. The main public entrance on the north side of the building is more unconventional in appearance but is equally positive in its approach. One ascends, rather than descends, along the walkway to arrive at the second-level entry. Once inside, the vaulted shape of the ceiling creates an open feeling, with glimpses of the plant-filled central atrium just ahead.

Even though the Terratech Center is predominantly earth covered and set into a north-facing slope, it is a very light and open building on the interior. The long, narrow plan, in which each of the two steel vaults with window walls face the central atrium area, enables every point in the building to be no more than 30 feet from a window. Sunlight penetrates directly into the south-facing windows and is reflected by the white exterior surfaces through the north-facing windows. In the north half of the building, a series of round skylights provides daylight along the north wall. Although exterior views beyond the limits of the building are limited, the inward orientation to the courtyard filled with plants provides an attractive focus. The garden court is available for relaxation and informal meetings, providing an outdoor atmosphere year-round.

Important concerns in developing the interior design of the building were maximizing the natural light coming from the window wall while maintaining acoustical privacy in individual office areas. The upper floor within the steel vaults has a 14-foot-high curving ceiling that is dynamic spatially and can aid in reflecting light. The ceiling is, however, acoustically undesirable in an open-plan office. The curved ceiling was therefore sprayed with a cellulose material that absorbs sound, reflects natural light, and provides fire protection for the steel structure. This enables spaces to be divided using only low acoustical partitions for privacy. In some cases glass partitions are used to permit view and light to penetrate to areas

away from the windows. Because the earth berms effectively reduce outside noise, the interior spaces were so quiet that acoustical privacy was hard to achieve. For this reason a background noise level is piped into the spaces at a frequency that assists in masking voices at a certain distance.

Building Technology and Costs

The selection of the steel vault structure used in the Terratech Center was based on the inherent capability of a vault shape to support large earth loads more efficiently than conventional flat roof systems. Typically, 1 to 2 feet of earth

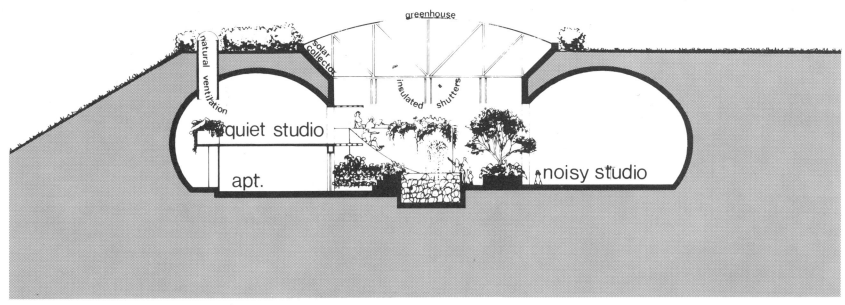

Section

154

over a flat roof structure can provide some cooling benefits and additional mass while permitting grass and small shrubs to grow. With greater amounts of earth cover, however, energy-related benefits can be increased year-round.

The simplest and most easily constructed vault forms are tubes or tunnels open only on the ends. By opening the vaults longitudinally as they are in the Terratech Center, the system becomes more complex both in design and construction. Basically, the two vaults require lateral forces at the top to resist the thrust from the earth loads against the sides. This is achieved by placing compression members between them, enabling the force from one vault to resist the force from the other. The structural design had to compensate for the fact that the force on the steeply bermed north side was not identical to that on the fully buried south side. In addition, backfilling and compaction with a system like this is critical to prevent great imbalances from occurring when loading different areas of the structure.

Critical elements of the structural system are the large concrete end walls, which stiffen the vaults along the edge and help to resist thrust and overturning. Since the two vaults are not directly across from each other over their entire length, the extended ends of the building tend to rotate. These forces are offset by diagonal braces extending across the courtyard space between the vaults. In spite of some of the complex engineering and detailing required in this experimental application, the use of vaulted structures

Right: Glass-enclosed central courtyard, photograph by Saari and Forrai.

for a wide variety of functions has significant implications for underground buildings.

Because of the curving, corrugated surface of the steel vaults penetrated by connecting bolts at regular intervals, most waterproofing and insulation products were not suitable. A liquid rubber material that conformed to the irregular surfaces was sprayed over the steel, and polyurethane foam insulation was then sprayed over the waterproofing. Since insulation requirements are greatest near the surface, the polyurethane was sprayed in a 3-inch layer over the top of the vaults, tapering to a 1-inch thickness on the sides. The insulation was then protected by another waterproofing layer, since it is not intended to be directly exposed to moisture.

Total construction costs for the Terratech Center were $1.1 million ($75 per square foot), which is within the range of high-quality conventional commercial office space. In addition to the unique structural system, this project included a wide range of unconventional details. Because of the experimental nature of the entire project and the impact of changes made during the construction process, it is difficult to use these costs for any valid comparison with conventional buildings or simpler applications of the steel vault structure. For example, the architects have subsequently used a similar structural system to provide a naturally cool underground warehouse for storing cheese. The warehouse structure cost only $30 per square foot to construct.

Energy Use Considerations

One of the original purposes of the Terratech Center was to test a variety of energy-conserving concepts. The primary

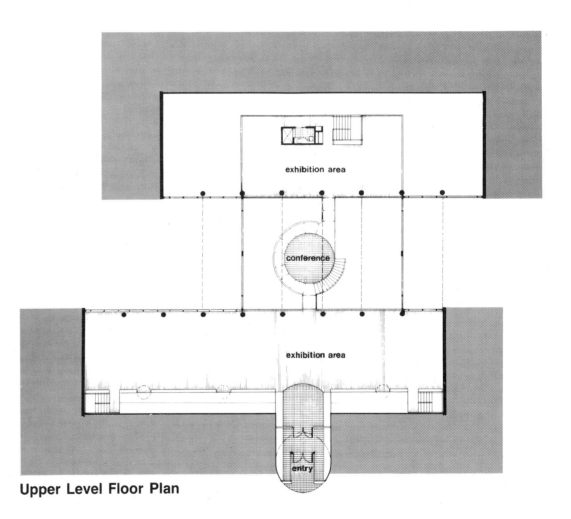

Upper Level Floor Plan

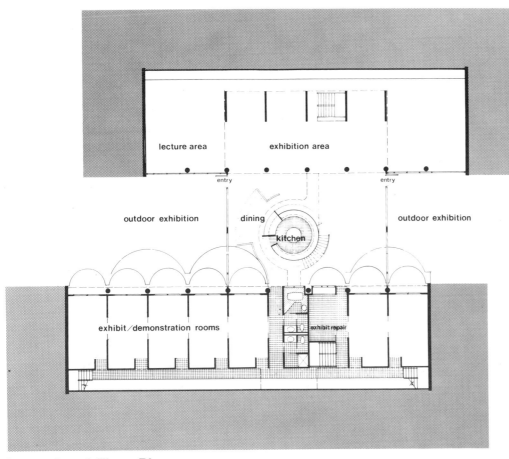

Lower Level Floor Plan

energy-related strategies involve placing the building underground while benefiting from solar energy as much as possible. Because the north-facing slope prevents all windows from being oriented to the south, only the northern half of the building and the atrium receive direct solar radiation. The roof of the atrium consists of all-plastic double-wall translucent panels, which permit sunlight to enter while maintaining some insulating value. In addition to passive solar collection, 780 square feet of flat-plate solar collectors are mounted on the roof edge. Heated water from the collectors is stored in a 22,000-gallon tank beneath the structure.

Since the north half of the building receives direct solar radiation all day long and the south half never receives any, their energy requirements differ greatly. Most of the time, the north half requires cooling and the south half requires heating. By using several small heat pumps, excess heat can be drawn from overheated to underheated spaces. Additional heat is available from the solar collectors, and a gas-fired boiler serves as a backup system.

During portions of the year, natural ventilation is used for cooling and providing air change. All office windows are operable, and openings in the atrium roof permit heat to be expelled, drawing air from other areas of the building. When necessary, cooling is provided by a conventional air-conditioning system.

One interesting concept demonstrated by this building is the mix of commercial spaces with residential units. In terms of energy use, commercial office spaces often are overheated as a result of lights, people, and machines, whereas residential spaces generally require more heat since

they do not have great internal loads. By combining the two types of spaces, the excess heat from one can be used to provide heat for the other. In this particular building, the ratio of office space to residential space is too high to affect energy use dramatically. The principle, however, is a valid one. Such a concept is not limited to single structures that contain both functions but can also be applied to neighborhood planning, using district heating and cooling systems.

Another contribution to energy conservation is found in the design of the lighting system. The fluorescent fixtures with eggcrate reflectors that are hung from the ceiling produce adequate lighting levels using less then 1 Watt per square foot. All energy systems in the building are controlled and monitored by a microcomputer.

For the years 1980 through 1982, the total energy use in the building varied considerably. In 1980, with executive offices in the majority of the spaces, the total use was 92,474 Btu/sq ft/yr. Because the building was unoccupied during three months in 1981, the total energy use was reduced to 81,424 Btu/sq ft/yr. Two small computers and extensive computer terminals installed in 1982 increased the electrical use, resulting in a total energy use of 115,593 Btu/sq ft/yr. Although the figures generally appear to be higher than one would anticipate, the building has some unusual characteristics that tend to distort the energy consumption. Clearly,

Above: Corrugated steel shell structure during construction, photograph by Steve Bergerson. Below: Concrete retaining walls viewed from the west end of the building, photograph by Richard Cottrell.

electrical usage for computers is a contributing factor. Heating and cooling the glass-enclosed garden court, however, appears to be the largest single component of energy use in the building. According to estimates, without heating and cooling the atrium, total energy use for the building would be 30 to 50 percent less—in the range of 40,000 to 60,000 Btu/sq ft/yr.

Project Data

Project: Terratech Center

Location: St. Paul, Minnesota

Owner: Control Data Corporation

Building type: Office building and residential unit

Completion date: 1979

Project size: 14,750 sq. ft. (includes 1,725 sq. ft. in central garden court)

Construction cost: $1,100,000

Structure: Corrugated steel vault roof with reinforced concrete end walls provides main enclosures; steel structure braces vaults and supports roof over garden court; intermediate floors are bar joist and wood deck; slab-on-grade and slab-on-steel deck floors

Earth cover: 50 percent of exposed exterior walls are covered, including the vaulted areas; 100 percent of roof is covered to a minimum of 3 ft. deep, not including the garden court

Insulation: Polyurethane sprayed onto vault structure 3 in. thick on top tapering to 1 in. thick on sides

Waterproofing: Sprayed-on liquid rubber membrane on vault

Heating system: Solar-assisted heat pump with gas-fired boiler as a backup source

Cooling system: Conventional closed-loop refrigerant air-conditioning system

Lighting: Fluorescent fixtures with eggcrate reflectors on movable track

Energy use:

1980: 92,474 Btu/sq ft/yr
Electricity 695×10^6 Btu (203,640 kWh)
Natural gas 669×10^6 Btu (669×10^6 cu ft)
Total $1,364 \times 10^6$ Btu

1981: 81,424 Btu/sq ft/yr
Electricity 693×10^6 Btu (203,160 kWh)
Natural gas 508×10^6 Btu (508×10^6 cu ft)
Total $1,201 \times 10^6$ Btu

1982: 115,593 Btu/sq ft/yr
Electricity 952×10^6 Btu (279,000 kWh)
Natural gas 753×10^6 Btu (753×10^6 cu ft)
Total $1,705 \times 10^6$ Btu

Note: Building was unoccupied during three months in 1981, accounting for reduced energy use. Increased use in 1982 is partially attributable to additional office machine and computer terminal use. Energy use per unit area based on 14,750 sq. ft., which includes garden court. Estimates are that garden court requires 30 to 50 percent of total energy use.

Heating degree days: 8,159

Cooling degree days: 585

Occupancy schedule: 60 hours per week in office areas, 168 hours per week in living unit

Credits

Architect: Criteria Architects Inc., Afton, Minnesota

Structural engineer: Wilhelm Reindl

Mechanical engineer: Horwitz Inc.

Interior design and lighting: Office Interiors Inc. and Orfield Associates Inc.

Contractor: Criteria Builders Inc. and Kraus-Anderson

Photographs: Gerald Allan, Saari and Forrai Photography, Steve Bergerson, and Richard Cottrell.

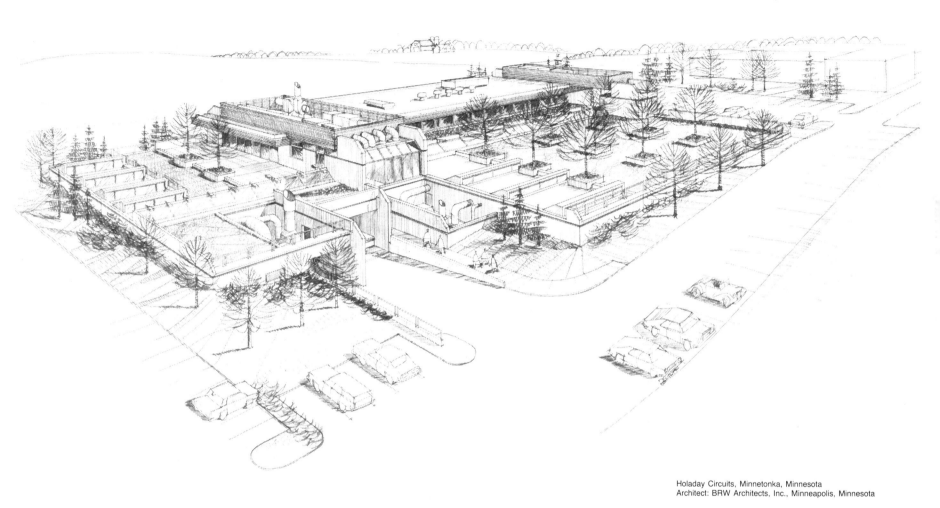

Holaday Circuits, Minnetonka, Minnesota
Architect: BRW Architects, Inc., Minneapolis, Minnesota

Chapter 6: Manufacturing and Storage Facilities

Great Midwest Underground

Kansas City, Missouri

In contrast to the majority of underground buildings, which are placed in soil at relatively shallow depths, very extensive mined space development exists in the Kansas City, Missouri, area that is 90 to 210 feet below the surface. Over 216 million square feet of space has been mined out of several sites since the 1940s to provide high-quality limestone rock for construction and other purposes. Within the abandoned mines, approximately 22 million square feet of space is presently utilized for warehouses, cold storage, manufacturing, and office space [6.1]. Although mined space development in Kansas City is the product of unique geological, geographical, and economic conditions, it illustrates the potential for such development in other locations. In addition, the development demonstrates a number of unique characteristics as well as design and planning issues associated with mined space.

The various mined space developments in the Kansas City area have many unique features and uses; the general characteristics in most cases, however, remain the same. In order to provide a more detailed examination of mined space, one development representing fairly typical conditions has been selected—the Great Midwest Underground. As with all mined space in the Kansas City area, it is located within the Bethany Falls layer of limestone, which is overlain by 50 to 200 feet of other rock layers (mostly limestones and shales). The Bethany Falls limestone layer is exposed in deep valleys in the surrounding terrain, permitting direct horizontal access to the mined space. Both rail and vehicular access is provided into the space, since existing rail lines and highways are located in the valleys.

In the Great Midwest development, as in other developments in the area, the lower 12 to 13 feet of the Bethany Falls layer is mined out, leaving an 8- to 9-foot solid limestone roof supported by massive pillars. Using the room-and-pillar method of mining, 25- by 25-foot pillars are left with 40-foot spans in between, producing a gridwork of space that provides long, straight openings for roads, corridors, or assembly lines.

As of December, 1982, the Great Midwest Underground included a total mined out area of 18.5 million square feet (not including support pillars). Of this total, 2.9 million square feet are developed and leased, another 2.1 million square feet have been developed as common areas for roads, loading docks, and parking, and 1.9 million square feet are available for immediate development. Included in the complex are 3.14 miles of roads and 1.88 miles of railroad tracks. Generally reflecting space utilization in the Kansas City area, 85 percent of the leased area in the Great Midwest Underground is for storage and warehouse uses, 11 percent is for manufacturing, and 4 percent is for office space. A unique aspect of the development is the provision of foreign trade zone status for a portion of the mined area, which provides a number of economic benefits since products can be imported, assembled, stored, and exported without application of custom duties.

Originally the mines in the Kansas City area were created for a single purpose, to provide limestone. Once a few pioneers began to use the abandoned space for

Opposite: Great Midwest corporate office entrance viewed from the underground roadway.

other activities, an increasing awareness of the advantages of placing certain functions deep underground developed. Today there is a long list of benefits to the tenant of the underground space, to the developer, and to the entire community. Although the Kansas City developers can profit from both rock extraction and leasing the space for secondary use, it is conceivable that the benefits of such space will cause it to be mined regardless of the profitability of the mining operation in the future [6.2, 6.3].

A primary advantage of mined space in Kansas City is lower construction costs: the raw shell is provided at essentially no cost, thus enabling developers to offer lower lease rates than surface facilities. Limited exposure to the outside makes it easier to provide tight security, and products and records are safe from tornadoes and other external disasters. Since there is no building exterior and protection from natural disasters is provided, maintenance and insurance costs are lower as well. An advantage for

storage and manufacturing is the virtually unlimited weight that can be supported on the rock floor. The deep, solid rock enclosure also provides a great reduction in outside noise and vibration. One of the pioneering companies in using mined space in Kansas City, Brunson Instrument Company, found this characteristic a particular asset for the manufacture of precision instruments.

One of the most appealing benefits of mined space is the significantly lower operating costs. At a depth of 150 to 200 feet, the temperature remains constant at approximately 60°F year-round, resulting in no heating and reduced cooling and dehumidification needs. These conditions are an asset for cold or cool storage and enable much closer control of temperature and humidity, when necessary, at lower cost. In addition, temperatures can be maintained for long periods of time with little or no input of outside energy.

From the developer's point of view, there are economic benefits in creating two layers of development on the same piece of land. The Great Midwest Underground is only part of a total master plan that will include industrial, commercial, residential, and recreational uses on the surface over the mines. This can benefit the community by increasing land-use efficiency, resulting in a higher tax base and more efficient use of existing roads and utilities. Generally, energy used for transportation can be reduced with more compact development, which includes housing on the surface and workplaces below. In addition, a number of environmental

Left: Entrances to mined space cut into the limestone bluffs.

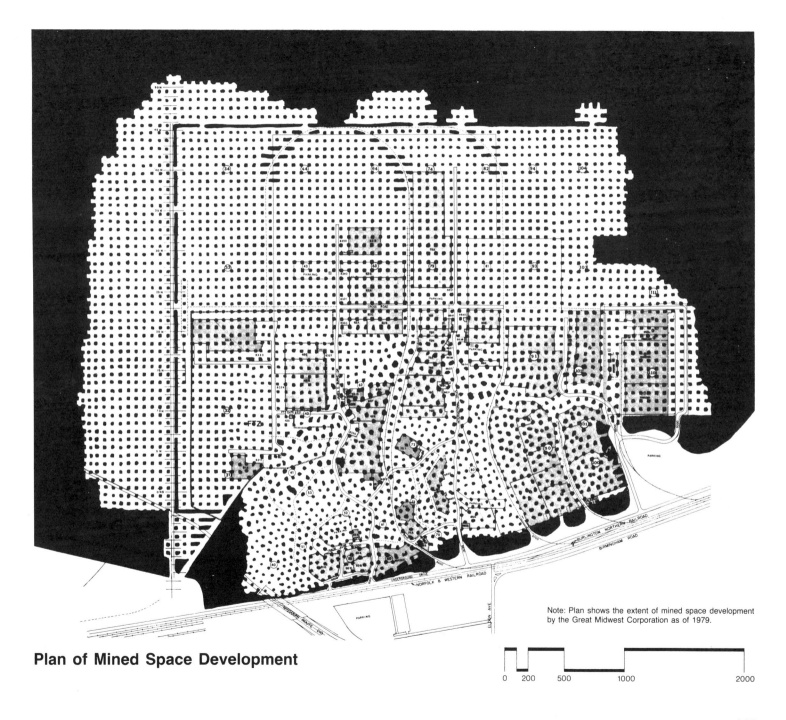

Plan of Mined Space Development

Note: Plan shows the extent of mined space development by the Great Midwest Corporation as of 1979.

0   200   500   1000   2000

165

benefits are inherent in utilizing mined space. For example, the impact of unsightly or noisy functions such as manufacturing or warehouses that occupy large land areas is virtually eliminated. The unobtrusive nature of the activities in mined space is reflected in current zoning ordinances in Kansas City—whatever use is permitted at the mine entrance can occur in the entire mine regardless of what is occurring on the surface above.

Because so little of a mined space development is evident from the surface, the exterior image might seem to be an irrelevant concern. On the contrary, the exposed entry portals become very critical simply because they are the only exterior elements. Before marketing secondary use of mined space in Kansas City became a major concern, entry portals were surrounded by parking lots and billboardlike signs, giving a generally barren, makeshift, industrial character. More recently, portals such as the main entrances to the Great Midwest Underground have been designed to create a positive image. There is no attempt to disguise the bluff or make the entry appear part of a false facade. Instead, the natural bluff with vegetation above is the main image. The entrance remains simple in design, highlighted by clear, uncluttered graphics and a colorful row of flags symbolizing the foreign trade zone. For the current use of the mined space, this seems an appropriate image—the individual images projected by different commercial tenants occur inside along the roadways. Potential tenants that require a high degree of visibility have alternatives: using mined space integrated with surface developments above, to achieve the benefits of both; or not locating their functions in mined space.

Special Design Concerns

In designing underground buildings near the surface, offsetting potentially negative associations with below-grade, windowless spaces frequently causes concern. In most cases, however, many techniques may be used to alleviate these concerns. The very deep and isolated nature of mined space presents the same, if not greater, concerns but offers fewer options to resolve them. It is therefore important to be sensitive to the design of mined space and equally important to identify functions that are appropriate in this type of space. Most concerns over creating an acceptable environment apply only to a limited extent for storage functions, which are the main use in Kansas City; however, they cannot be overlooked in offices and manufacturing, where many people spend the entire day.

The exterior image of the entrance to a mined space development has been discussed. The negative or positive feelings associated with entering such a space are also worthy of some concern. Physically, it is not possible to change the basic size and shape of the mine—one enters a relatively small opening, passes through a tunnel, and drives along roadways inside the complex, passing regular rows of massive rock pillars. Individual tenant areas for offices, factories, or warehouses usually have parking areas in the mine and individual facades with entrances set between pillars.

The potentially negative aspects of this entry sequence are the darkness compared with the outside, the lack of variety along the interior roadway, and lack of orientation. One inherently positive aspect of entering mined space in most Kansas

City developments is the horizontal access—the interior roads are an extension of the surface roads without any conspicuous downward movement inside the mine. At least one development relies on vertical access through elevators from the surface above, which can evoke more negative associations; however, its downtown location is an offsetting asset. In spite of these concerns, all mined space development in the Kansas City area has the potential of creating positive associations simply because it is unusual and unique.

Within the offices and manufacturing facilities, there is no natural light and outside view. Opportunities to provide exposure to the outside would depend on large-scale development of the surface with deep shafts penetrating to the mined level or the use of an optical system to transmit light and view from portals or through shafts. Since these alternatives are unlikely in the near future, the interior environments must be designed to compensate for these perceived deficiencies as much as possible.

In various offices and display areas within the Great Midwest Underground, several design techniques are employed to create a varied and stimulating environment. To take advantage of the unique character of the mined space, limestone walls remain exposed even within offices but are painted white to lighten the interiors. Glass walls between spaces permit long extended views through the complex, providing spatial relief and interest when viewed from the roadway. Lighting is sometimes used dramatically along with bright colors. One highlight within the development is the Great Midwest offices, with brightly colored flags hanging over the entry. Such unique or special places within the development help to create variety and surprise as well as give orientation and a sense of arrival.

A final set of special concerns over the use of mined space relates to fire safety. The same fire exit requirements applied to conventional buildings simply cannot be applied to mined space as it exists in the Kansas City area. Many locations within the mines are very remote from the portal openings with no provision for escape through vertical elevator shafts. Until recent years secondary use of the mined space existed without conformance to building codes. Safety concerns were not acute because the occupancy was low in a warehouse, escape paths—though long—were many, fire from external sources posed no threat, and except for their contents, the spaces were completely fireproof. Now standards have been developed and adopted that establish the Kansas City mined space as a unique category of building in the code. Included are provisions for smoke venting, exit requirements, and sprinkler systems. Similar to other developments, the Great Midwest Underground utilizes a sprinkler system over the entire leased area [6.4].

Building Technology and Costs

It is more accurate to describe the construction of the deep underground space in Kansas City as mining technology than as building technology. Instead of creating a structure, openings made in the rock serve as a natural structural

Right: Roadway through undeveloped mined space.

enclosure. Converting the space for secondary uses consists of building nonstructural partitions and providing lighting, power, ventilation, sprinklers, and interior finishing.

The width, height, and layout of the mined space are basically determined by the geology, combined with safe mining practices. When the limestone mining in Kansas City began, no provision was made for later use or absolute safety from falling rock. Pillars were left in a

haphazard pattern, and ceilings were arched to within a few feet of the top of the Bethany Falls layer in order to remove as much limestone as possible [6.2]. The current practice is to remove only the lower 12 to 13 feet of limestone, up to a flat bedding plane. This natural break leaves 8 to 9 feet above, forming a structural rock roof overhead, and results in a flat ceiling with little danger of falling rock. When necessary, rock bolting is used to ensure the structural integrity of the

Loading dock for underground warehouses.

Another concern with mining practices involves opening up spaces too close to the bluff and entry portal area. By mining a short tunnel entry and opening large spaces near the bluff, lateral forces are introduced that can cause rock slabbing near the entry portals. This degradation can eventually cause unsafe conditions in some circumstances; it could be avoided by creating longer access tunnels (150 to 200 feet), which would leave a substantial rock mass between the mined space and the bluff.

The cost of mined space development can vary greatly, depending on the function and the requirements of the tenant—just as it varies above grade. In general, though, according to the Great Midwest Corporation, basic warehouse facilities cost from 30 to 50 percent less than similar buildings above grade do (including site development costs in both cases). The basic difference is that, since the mining is a separate profit-making venture, no costs are attributed to the structural shell. According to figures published in 1979, the cost of creating warehouse space underground in Kansas City was $4.50 to $5 per square foot [6.5].

Energy Use Considerations

Because of the greater depth and isolation from the surface, mined space presents unique opportunities for energy conservation that are available to a more limited degree in underground buildings near the surface. The constant 60°F temperature is virtually uninfluenced by the time of year or outside conditions. This is an acceptable temperature for many warehouses with no heating or cooling

ceiling. In current practice the pillars are left in an organized grid to facilitate secondary uses. Both the older and newer methods of mining are in evidence within the Great Midwest property, although the older areas in use have been made safe with rock bolting. In general, pillars range from 20 to 30 feet square and spans between pillars range from 40 to 60 feet in the Kansas City area.

Because the Galesburg shale layer overhead prevents water seepage, there are few problems with leakage or moisture.

Problems have occurred, however, with heaving of the shale layer that forms the floor of the mined space. Two to five years after mining, expansion can occur, causing buckling. The cause of shale heaving is not clear, and the only permanent solution employed so far is to remove the shale as well as the limestone. This approach eliminates the problem but increases costs, since there is no market for the shale. Even when the shale is left in place, it may be removed to create greater ceiling heights for roadways and railroad tracks.

input. People, lights, and machines in offices or manufacturing spaces often raise the temperature to the comfort zone. Cooling and dehumidification of outside ventilation are the major energy requirements but are still estimated to be 50 percent less than for similar functions above grade. The constant temperature is also a definite benefit for cold or cool storage. Once the rock is brought down to a lower temperature, its mass can maintain the temperature for a relatively long period of time; this can protect frozen goods in cases of equipment failure. According to the largest cold storage facility in the Kansas City area, Inland Storage Distribution Center, the interior temperature rises only about 1°F in twenty-four hours without any refrigeration equipment running.

Similar to above-grade buildings, actual energy use varies in the mined space depending on the function and the habits of the occupants. Because of this variation, Great Midwest Corporation described energy use within the broad range of 25 to 85 percent less than utility costs for similar buildings on the surface. According to a study by Dr. Truman Stauffer, energy savings in underground facilities in Kansas City average 47 to 60 percent for manufacturing operations, 60 percent for service facilities, and 70 percent for warehouses [6.6]. Although reduced energy use for heating and cooling is impressive, it is offset slightly by increased energy requirements for artificial lighting over roadways, entrance tunnels, and loading docks. One suggestion to improve energy conservation even further involves the use of longer entrance tunnels. Passing through a longer tunnel, warm air from the outside would be cooled and humidity reduced by condensation before it reached occupied areas.

Project Data

Project: Great Midwest Underground

Location: Kansas City, Missouri

Owner: Great Midwest Corporation

Building type: Warehouse, manufacturing, and office space

Completion date: Continuous mining and secondary development of space

Project size:

Total leased area	2,924,000	sq. ft.
Developed in common	2,067,000	
Prime developable area	1,948,000	
Undeveloped space	11,600,000	
Total mined area (less pillars)	18,539,000	sq. ft.

Note: Figures reflect project size as of December, 1982.

Construction cost: Raw mined space provided at no cost as it is a separate profit-making mining operation; finishing costs vary depending on tenant requirements

Structure: Self-supporting limestone roof on 25 ft. square limestone pillars placed 65 ft. on center

Earth cover: Entire envelope of space in direct contact with bedrock

Insulation: None

Waterproofing: None

Heating system: None

Cooling system: Conventional closed-loop refrigerant air conditioning system

Lighting: Primarily fluorescent

Energy use: Information not available

Credits

Design and construction: Great Midwest Corporation, Kansas City, Missouri

Photographs: Paul S. Kivett

Holaday Circuits

Minnetonka, Minnesota

Architect: BRW Architects

Set into a sloping site in a suburban office park, this partially underground building is the headquarters for Holaday Circuits, a firm that designs and fabricates electronic circuit boards. Contained in the building are 8,000 square feet of office space on the upper level and 27,000 square feet of manufacturing space on the lower level. These two distinct functions are treated differently in the overall building design. The office area is much like any conventional above-grade building, completely visible from the exterior with extensive windows providing light and view. The larger manufacturing area is entirely below grade, with an earth-covered, landscaped roof. The sloping site allows for grade level access to both levels and enables the manufacturing level to be exposed on one end of the site, where the loading dock is located.

The partially underground design resulted from site-related factors, including a significant reduction in land required as well as the client's strong commitment to energy conservation. By placing a large portion of the building below grade and landscaping the earth-covered roof to provide usable outdoor space, a greater percentage of the site could be covered by the building than the local zoning ordinances normally allow. This enabled the client to purchase significantly less land than would have been required for a conventional above-grade building of the same size.

The underground design not only provides economic benefits for the owner, but it is desirable for the community and the general environment as well. The community as a whole benefits from more efficient land use since less extensive roads and utilities are required to support higher densities. Also, instead of a relatively massive industrial structure with large lawns around it to diminish its impact, the building scale is reduced considerably and the forms are softened even further by earth berms and plant materials.

Manufacturing and storage space underground represent particularly appropriate uses for windowless subsurface space. By combining these larger functions with a relatively small above-grade office component, much of the roof can be landscaped. Compared with many other underground buildings, however, this facility still maintains many characteristics of conventional buildings. For example, the exposed portions provide a definite, positive image for the company, which is enhanced by extensive landscaping. Also, the entry is a dominant, clearly distinguished form, and the building edges are defined by walls and berms. This partially underground building illustrates one of many earth-integrated design concepts resulting from specific site conditions, building function, and special requirements of the client. In this case the building form is not that of a "nonbuilding," nor does it merge completely with a surrounding natural landscape; it combines suitable elements from both above- and below-grade structures.

Building Technology and Costs

The distinct architectural treatments of the office and manufacturing components of the building are reflected in the different structural systems as well. The structure of the above-grade office area consists of steel-framed roof and walls resting on the heavier masonry walls and precast concrete roof deck of the manufacturing space below. Although an earth-covered

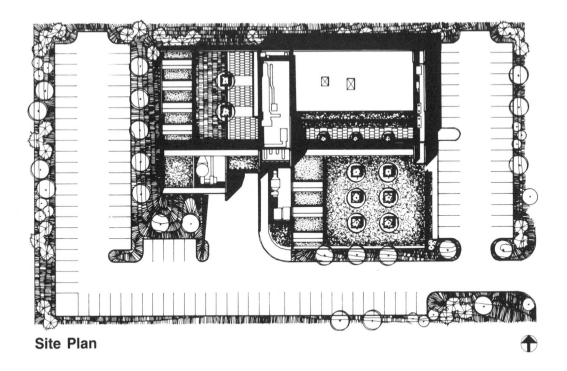

Site Plan

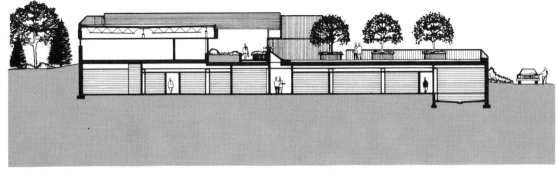

Section

roof is more expensive than a conventional roof, the total cost of construction was considered to be comparable. Similar to many manufacturing facilities, a high percentage of the cost of construction—40 percent in this case—is for mechanical and electrical systems that are mostly associated with the fabrication processes.

Energy Use Considerations

By placing the majority of the building below grade with earth-covered walls and roof, heat loss and heat gain are reduced. The extensive plant materials on the roof also assist in shading the building, further reducing heat gain from the sun. It should be noted, however, that in many manufacturing facilities, including this one, the largest component of energy use is that required by the manufacturing processes themselves, not the building heating, cooling, or lighting. Heat recovery devices are therefore installed on the industrial air systems in this facility.

The Holaday Circuits building employs a special system to provide some natural light to the below-grade spaces while reducing the amount of artificial light required. Skylights penetrating the earth-covered roof provide natural light to areas of the building that do not require constant and unchanging light levels. These include circulation spaces and certain production and storage areas. When the amount of

Opposite, above: View of the landscaped roof showing skylights in the foreground and offices in the background. Lower left: Corridor on the manufacturing level with continuous skylights overhead. Lower right: Walkway to the office entrance on the landscaped roof.

light from the sun falls below an acceptable level, light-sensitive devices automatically turn on artificial light. The artificial lighting for these skylight areas is located outside of the building so the same fixtures can both illuminate the inside areas and provide security lighting on the roof deck above.

Project Data

Project: Holaday Circuits

Location: Minnetonka, Minnesota

Owner: Holaday Circuits, Inc.

Building type: Manufacturing and office building

Completion date: 1981

Project size: 35,000 sq. ft. (8,000 sq. ft. office and 27,000 sq. ft. manufacturing)

Construction cost:

General	$1,300,000
Mechanical	588,000
Electrical	275,000
Total	$2,163,000

Structure: Masonry walls, precast concrete roof, and slab-on-grade floor for lower-level manufacturing space; steel-framed roof and walls for upper-level office space

Earth cover: 60 percent of total wall area covered; 75 percent of total roof area covered with 14 in. of earth

Insulation: Extruded polystyrene, 2 in. on earth-covered roof, 3 to 6 in. on exposed roof areas, 2 in. on walls to a depth of 6 ft; fiberglass batts, 6 in. thick on above-grade frame walls

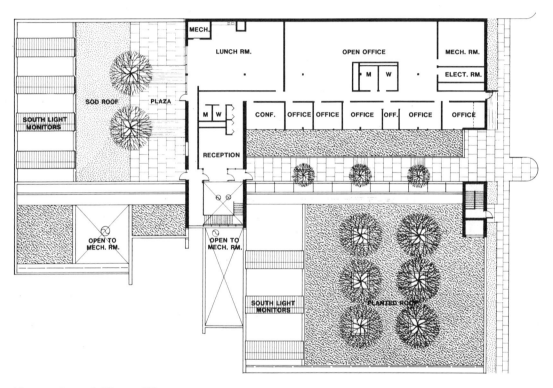

Upper Level Floor Plan

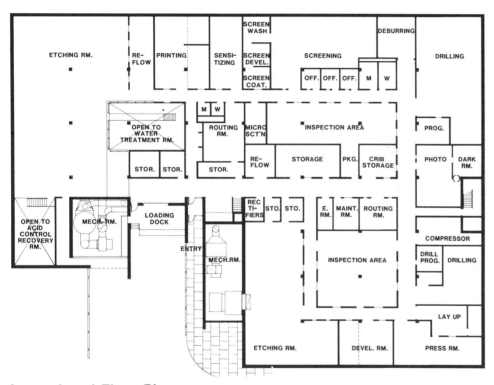

Lower Level Floor Plan

Labels within the plan:

ETCHING RM.

RE-FLOW

PRINTING

SENSI-TIZING

SCREEN WASH

SCREEN DEVEL.

SCREEN COAT.

SCREENING

DEBURRING

DRILLING

OFF. OFF. OFF. M W

OPEN TO WATER TREATMENT RM.

M W

ROUTING RM.

MICRO SCT'N

INSPECTION AREA

PROG.

STOR. STOR.

STOR.

RE-FLOW

STORAGE

PKG.

CRIB STORAGE

PHOTO

DARK RM.

OPEN TO ACID CONTROL RECOVERY RM.

MECH. RM.

LOADING DOCK

REC TI-FIERS

STO. STO.

E. RM.

MAINT. RM.

ROUTING RM.

COMPRESSOR

ENTRY

MECH. RM.

INSPECTION AREA

DRILL PROG.

DRILLING

LAY UP

ETCHING RM.

DEVEL. RM.

PRESS RM.

Waterproofing: 60-mil. rubberized asphalt and polyethylene film below grade; built-up roof on exposed roof area

Windows and skylights: 1,370 sq. ft. of windows in office area, 890 sq. ft. of skylights over corridors, and 520 sq. ft. of light monitors over production area

Heating system: Gas-fired forced air

Cooling system: Air-cooled water chiller with forced-air delivery

Lighting: Quick-connect fluorescent

Energy use: Information not available

Heating degree days: 8,159

Cooling degree days: 585

Occupancy schedule: 80 hours per week in manufacturing area, 40 hours per week in office area

Credits

Architect: BRW Architects, Inc., Minneapolis, Minnesota (formerly Myers and Bennett/BRW)

Structural engineer: BRW, Inc.

Mechanical engineer: Oftedal, Locke, Broadston and Associates, Inc.

Electrical consultant: Cramer Electric Co.

Contractors: Acton Construction Co., Inc., general; Loop Beldon Porter, mechanical; Cramer Electric Co., electrical

Photographs: George Heinrich

Fort Snelling Visitor Center (proposed design), St. Paul, Minnesota
Architect: BRW Architects, Inc., Minneapolis, Minnesota

Chapter 7: Visitor and Interpretive Centers

Highway Rest Area Buildings

Blue Earth, Minnesota

Architect: David Kane and James Cox

Anchor Lake, Minnesota

Architect: Damberg and Peck Architects

Enfield, Minnesota

Architect: Pauly and Olsen Associates

In Minnesota, as in other states that contain interstate highways, rest areas are provided for motorists at intervals of approximately fifty miles. These rest areas provide a place to park off the highway and access to restrooms, telephones, and travel information contained in relatively small buildings ranging from 1,100 to 1,800 square feet. In addition to these basic functions, rest areas attempt to provide a pleasant environment and some recreational opportunities for the traveler; thus, most designs include picnic and playground areas and trails taking advantage of views and natural features of the site.

Sites for the rest areas are selected by landscape architects at the Minnesota Department of Transportation based on a number of criteria. Features that are sought in site selection are rolling topography, views, water, and tree cover. The sites are then designed to preserve and enhance these elements, maintain any wildlife on the site, and interpret these features for the traveler. Both to meet the goal of harmonizing with the natural setting and to enhance energy efficiency in building design, earth-integrated structures have been built at some rest area sites. So far three sites have been chosen for earth sheltered designs in Minnesota. The resulting designs include an almost completely earth-covered building at the Enfield Rest Area, a partially bermed and covered building at the Anchor Lake Rest Area, and two nearly identical bermed and covered buildings on either side of the highway near the town of Blue Earth. To varying degrees the buildings utilize passive solar techniques to reduce energy consumption as well.

Although the rest area buildings are relatively small and serve mainly simple utilitarian purposes, they must be designed to function efficiently and attractively since a typical building serves 400,000 to 600,000 visitors per year and represents a part of the state's image to potential tourists. The buildings are operated continuously throughout the year; however, only about 5 percent of the visitors use the rest areas in the winter months from November to March. Since the basic spaces in the building—a lobby with phone and travel information, toilets, and a mechanical/custodial room—do not have absolute requirements for windows and little time is actually spent in these areas, there are no great problems to be overcome in placing them partially or completely below grade. Because the spaces are small, however, it is visually desirable to provide windows or skylights at least in the lobby area to provide natural light and alleviate any feeling of claustrophobia.

Since a major emphasis of the overall rest area design is to provide recreation opportunities in a natural setting on the site surrounding the building, the exterior design of the buildings is probably more critical than the interior design. Not only should the buildings harmonize with the site since they are often the only structure building on the landscape, but they must also be easily recognized and the entrance must be clearly perceived by the visitor. In spite of the similar requirements for each building, the state of Minnesota aims to create diverse rest area designs that utilize indigenous materials. It is particularly interesting that even with the additional program requirements of designing earth sheltered buildings, the three architects

Opposite: Enfield Rest Area.

developed very unique designs, each with distinct exterior forms, materials, and degrees of earth integration.

Costs

The initial construction costs of the rest area buildings range from $98 per square foot at Enfield to $145 per square foot for the Blue Earth structures. The highest total cost—$232,000 for the Anchor Lake building ($129 per square foot)—is partly attributable to the extra costs of winter construction. Although these costs appear to be significantly higher than for most conventional construction, it is not their earth sheltered design that is mainly responsible for the increased costs but several other factors related to this particular building type. According to the Minnesota Department of Transportation, the cost of rest area buildings throughout the state ranges from $100,000 to $275,000. One major reason for these high costs for such relatively small buildings— 1,100 to 1,800 square feet—is that being predominantly bathrooms, mechanical costs are quite high per unit area. Also, the building locations are often remote, increasing contractor's costs. Although additional structure and waterproofing represent a cost increase in the earth-covered buildings, they are not generally considered to be significantly more expensive than conventional structures.

Unfortunately, the exact cost figures for the rest area buildings cannot be relied upon as accurate reflections of the true construction costs. The main reason for this is that the buildings are usually a

Above: Blue Earth Rest Area. Below: Anchor Lake Rest Area.

small part of a package bid including all of the road, utility, and other site work surrounding the actual structure. The entire package can exceed $1 million per rest area. Consequently, the stated cost of the building is sometimes not the true cost but simply an adjusted cost to facilitate regular periodic payments to the contractor. This process, referred to as unbalanced bidding, results in the wide disparity in reported costs for apparently similar buildings.

Energy Use

In all three of the rest area designs, various degrees of earth berming and earth covering are utilized in part, to reduce energy consumption. The lowest total energy consumption—111,300 Btu/sq ft/yr—is achieved in the Enfield structure, which is the most completely earth covered on both roof and walls. The two Blue Earth buildings are close to Enfield in performance at 118,700 Btu.sq ft/yr and 126,500 Btu/sq ft/yr respectively. The highest energy consumption of the earth sheltered buildings is at Anchor Lake—167,400 Btu/sq ft/yr. The higher figure for the Anchor Lake structure is assumed to be related to the lack of thermal breaks, permitting the concrete structure to conduct heat directly outside. It should also be noted that Anchor Lake is somewhat further north, exposed to a more severe winter than the other buildings. The total energy use figures for these buildings include energy for lighting, pumps, mechanical equipment, and heating water; there is no cooling system and therefore none of the energy is attributable to cooling. Although conventional rest area buildings are not usually mechanically cooled, the passive cooling effect of these earth sheltered structures is considered a

benefit since they are more comfortable in summer and other cooling techniques are not necessary.

Although the total energy consumption for these buildings seems relatively high compared with energy-efficient standards for either residential or nonresidential structures, they are actually quite efficient for this building type in this climate. Rest areas, being mainly large public bathrooms, have a very high energy use per square foot for a number of reasons. Building codes require bathrooms to be well ventilated, resulting in significant heat loss in winter as warm air is replaced by colder fresh air. Although all of the structures include heat-exchange devices to recover heat from the exhaust air to preheat fresh makeup air, the amount of ventilation required still results in considerable losses. In addition to ventilation, energy use is relatively high because of hot water requirements, lights that are constantly in use, frequent opening of doors, and electrical energy required for lift pumps in some locations. In more typical buildings, the energy-intensive requirements of the bathrooms are combined with the more moderate demands of much larger spaces to produce a lower energy use per unit area. To more clearly understand the relative performance of these earth sheltered buildings, they can be compared with older as well as newer conventional rest area buildings. The older rest area buildings in the Minnesota system have considerably higher energy consumption figures than any of these examples do —as high as 250,000 Btu/sq ft/yr in one case. This represents 2.25 times the consumption at the Enfield Rest Area. An even more revealing comparison can be made between the earth-covered Enfield Rest

Area and a nearby conventional rest area building with the same layout and area. The total energy use for the same period in the above-grade building is 273.4 x 10^6 Btu, which translates into 160,800 Btu/sq ft/yr—44 percent more energy use than the otherwise identical earth sheltered building. Clearly, the use of earth contributes to reducing the energy use in these structures. There is, however, a limit to how much the thermal envelope of the structure can reduce energy use when heat loss is dominated by ventilation requirements.

Aside from helping to reduce operating costs, there is another important advantage of earth sheltered rest area structures that cannot be equaled by conventional construction. A building placed in the earth will maintain a temperature for a long period of time with no heat input; if the heat is cut off, it generally will slowly drop in temperature only to a point approximating the ground temperature, which is much more moderate than outside conditions. This is a valuable asset in rest area buildings, which are in remote locations without maintenance personnel constantly present. Power outages periodically occur in remote locations, and the extensive plumbing in these structures is subject to damage from freezing. This advantage was clearly demonstrated in one of the Blue Earth buildings when, during a severe winter storm, electric power was cut off for five days, leaving the building without heat while outside temperatures were below zero (°F). During this period the building temperature dropped sixteen degrees and stabilized at about 50°F. A small space heater was able to maintain the temperature at this point until electric power was restored.

Blue Earth Rest Areas

Placing two rest areas on Interstate 90 near Blue Earth, Minnesota afforded the opportunity to preserve a wooded, 130-acre site along the Blue Earth River. The specific locations for the two nearly identical rest area buildings were chosen in part because the southwest-facing bluffs provide opportunities for earth sheltered, passive solar designs. The two structures differ only in that the plan of one is the mirror image of the other and that the building for eastbound traffic is oriented directly south while the building for westbound traffic is oriented slightly south of west.

The buildings are set into the top of the bluff, each with an observation deck on the roof and adjacent picnic areas that are an extension of the building forms and details. The rest rooms and mechanical/custodial space are completely earth covered, whereas the lobby, with a view of the river valley and surrounding woodlands, is exposed along the bluff edges. The most prominent exterior elements of the buildings are the limestone walls and the freestanding wooden roof structures providing shade over the view deck and picnic areas. The limestone, which is native to this area, reflects natural earth-tone colors of the site and has been used on all rest area buildings along this southern Minnesota route.

Since the buildings are set into the bluff, they are partially earth bermed and covered, with one elevation completely exposed for passive solar gain. The dark quarry tile floors and massive stone cavity walls retain the sun's heat as it enters the lobby windows. The heat is radiated back into the space and circulated by the heating system throughout the building

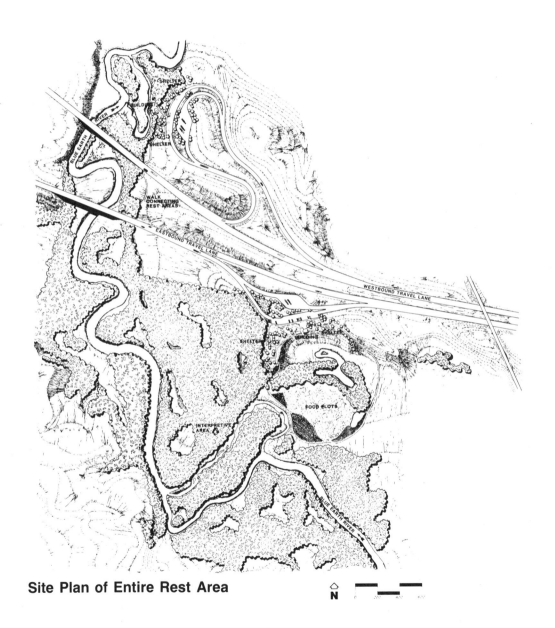

Site Plan of Entire Rest Area

N

during nighttime hours. In the energy use figures shown on the adjacent page, the westbound building uses slightly less energy than the eastbound building in spite of the direct southerly orientation of the latter. This difference, however, is not related to orientation but to the inclusion of the energy required to operate a major lift pump in the figure for the eastbound building.

Project Data

Project: Blue Earth Rest Areas

Location: Interstate 90 near Blue Earth, Minnesota

Owner: Minnesota Department of Transportation

Building type: Highway rest areas (2 identical buildings)

Completion date: 1979

Project size: 1,100 sq. ft.

Construction cost: $160,000 per building

Structure: Precast, prestressed concrete plank roof with reinforced concrete topping sloped for drainage—12-in. by 48-in. planks; reinforced concrete walls—8 in. thick; 4-in. slab-on-grade floor

Earth cover: 40 percent of exterior walls are earth covered; 34 percent of the roof is covered with an average thickness of 3 ft. of earth

Insulation: Extruded polystyrene, 4 in. on roof, 2 in. on entire wall area

Waterproofing: Rubberized asphalt waterproof membrane

Heating system: Electric forced-air furnace

Cooling system: No mechanical cooling

Lighting system: Primarily fluorescent fixtures

Energy use:

Westbound building:118,818 Btu/sq ft/yr
Electricity 130.7 x 10^6 Btu (38,290 kWh)

Eastbound building: 126,727 Btu/sq ft/yr
Electricity 139.4 x 10^6 Btu (40,820 kWh)

Note: Energy use figures are for the period from July 1981 through June 1982.

Heating degree days: 8,227 (Rochester)

Cooling degree days: 474 (Rochester)

Occupancy schedule: 24 hours per day, 365 days per year

Credits

Architect: David Kane, Austin, Minnesota; James Cox, Marine on the St. Croix, Minnesota

Structural engineer: TSP Engineers

Mechanical engineer: TSP Engineers

Landscape architects: Minnesota Department of Transportation

Contractor: Robert W. Carlson Construction

Photographs: Neil Kveberg

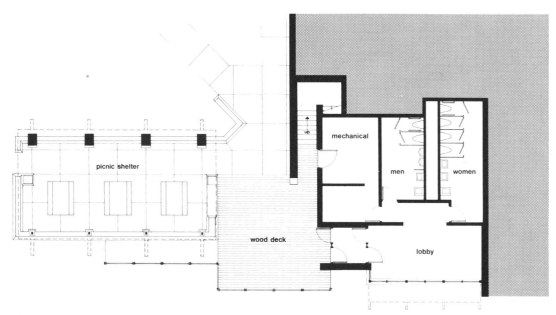

Floor Plan

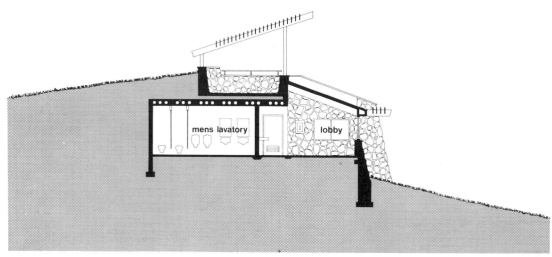

Section

Anchor Lake Rest Area

The Anchor Lake Rest Area along Highway 53 near Eveleth, Minnesota, is one of the larger buildings in the system because it serves as a more complete tourist information center than the other rest areas. The site provides an excellent opportunity for an earth sheltered, passive solar building. By setting the building into a steep bluff, it is protected from cold northwest winter winds while maintaining exposure to the south. The rest rooms and mechanical space are completely earth bermed and covered, while the lobby has an exterior view. Above part of the lobby, a roof deck provides views of northern Minnesota's forest lands.

The exterior character of the building is dominated by the rough-textured concrete parapet forming balconies on the roof deck. In spite of these strong, man-made forms, other elements—their horizontal nature, the large overhangs, and the dark glass below—all contribute to blending the building into the landforms. A skylight projects up from the roof to create a contrasting vertical element and provides sunlight and solar heat to the interior.

The energy performance of the Anchor Lake building is considered reasonably good by the standards of more conventional rest area buildings in the state. Several modifications are currently being made to improve the efficiency of the lighting and mechanical system, however. In addition, the architect acknowledges that the performance could easily be improved with the addition of thermal breaks in the design to reduce heat conduction through the exposed portions of the concrete structure.

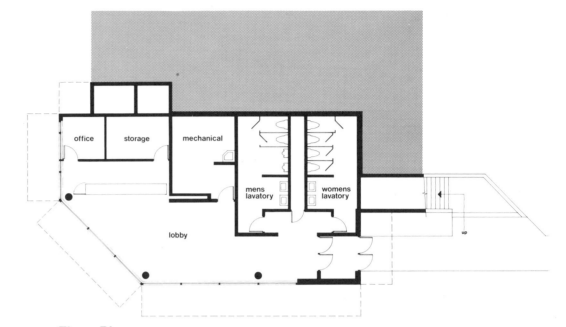

Floor Plan

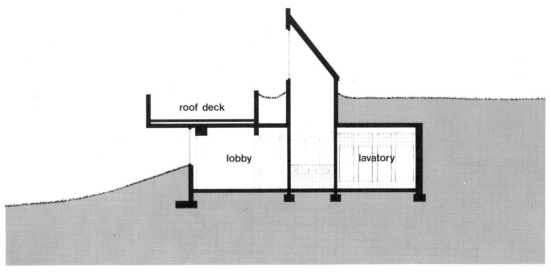

Section

186

Project Data

Project: Anchor Lake Rest Area and Information Center

Location: Highway 53, near Eveleth, Minnesota

Owner: Minnesota Department of Transportation

Building type: Highway rest area

Completion date: 1979

Project size: 1,800 sq. ft.

Construction cost: $232,000

Structure: Cast-in-place reinforced concrete roof—8 in. thick; reinforced concrete walls—12 in. thick; 4-in. slab-on-grade floor

Earth cover: 41 percent of exterior walls are completely earth covered; 46 percent are covered to a height of 40 in.; 36 percent of roof is covered with a minimum of 3 ft. of earth

Insulation: Extruded polystyrene, 2 in. under soil on earth-covered portion of roof, 3 in. under exposed portion of roof, 2 in. on upper 4 ft. of walls with 1-in. thickness on remainder of walls

Waterproofing: Rubberized asphalt waterproof membrane

Heating system: Propane forced-air furnace

Cooling system: No mechanical cooling

Lighting system: Fluorescent and incandescent track lights

Energy use: 167,500 Btu/sq ft/yr

Electricity	97.0×10^6 Btu (28,410 kWh)
Propane	204.5×10^6 Btu (2,235 gal.)
Total	301.5×10^6 Btu

Note: Energy use figures are for the period from July 1981 through June 1982.

Heating degree days: 9,756 (Duluth)

Cooling degree days: 176 (Duluth)

Occupancy schedule: 24 hours per day, 365 days per year

Credits

Architect: Damburg and Peck Architects, Virginia, Minnesota

Structural engineer: Damburg and Peck Architects

Mechanical engineer: Foster, Jacobs and Johnson, Inc.

Landscape architect: Minnesota Department of Transportation

Contractor: Winkleman Enterprises

Photographs: Neil Kveberg

Enfield Rest Area

The rolling, wooded site of the Enfield Rest Area along Interstate 94 in central Minnesota includes a variety of hardwood species and small ponds. The almost completely underground design evolved from a desire to retain as many trees as possible, minimize the visual impact of the building, and enhance the energy efficiency of the structure as well. The large parking area is placed along the edge of the woods.

The exterior appearance of the Enfield building is the most unique of the three earth sheltered buildings in the Minnesota system. The brick-covered cylindrical forms of the retaining walls at the entry and light wells on the roof are the only visible elements of the building. The two large curving shapes, which create a striking image, enclose courtyards at the two entrances—one approached from the parking area and the other leading to the trail and pond beyond the building. The earth berms surrounding the structure blend it into the landscape, obscuring its true rectangular form.

Although the Enfield building is by far the most completely earth covered of the rest areas, the interior has a surprising amount of light from the light wells in the bathrooms and large skylights over the lobby. The circular design forms of the exterior are reinforced by curving brick details in the lobby interior.

The energy use at the Enfield building is the lowest of the earth sheltered designs and far less than most of the conventional buildings in the Minnesota system. Included in the energy-use figures for the Enfield Rest Area building are those for a conventional sister building with the

identical layout and area. The conventional building uses 44 percent more energy than the earth-covered structure does during the same time period.

Project Data

Project: Enfield Rest Area

Location: Interstate 94 between St. Cloud and Monticello, Minnesota

Owner: Minnesota Department of Transportation

Building type: Highway rest area

Completion date: 1980

Project size: 1,700 sq. ft.

Construction cost: $166,000

Structure: Precast, prestressed concrete plank roof with reinforced concrete topping sloped for drainage—12-in. by 48-in. planks; reinforced concrete walls—12 in. thick; 3 in. slab-on-grade floor

Earth cover: 85 percent of exterior walls are earth covered; 98 percent of roof is covered with a minimum thickness of 18 in. of earth

Insulation: Extruded polystyrene, 2 in. on roof, 2 in. on upper 4 ft. of walls and 4 ft. each side of each light shaft, 2 in. under floor near light shafts

Waterproofing: Bentonite-based waterproofing layer sprayed on at a thickness of ⅛ to ¼ in.

Aerial view of Enfield Rest Area

Heating system: Propane forced-air furnace

Cooling system: No mechanical cooling

Lighting system: Fluorescent fixtures

Energy use:

Earth covered building: 111,353 Btu/sq ft/yr

Electricity	91.3×10^6 Btu	(26,751 kWh)
Propane	98.0×10^6 Btu	(1,071 gal.)
Total	189.3×10^6 Btu	

Conventional building: 160,824 Btu/sq ft/yr

Electricity	56.5×10^6 Btu	(16,540 kWh)
Propane	216.9×10^6 Btu	(2,370 gal.)
Total	273.4×10^6 Btu	

Note: The above data is for the earth covered rest area at Enfield and a conventional rest area building near Enfield with the identical layout but no earth cover. Energy use figures are for the period from July 1981 through June 1982.

Heating degree days: 8,868 (St. Cloud)

Cooling degree days: 426 (St. Cloud)

Occupancy schedule: 24 hours per day, 365 days per year

Credits

Architect: Pauly and Olsen Associates, St. Cloud, Minnesota

Structural engineer: Pauly and Olsen Associates

Mechanical engineer: Gausman and Moore, Inc.

Landscape architect: Minnesota Department of Transportation

Contractor: Winkleman Enterprises

Photographs: Neil Kveberg

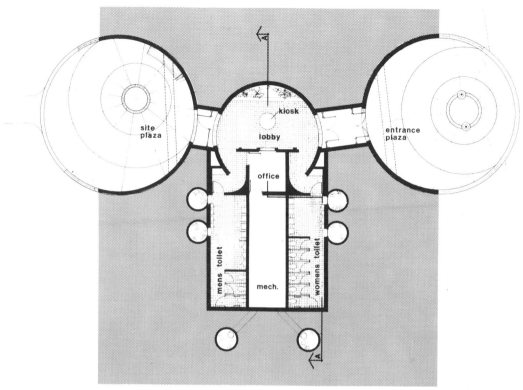

Floor Plan

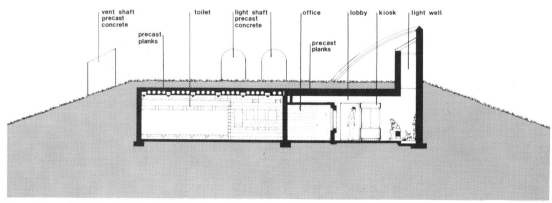

Section A-A

Kelley
Interpretive
Center

Elk River, Minnesota

Architect: Thorsen and Thorshov Associates

Visitor centers, designed to provide information to tourists about specific natural or historical sites, represent a unique building type. The main function of these structures is to focus attention on the surrounding site rather than on the building itself. For this reason interpretive centers are often placed partially or completely into the earth so that the character of the site or the historical setting is only minimally disturbed by the new structure.

An excellent example of the nonbuilding approach to visitor center design is located on the Oliver Hudson Kelley farm in central Minnesota. The almost completely underground interpretive center blends unobtrusively into the landforms of the site. Because the building separates the parking area from the farm and the visitor passes through it to reach the farm, the center serves as a transition between the automobile and horse-drawn era. Owned and operated by the Minnesota Historical Society, the Kelley farm site is the recognized birthplace of the organized agriculture movement in the United States. In addition to the restored nineteenth-century buildings, the site includes 189 acres of land—a large portion of which has been farmed continuously for over one hundred years.

The specific siting of the interpretive center and the organization of the building plan are designed to direct the visitor and serve as a gateway to the farm. As one approaches the site, the farmhouse is visible from a rise in the road; then the visitor is directed to the interpretive center and parking area. Approaching the center, the farmstead can be seen through the glass-enclosed lobby and circulation space of the newer structure. The major exhibition and audiovisual spaces are placed on one side of the central spine with various support functions on the other side. This arrangement permits all of these functions to be completely below grade yet always brings the visitor back into the central space with a view of the farm and a sense of orientation.

Viewed from the exterior, the only visible elements of the building are the steel and glass enclosure of the central lobby space and the bare concrete walls and forms around the entries at either end of the building. On this large, mostly flat site, the visible mass of the building is not imposing, and the earth-covered portions appear to be extensions of the natural grade on the site. Portions of the farm site are planted with native prairie grasses, and the plan is to extend these materials over the roof of the new structure. The long native grasses surrounding and covering the center should further integrate it into the character of the site.

Special Design Concerns

Locating the entry to an underground building and maintaining orientation in a mostly windowless structure are important design concerns. In the case of the Kelley Interpretive Center, there is little problem since the entrances are the main visible portions of the building and the site is organized to direct people to them. The one-level building is entered at grade, eliminating any negative feeling associated with descending into an underground space.

The glass-covered central spine of the building serves not only to orient the visitor and direct him to the farm beyond, but also to provide extensive natural light and the feeling of a high interior space. Although most of the exhibition and

support functions are well suited to windowless space, their location next to the central space gives the entire building a feeling of having ample natural light and exterior views. The colors used on the interior surfaces are designed to make a graduated transition to the native materials used on the farmstead.

Building Technology and Costs

The interpretive center is a reinforced concrete structure with approximately 90 percent of the roof and walls covered with earth. The large steel and glass skylight is the only exposed portion of the roof. The cost of this building, approximately $72 per square foot, is not unusually high for this type of building. Small buildings with relatively large requirements for plumbing, some special equipment, and high-quality interior finishing materials are likely to be similar in cost to the Kelley Interpretive Center, regardless of the placement above or below grade. A cost increase is undoubtedly attributable to the additional structure needed to support the earth load on the roof. This is somewhat offset, however, by the lack of exterior finishing materials that would be required to create an above-grade building harmonious with this historical setting.

Energy Use Considerations

The major architectural features of the Kelley Interpretive Center, the earth cover and the glass-enclosed central space, are also the main concepts for reducing heating and cooling energy use in the building. The central spine of the building runs from northeast to southwest, creating a southeasterly orientation for the skylight.

The skylight is designed to maximize solar gain and make use of the large concrete mass of the building structure. The orientation of the building enables earth berms to cover the entire northwestern face of the structure, serving to protect it from the direct winter winds that can be severe on open rural sites. In addition, the earth-covered roof contributes to reducing summer heat gain.

Actual energy use in the building was 139,333 Btu/square foot during 1982. This figure is somewhat higher than for larger energy-efficient buildings in this climate. It should be noted, however, that small public buildings often consume more energy per square foot than larger ones. This results from certain energy-consuming functions common to all buildings—heating water and ventilating bathrooms with

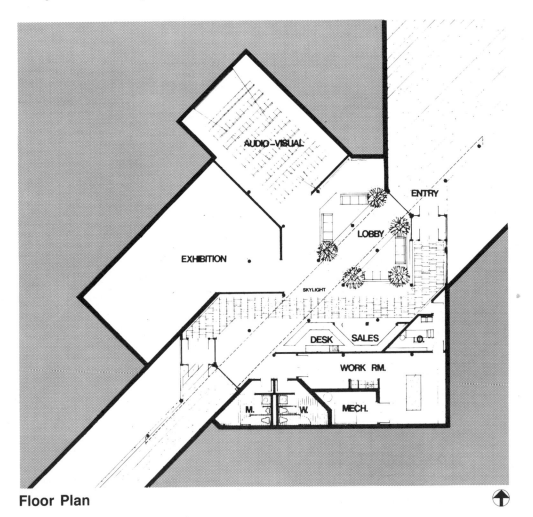

Floor Plan

outside air, for example—being attributed to a much smaller total building area. Another explanation for the energy use in this building is that no insulative devices cover the skylights at night, so that any heating gains in this climate may be lost to the cooler night air. Moreover, no shading protects the space from summer sun. Nighttime insulation in winter and shading devices in summer would appear to be potential future improvements.

Project Data

Project: Kelley Interpretive Center

Location: Elk River, Minnesota

Owner: Minnesota Historical Society

Building type: Visitor information center

Completion date: 1981

Project size: 6,000 sq. ft.

Construction cost:

General	$353,671
Mechanical	55,865
Electrical	19,760
Total	$429,296

Structure: Cast-in-place reinforced concrete roof and walls; slab-on-grade floor

Earth cover: 90 percent of total wall area covered; 90 percent of total roof area covered with a 2½- to 3½-ft-thick layer of earth

Insulation: Extruded polystyrene, 3 in. on roof, 3 in. on walls to a depth of 5 ft.

Waterproofing: Rubberized asphalt membrane on roof; bentonite-filled cardboard panels on the walls

Heating system: Oil-fired forced-air system

Cooling system: Conventional closed-loop refrigerant air-conditioning system

Lighting: Fluorescent, plus some decorative incandescent

Energy use: 139,333 Btu/sq ft/yr

Electricity 373×10^6 Btu (109,358 kWh)
Fuel Oil 463×10^6 Btu (3343 gal)
Total 836×10^6 Btu

Note: Energy use figures are for 1982.

Heating degree days: 8,868 (St. Cloud)

Cooling degree days: 426 (St. Cloud)

Occupancy schedule: 40 hours per week, 52 weeks per year

Credits

Architect: Thorsen and Thorshov Associates, Minneapolis, Minnesota

Structural and mechanical engineer: Bakke, Kopp, Ballou and McFarlin, Inc.

Contractor: Norman Berglund Construction Company

Photographs: Klara Komorous-Towey

Above: View through the central concourse of the building. Below: The glass-covered lobby area.

Benedictine Mission House, Schuyler, Nebraska
Architect: Astle/Ericson Associates, Omaha, Nebraska

Chapter 8: Special Use Facilities

Benedictine Mission House

Schuyler, Nebraska

Architect: Astle/Ericson and Associates

Set into the open, rolling countryside near Schuyler, Nebraska, the Benedictine Mission House demonstrates earth-integrated design that responds to both aesthetic and climatic forces on its site. The almost completely earth-covered roof enables the structure to merge with the surrounding landscape, and earth-bermed walls on the north and west protect the building from strong prevailing winter winds. The majority of the windows face south to maximize passive solar gain as well as to provide a scenic view of the Platte River valley. In the summer, breezes from the southeast are channeled through the building to provide natural ventilation.

Completed in 1979, the monastery is workplace, home, and place of worship for the fathers and brothers of the Benedictine Mission House, an order of German descent with a long history of missionary support. The major activity of the twelve monks in residence is to raise funds and provide support for remote missions in southern and eastern Africa, South Korea, and Latin America. To house all the required functions, the monastery actually encompasses several building types: a chapel, office space, a printing shop, gallery space, living units for monks and guests, and common dining, recreation, and meeting spaces.

The diverse functions of the 40,000-square foot monastery are placed in separate building masses or wings. The resulting plan arrangement sprawls over the site, mostly on one level, defining exterior spaces and providing light and view to virtually every part of the building. One enters the complex along the east side of a central courtyard, which is enclosed on the north by a row of guest rooms. They are in a wing that also includes the garages, mostly shielded from view. The commons area on the west side of the courtyard includes spaces for conference, music, recreation, dining, and kitchen. On the south side of the courtyard is the central entry hall, which also serves as a gallery space. From this area one can enter the office and print shop area, extending in a wing to the east, as well as the chapel, the dominant form of the complex and center of monastery life. Extending diagonally to the southwest on two levels are the living quarters of the monks. Entered from a single-loaded corridor, the rooms in this wing are stepped, creating variation in the facade. The upper level rooms are set back from those on the lower level, forming roof terraces.

Although the dominant image of the Benedictine Mission House is that of a structure completely integrated with its site, the building's exterior form and character consist of many diverse components. Approached from the north, the building almost disappears into the vast, barren landscape. Because it is shielded from view by the earth berms, the true extent of the complex is not evident. The portions of the building that are visible on the entry side maintain a low profile and merge with the earth at the ends of the building wings.

The most notable element in the complex is the chapel projecting above the level of the flat, earth-covered roof. Its form serves as a religious symbol identifying it as a parish house for the surrounding farm community. From the north the chapel roof interrupts the horizon but still remains relatively small in scale. On the south side of the building, the complete form of the chapel is revealed. The sloping forms of the roof are complemented by steeply sloping, geometric earth berms around the

base of the chapel. Although the south facade of the building remains low in profile and appears to fit closely with the terrain when viewed from a distance, it is far more complex and visually interesting than the other sides. Not only is it less covered with earth, but the concrete forms and articulation of the units in the living quarters combined with the dominant chapel form create an image of a more conventional building complex, particularly when viewed at close range.

Special Design Concerns

A goal in designing the Benedictine Mission House was to create an energy-efficient facility employing passive systems without compromising natural light and exterior view. In spite of the earth integration of the project, the majority of the exterior walls are exposed above grade, and the sprawling plan permits windows in virtually every space. In the very few spaces without windows—the music and recreation rooms in particular—domed or vaulted skylights provide natural light. Large skylights are also present over the corridors of the commons and office areas. Although completely above grade, the chapel is intentionally windowless; natural light enters the space from large areas of skylights in the roof.

With such an extensive array of windows and skylights, there is little need to use interior design to compensate for the lack of light and view inherent in some

*Above: Rooftop level view of the complex.
Below: Central common space in the administration area.*

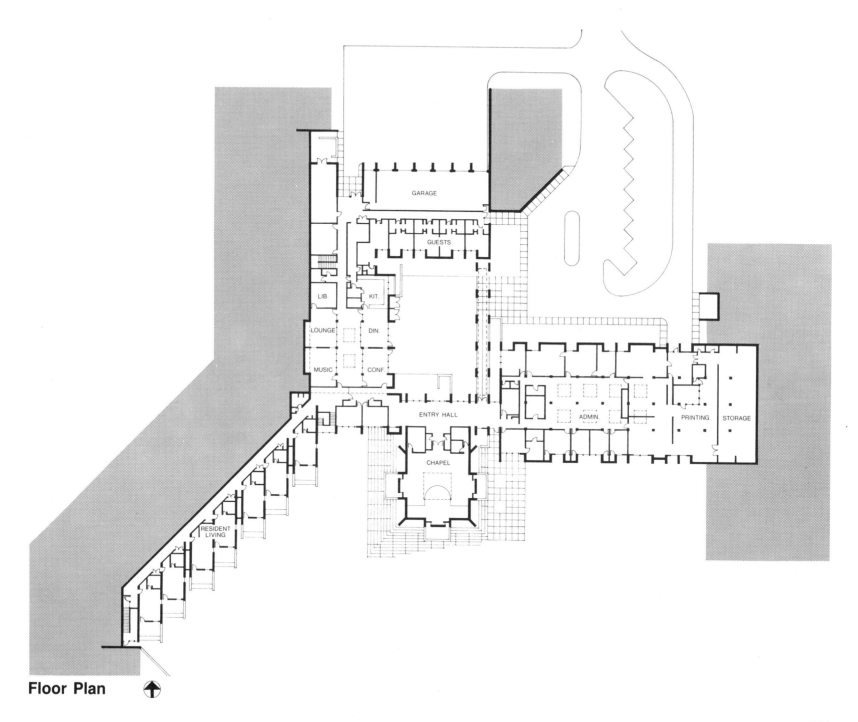

Floor Plan

GARAGE

GUESTS

LIB.

KIT.

LOUNGE

DIN.

MUSIC

CONF.

ENTRY HALL

ADMIN.

PRINTING

STORAGE

CHAPEL

RESIDENT LIVING

underground buildings. The interiors are simple in most areas, with sandblasted concrete walls and quarry tile floors or carpet; they are, however, also very warm, with extensive use of western red cedar, particularly in the chapel. Artwork from around the world is displayed in public areas, and large wooden planters and benches make corridors appear to be indoor atriums.

Unlike a flat site, where an underground building is either totally below grade or is built on grade with berms around it, both conditions may occur on a rolling site. This permits the natural grade to meet the roofline in places and descend to the floor level in others. The manner in which the Benedictine Mission House is nestled into the rolling landscape permits the building to be entered at grade quite easily. Thus, there is no transition to underground space to be concerned about in the design of the entry. As one approaches from the north, elements of the building appear and disappear in the landscape, but once near the complex, one is directed unmistakably to the entry courtyard.

Building Technology and Costs

The entire structure of the building, except for the chapel, is cast-in-place reinforced concrete. The structure supporting the earth-covered roof is designed to hold a combined live and dead load of 500 pounds per square foot. Rubberized asphalt (180-mil. thickness) is applied in liquid form over the concrete roof slab, the inside of the parapet walls, and the upper 2 feet of the below-grade walls. Polystyrene insulation is placed over the entire roof and upper 4 feet of the below-grade walls at a thickness of 2 inches. In the chapel, which is the only part of the building without earth covering the roof, cedar beams support the lighter wood framework on the ceiling. The $3 million total cost of the building ($75 per square foot) includes sitework, parking area, landscaping, interiors, signage, and fees.

Energy Use Considerations

Although aesthetic concerns significantly influenced the decision to place the monastery partially into the earth, both client and architect were strongly committed to energy conservation as well. Protection on the north and west side with earth berms is particularly important on an open site with no surrounding trees or buildings to divert or diminish the effect of winter winds. The majority of the windows not only face south, but have carefully designed overhangs that permit the winter sun to enter but shield the hot summer sun.

The extended plan arrangement results in a large exposed surface area that is large in relation to the floor area, a condition not optimal for winter heating. On the other hand, the plan is ideal for promoting cross-ventilation in summer. The building shape funnels southeast summer breezes through low exhaust openings in the roof to provide excellent natural ventilation. Separate mechanical and electrical zoning of the different wings and functions in the building reduce energy requirements in unused areas. Heating is supplied from an oil/propane-fired boiler in a conventional manner. In the summer, chilled water is taken directly from the groundwater at a temperature of 55°F and used in cooling coils in the HVAC system, and then drained back into the ground. Only during extremely hot periods is additional cooling

of the water with a conventional condensor unit necessary.

An energy analysis of the Benedictine Mission House was done in 1981 using the DOE-2.1 computer program [8.1]. According to the analysis, the predicted energy use of the building as designed was 53,750 Btu/sq ft/yr. Of this total, 44 percent of the energy use was for heating, 12 percent for cooling, and 44 percent for electricity. If the earth berms were removed from the building, the computer model indicated that total energy use would increase by 16 percent. Although such computer simulations have inherent limitations and actual operation of the building can vary significantly, it is a relative indication that the Benedictine Mission House is very effectively designed with respect to energy use.

Project Data

Project: Benedictine Mission House

Location: Schuyler, Nebraska

Owner: Benedictine Mission House

Building type: Monastery

Completion date: 1979

Project size: 40,000 sq. ft.

Construction cost: $3,000,000

Structure: Cast-in-place reinforced concrete roof and walls; western red cedar roof beams in chapel; concrete slab-on-grade floor

Earth cover: 40 percent of exterior wall area is covered; over 90 percent of roof is covered with 18 to 20 in. of earth—only chapel roof and skylights are exposed

Insulation: Extruded polystyrene, 2 in. on roof, 2 in. on below-grade walls to a depth of 4 ft.

Waterproofing: Liquid-applied rubberized asphalt membrane on roof, parapets, and upper 2 ft. of below-grade walls at 180-mil. thickness; fiber-reinforced asphaltic waterproofing troweled on remaining wall area

Heating system: Oil/propane-fired boiler

Cooling system: Cool groundwater is supplied to air handling and fan coil units, conventional condensor unit chills water further during extremely hot periods

Lighting: Track, down, and spot incandescent lights

Energy use: 53,750 Btu/sq ft/yr projected

Heating	23,580 Btu/sq ft/yr
Cooling	6,650 Btu/sq ft/yr
Electrical	23,520 Btu/sq ft/yr

Heating degree days: 6,981 (Norfolk)

Cooling degree days: 925 (Norfolk)

Credits

Architect: Astle/Ericson and Associates, Omaha, Nebraska

Structural engineer: Ketchum, Konkel, Barrett, Nickel and Austin

Mechanical engineer: Raymond G. Alvine and Associates

Consulting soil engineers: Woodward/Clyde Associates

Contractor: Knudson, Inc.

Photographs: Gordon Peery

Yates Fieldhouse

Georgetown University
Washington, DC

Architect: Daniel F. Tully Associates

Covering nearly 3.5 acres, the Yates Fieldhouse on the campus of Georgetown University in Washington, DC, represents a creative solution to a number of difficult problems. By placing the entire structure underground, the available land is used efficiently on the crowded campus. Not only does the enormous mass of the building almost disappear, but the entire rooftop is used as an outdoor recreation area—in the same space a football field occupied before the fieldhouse was built. In addition to saving space on the campus, the underground design saved the university considerable time and effort. In Washington, DC, all new buildings must receive the approval of the National Commission on Fine Arts—a process that takes an average of two years—unless the building is 85 percent below grade.

Regardless of its location, above or below grade, a fieldhouse containing running tracks, tennis courts, and basketball courts presents difficult structural requirements because of the long spans and high spaces involved. Placing the building underground introduces an additional difficulty—the depth required for many conventional long-span systems such as trusses or concrete barrel vaults would force the floor level to be quite low in relation to the surface. This would make access more difficult and would increase the cost of the exterior building walls, since they must be higher and stronger to resist earth loads. To overcome these problems, the roof system at the Yates Fieldhouse consists of concrete shells shaped in hyperbolic paraboloids (hypars). This system enables the floor level of the building to be only 35 feet below grade while permitting a 34-foot interior ceiling height over the center of the court areas. In addition, the hypars are less costly than

other systems, and they create a dynamic interior environment. Because a flat playing field and track was required on the roof, the hypars support the flat slab using a patented structural technique described in greater detail in a later section.

Because of the sloping terrain, the south and west walls of the fieldhouse are partially exposed, permitting the main entry to occur through a sunken courtyard located at the southeast corner of the building. The rooftop playing field and track, covered with synthetic turf, is an extension of the existing grade on the northern and eastern side of the site. The 142,275-square foot building contains a four-lane, 200-meter indoor track; twelve multiuse courts; four handball and four squash courts; and an eight-lane swimming pool with diving well. In addition, 25,600 square feet of exercise/dance space are provided, as well as office and meeting room spaces, lockers for 2,000 people, and facilities for pole vaulting and long jumping, plus golf and batting cages. The exterior dimensions of the entire building are 390 feet by 325 feet, with the main space that contains the multiuse courts and track being 390 feet by 260 feet—divided by only five columns in the center.

Viewed from the exterior, the huge mass of the Yates Fieldhouse is not apparent—precisely the goal of the architect in placing it underground. Compared with many smaller subsurface buildings that completely blend into the surrounding landscape, however, the fieldhouse is distinguishable from its surroundings. Rather than a landscaped roof, it has a functional hard surface covered with synthetic turf. The partially exposed walls on the south and west

sides of the building define the building edge but do not create the dominating effect that such a large building on grade would. Approached from the north or west, the building edges and scale are not as evident. In general, the character of the exposed surfaces of the building can be described as simple and functional. The most carefully articulated and landscaped portion of the building exterior is the entry court. The use of brick, large areas of glass, and tiers of plants around the courtyard create an inviting image. Even though the roof is a vast flat area covered by synthetic turf, it remains an outdoor open space on a crowded campus.

Special Design Concerns

Tennis courts, basketball courts, and other athletic facilities represent very appropriate below-grade functions. Not only are exterior views not required, but natural light is actually considered undesirable in some cases. Artificial lighting can be designed to be more uniform; moreover, glare and blind spots, which can occur with natural lighting, are eliminated. In the Yates Fieldhouse, light reflected off of the hyperbolic paraboloid roof structure indirectly illuminates the main court spaces. In addition to providing uniform illumination, the sculptural forms of the roof structure are highlighted. The fieldhouse is not entirely windowless—large areas of glass provide exterior views from the lobby area and from the swimming pool.

Because recreation spaces are often windowless even built above grade and because the interior spaces are required to be large, high volumes, interior design that offsets negative associations with the underground is unnecessary. Nevertheless,

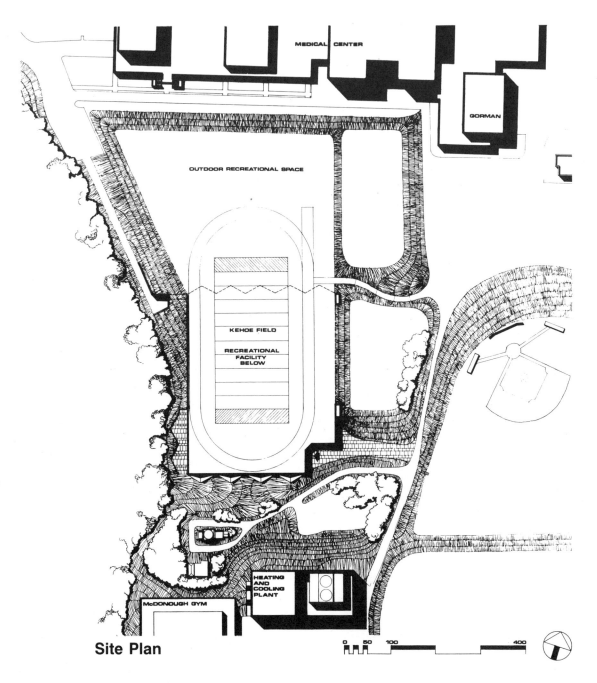

Site Plan

the interiors of the Yates Fieldhouse, dominated by the dynamic forms of the roof structure, provide an attractive, light, and spacious environment.

Most of the spaces in the building are on one level at a depth of 35 feet from the surface. Only in one small portion of the building along the south wall are there two levels. Because of the lower ground level on the southern part of the site, the upper level approximately equals existing grade. Rather than descending into the open courtyard outside the building, one enters at the upper level on a balcony overlooking the courtyard. By entering on the upper level and descending to the lower level on a large open staircase within the building, the visitor is exposed immediately to views overlooking the two-story lobby, the handball courts, and the huge space containing the tennis courts and track. The transition to the below-grade main floor is facilitated and made interesting by these large spaces and expansive views of the interior spaces.

Building Technology and Costs

The structural system used in the Yates Fieldhouse is unique not only in its appearance and ability to provide long spans and high spaces at minimum depth, but also in its detailed structural design. The eighteen structural shells forming the roof include eleven that are 130 feet by 65 feet; these form the basic module. Of the remaining shells, five are half-shells cantilevered 65 feet from an end wall, one is 65 feet by 97.5 feet, and one is 65 feet by 65 feet. Resting on 17-foot-high columns that are 3 feet by 5 feet, the 5-inch-thick hyperbolic paraboloid shells rise 18-feet from the top of the column to the flat roof.

Tennis courts covered by hyperbolic paraboloid roof structure.

The hyperbolic paraboloid shell system provides the long spans—130 feet in this case—with little depth (1 foot) required at the high points over the center of the courts. Also, hypars are generally considered cost-effective with their favorable weight-to-strength ratio. Problems arise, however, in using the hypar shapes to support a completely flat roof. In the design for Yates Fieldhouse, the architect and engineers developed a new structural technique integrating the hypars with the flat slab, which results in an extremely efficient and economical structure in which

shells and slab work together. The flat slab acts as a horizontal diaphragm to control the tendency of each shell to deflect. Edges of the hypars are post-tensioned, and shear stresses in the hypar are partially transmitted to the diaphragm.

The 3.5-inch-thick concrete roof slab is poured over fluted metal decking and then supported on a grid of pipe columns and light steel beams above the hypar shell. The pipe columns are 7 to 8 feet apart and are adjusted to different lengths to rest on the curving form of the shell.

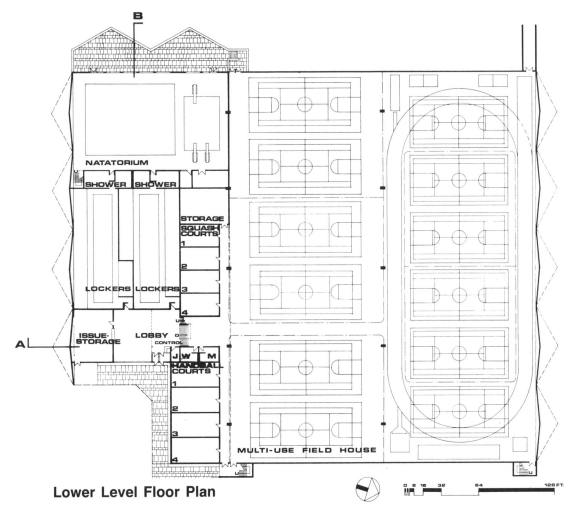

Exterior walls are cast-in-place reinforced concrete and waterproofed with troweled-on bitumastic material. Below-grade walls are insulated to a depth of 4 feet with 1 inch of polystyrene insulation (2 inches in the pool area). A waterproof polyurethane layer covers the concrete roof slab and is overlain by a ⅝-inch layer of polyurethane foam and the synthetic turf. The ⅝-inch polyurethane foam acts as a cushion and provides insulating value as well.

The designer of the fieldhouse and the contractor who is affiliated with the architect in building these unique structures noted several difficulties during construction. Construction access was more complicated on this site, and concrete roof forms that could be lowered several feet to move them around inside the building had to be developed. This type of construction proved to be rather weather-sensitive, resulting in delays. Earth

Lower Level Floor Plan

NATATORIUM

SHOWER SHOWER

STORAGE

SQUASH COURTS

LOCKERS LOCKERS

ISSUE-STORAGE

LOBBY CONTROL

HANDBALL COURTS

MULTI-USE FIELD HOUSE

0 8 16 32 64 128 FT.

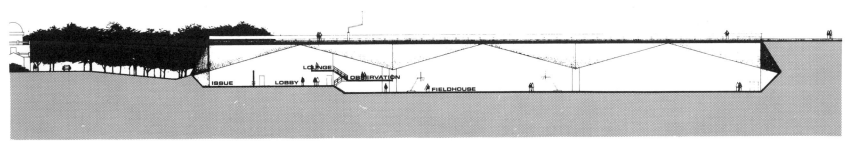

ISSUE LOBBY LOUNGE OBSERVATION FIELDHOUSE

Section A

moving and backfilling operations were more sophisticated and critical than with conventional construction.

In spite of these problems and the unusual nature of the structure, the total cost of the building—$47.26 per square foot—proved to be very acceptable. Compared with a conventional building, the architect estimates that certain higher cost items—excavation, wall structure, and heat recovery systems—were offset by lower costs for exterior finishing materials and the roof structure. According to a study of alternate structural systems done during the building design in 1977, the concrete hypar roof cost $11.75 per square foot, compared with $14.50 per square foot for precast concrete "tees" and girders, the next lowest cost system. In the same study, long-span steel construction cost $15 per square foot, and wide flange beams, $16.80 per square foot.

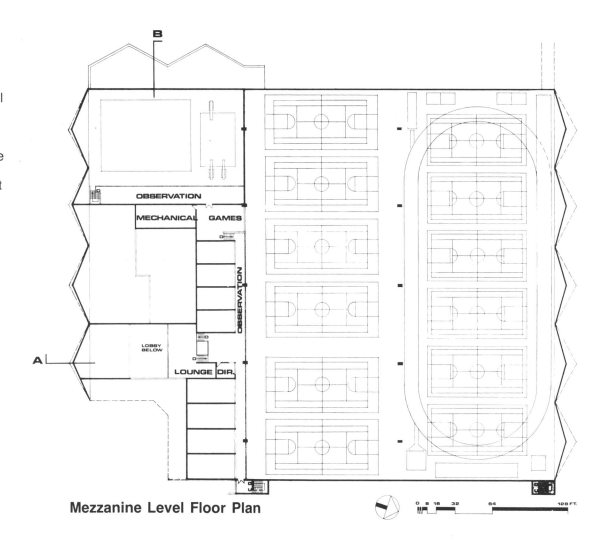

Mezzanine Level Floor Plan

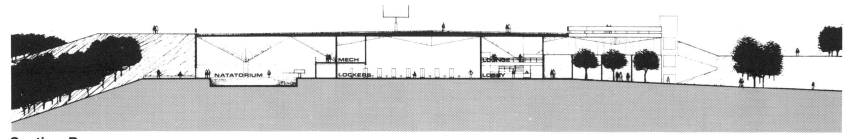

Section B

Energy Use Considerations

Locating the Yates Fieldhouse predominantly underground places it in a more moderate environment. With ground temperatures at approximately 60°F at a depth of 15 feet or more in Washington, DC, the structure can benefit in both the heating and cooling seasons. Additional energy for heating and cooling is saved by the use of heat wheels for waste heat recovery and humidity stabilization from the exhaust air system. During summer the exhaust from the building is both cooler and drier than outside air. In winter, exhaust air from the pool and locker rooms is not only warmer than outside air, but more humid, making heat recovery particularly effective. Heat wheels recovering sensible as well as enthalpic energy are approximately 85 percent efficient. The cavities inside the hyperbolic paraboloid shells are used for mechanical and electrical equipment but also serve for passive solar collection. In winter, sun-heated air is circulated through 2-foot-diameter holes in the shells. The holes are plugged in summer.

Actual energy consumption figures for the building are not available since energy is supplied to all buildings on campus through a central system that is unmetered. At the time of design, the architect estimated that the below-grade location reduced energy consumption 20 percent, and the heat recovery system further reduced energy consumption to one-third that of a conventional building without these features.

Above: Entrance courtyard. Below: View from the mezzanine level of a squash court in the foreground and tennis courts in the background.

Project Data

Project: Yates Fieldhouse

Location: Washington, DC

Owner: Trustees of Georgetown University

Building type: Multiuse recreational building

Completion date: 1979

Project size: 152,275 sq. ft.

Construction cost: $7,197,200

See construction cost table for detailed breakdown.

Structure: Roof system of concrete shells shaped in hyperbolic paraboloids support flat concrete slab roof poured over metal deck; slab acts as diaphragm, stiffening hypars, and is supported by light metal framing and pipe columns resting on shells below; cast-in-place reinforced concrete walls; 6-in. slab-on-grade floor

Earth cover: 85 percent of exterior wall area is covered; no earth cover on roof

Insulation: ⅝-in.-thick layer of polyurethane over roof slab and 4 in. of fiberglass under roof deck; 1-in. polystyrene on below-grade walls to a depth of 4 ft.; 2-in. polystyrene in pool area

Waterproofing: Liquid-applied polyurethane membrane on roof deck; trowel-applied bitumastic waterproofing on below-grade walls

Heating system: Hot water is provided from heat exchangers within building which interface with central steam supply system

Cooling system: No mechanical cooling; cooling provided by high-volume ventilation system and dehumidification by electric air-cooled condensing units

Lighting: Metallic halide indirect lighting

Energy use: Information not available

Heating degree days: 4,211

Cooling degree days: 1,415

Occupancy schedule: 18.5 hours per day, 7 days per week, 52 weeks per year

Credits

Architect: Daniel F. Tully Associates, Inc.

Structural engineer: Daniel F. Tully Associates, Inc.; William C. Hale, P.E.; Walter H. Weidner, Jr., P.E.

Mechanical engineer: TCI/Lambda

Contractor: Creative Building Systems, Inc.

Photographs: Edward Jacoby/APG

Construction Costs for Yates Fieldhouse

General conditions	$423,000
Earthwork	433,000
Paving	21,000
Pile foundations	195,000
Concrete foundations	858,000
Concrete superstructure	1,181,000
Horizontal concrete diaphragm	353,000
Masonry	165,000
Structural steel	64,000
Carpentry	14,000
Dampproofing and insulation	86,000
Door frames, glazing	97,000
Studs, drywall	6,200
Ceramic tile	24,000
Flooring	245,000
Painting	53,000
Showers, accessories	4,000
Lockers, benches	31,000
Fire alarms, extinguishers	53,000
Swimming pool	200,000
Athletic equipment	26,000
Squash and handball courts	102,000
Plumbing	85,000
Heating, ventilating, and electrical	911,000
Landscaping	52,000
Elevators	33,000
Synthetic turf	302,000
Synthetic track	355,000
Egress tunnel	11,000
Site utilities	175,000
Overhead, profit, and design fees	500,000
Change orders	139,000
Total	$7,197,200

Moscone Convention Center

San Francisco, California

Architect: Hellmuth, Obata and Kassabaum

Located on an 11.5-acre site near downtown San Francisco, the Moscone Convention Center is one of the largest and most impressive structures of its kind in the world. The 650,000-square foot building is almost entirely below grade except for a relatively small entrance pavilion on the surface. Seen by many as a catalyst to future development in the area and a means of increasing tourism, the convention center was opposed by groups resisting the development in general and the enormous scale in particular. Placing the massive convention center underground with future development potential on the roof was recommended by a committee selected to resolve the long-running controversy over the project.

Completed in 1981, the center occupies an oversize city block, 840 feet by 525 feet and serves as the focal point of future redevelopment of the 87-acre Yerba Buena area. The 275,000-square foot main exhibit hall is the largest column-free exhibition space in the United States. The 275-foot-long concrete arches spanning the exhibition space are designed to support extensive future development on the roof. Development as heavy as a three-story building or mounds of earth 7 feet deep can be placed on the 8-acre roof, which currently remains unoccupied. At least part, if not all, of the rooftop is intended for use as a park. On the sloping site, the main exhibition floor is located from 16 to 30 feet below grade. Surrounded by earth berms, the rooftop is actually above existing grade, as the huge arches rise to provide a 37-foot-high space in the main exhibition area.

The convention center is entered through a 30,000-square foot glass-enclosed pavilion on the surface—the only above-grade portion of the complex. The two lower levels are reached by escalators, elevators, and stairs from the entrance lobby. As many as thirty-one individual meeting rooms can be created with partitions on the mezzanine level. On the lowest level, in addition to the main exhibit hall, is a 30,000-square foot main ballroom. Like the main exhibit hall, the ballroom can be subdivided into three separate spaces with acoustical partitions. Also included in the building is a kitchen that can serve 6,000 people and twelve loading docks reached by ramps on the building perimeter. The main exhibit hall can hold 20,000 people, with an additional 4,000 in other spaces.

Because the final development on the building roof has not yet occurred, the complete exterior form and character of this building has not yet been established. If the entire rooftop is landscaped as a park, the dominant image will be a welcome open space in the center of the city with a glass-enclosed pavilion on one side. A different image altogether may be created if building forms are placed on the roof. The exterior image will then depend on the design of the new buildings, and the glass-enclosed lobby will not be as prominent a form when combined with other masses on the site. Nevertheless, the existing above-grade lobby with its large, exposed truss roof will continue to present a striking image for the center under any circumstances. Even if the rooftop is completely landscaped, the site will maintain a very urban character, well defined by the surrounding streets. Very

Opposite: Aerial view of the Moscone Convention Center showing the above-grade entrance pavilion and undeveloped roof area, photograph by Peter Henricks.

definite edges are created on the perimeter of the site by shafts for intake and exhaust air, stairways, retaining walls, and steep berms in some places. In spite of these elements, the goal of diminishing the visual impact of such an enormous complex has been achieved, and the potential for a large, well-designed open space on the site exists.

Special Design Concerns

Since exhibition areas and meeting rooms do not require natural light and view, such spaces are quite appropriate in underground space; in fact, windows are often undesirable in those spaces. There are, however, legitimate concerns over any negative associations with descending into an underground building or finding dark, confined interior spaces. These potential problems are carefully resolved in the design of the Moscone Convention Center.

Entering the building at grade is similar to any conventional structure. The descent to lower levels by escalators and stairs occurs in a 60-foot-high atrium space filled with natural light from the glass-enclosed lobby above. There are glimpses of the San Francisco skyline in this entrance area; at various levels, walkways and balconies overlook the larger spaces below. On the lowest level, the entrance area to the main exhibit hall and ballroom is open to the lobby above and receives natural light from skylights overhead. Inside the main exhibit hall, the enormous space framed by the long curves of the concrete arches creates a light and airy feeling even though there are no windows.

An important design concern in underground buildings is providing life safety and, in particular, adequate fire

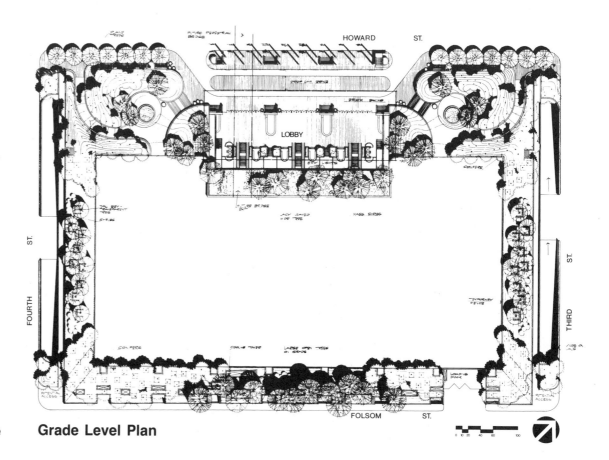

Grade Level Plan

egress. In most cases subsurface structures are quite similar to above-grade buildings. It is only when the occupied spaces are unusually deep or extremely large—as in the case of the Moscone Convention Center—that unique problems arise. Since, at certain times, the building would have as many as 24,000 people, and since large auditoriums can be vulnerable to disaster in case of fire, the center is designed to be at least equal to an above-grade building in safety, incorporating many sophisticated systems. Most remarkable is the number and scale of the exits available: 100,000 square feet of exit ramps and stairs are included in the building. Four 27.5-foot-wide ramps are located at the corners of the structure, and eighteen 20-foot-wide exit stairs are located on the perimeter of the building. In addition to swift egress, the building includes an extensive sprinkler system, smoke detectors, and an emergency reporting system. Since roof vents will not automatically assist in evacuating smoke in an underground building, large fans can be activated for this purpose.

Building Technology and Costs

One of the most challenging problems in placing the Moscone Convention Center underground on this site was preventing leakage and structural damage from water. The natural groundwater table is 10 feet above the lower floor level of the building. A massive concrete foundation mat—averaging 7 feet in thickness—provides weight to counteract

Above: Main entrance of the Moscone Convention Center. Below: Main exhibit hall, photographs by Peter Henricks.

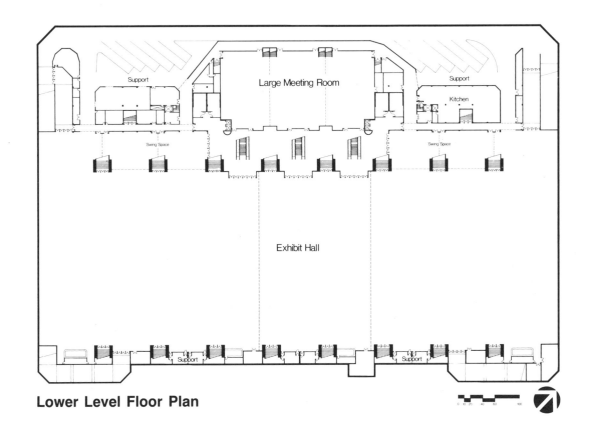

Lower Level Floor Plan

0 10 20 40 60 100

hydrostatic pressure. The mat covers a 550- by 850-foot area and contains 120,000 cubic yards of concrete. Within the concrete mat is a waterproofing layer composed of a bentonite-based mixture that expands and seals when wet. On the walls the same bentonite-based mixture was sprayed directly on the shoring; reinforced concrete walls were then formed against the shoring and waterproofing. The concrete roof slab is waterproofed with a sprayed-on elastomeric membrane.

The sixteen concrete arches spanning 275 feet over the main exhibit hall were formed and then post-tensioned. Post-tensioning cables in the foundation mat resist 5,300 tons of thrust for each arch. By placing the arches in eight pairs, spans of 60 feet between the pairs and 20 feet within the pairs must be bridged. Precast tees are used in the longer spans, and an 8-inch concrete slab with no expansion joints is poured over the entire roof structure.

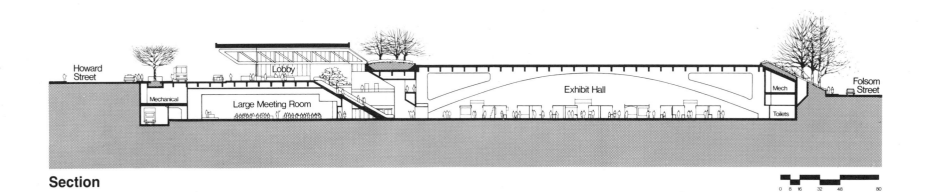

Section

0 8 16 32 48 80

A separate structural system is used to support the roof over the above-grade lobby area. Four 120-foot-long tubular steel trusses placed 90 feet apart are the main visible support for the roof. Spanning between these large trusses are 5-foot-deep steel girders supporting the roof deck. The four tubular trusses are supported on one end by the arch abutments and on the other by steel X-bracing resting on post-tensioned concrete box beams below. These large box beams (11 by 20 feet) serve as fire exit tunnels and support the roof of the main ballroom on the lower level.

Many aspects of the construction process and features included in the building are almost unprecedented in their size and scope. For example, as much as 1,500 to 2,500 cubic yards of concrete were placed in a single pour—quantities usually seen only in dam construction. Not only is the building designed to support extensive loads from above and resist hydrostatic pressures, but it must also resist earthquake loads. Designed to resist seismic forces 25 percent higher than required by the San Francisco code, the structure would move only an estimated $7/8$ to $1 3/8$ inches if a catastrophic earthquake took place.

Lighting and utility systems are designed to provide a great deal of flexibility. Metal halide, quartz halogen, and quartz down lights are placed in arrays with a variety of possible arrangements available to exhibitors. In the main exhibit hall, a unique network of tunnels and raceways under the floor can provide electricity, telephone, water, waste, compressed air, and gas to every location in the space.

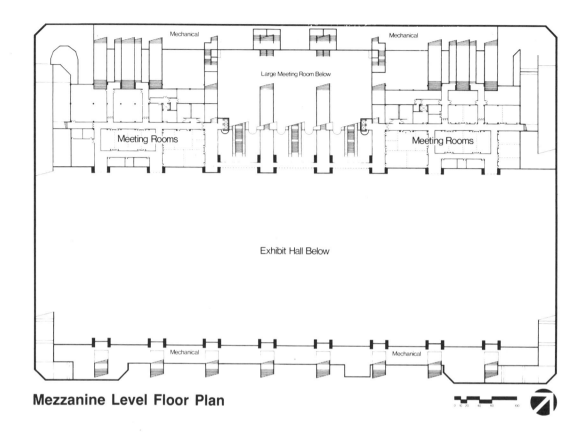

Mezzanine Level Floor Plan

The total cost of the Moscone Convention Center project was $126.5 million. A breakdown of the items attributed to actual construction contracts for the building (totaling $100.7 million) is shown in a table at the end of this section. A project of this scale with so many unique structural requirements almost defies comparison with smaller buildings or an equivalent convention center built above grade. It has been estimated by the designers, however, that approximately $20 million of the total could be attributed to the underground placement of the center along with the structural requirement of supporting rooftop development. This extra cost has to be weighed against the value of the space preserved for future development, the value to the total environment of placing the massive structure out of sight, and the perception that without building the center underground it may not have been built at all.

Energy Use Considerations

During an eleven-month period from July 1982 through May 1983, the building consumed 41.4×10^9 Btu (63,230 Btu/square foot). Based on these figures, the annual consumption would be approximately 69,000 Btu/square foot. One consideration in examining these total energy use figures is that they include electricity consumed for lighting and equipment that are part of the displays and exhibitions. Energy use for these special purposes is not separately metered at this time.

An important consideration in designing an HVAC system for a convention center is the tremendous variation in the number of occupants and the times when the building is occupied. A key to reducing energy use is providing the capability to heat and cool different zones of the building independently, making it possible to shut down certain areas when not in use. In the Moscone Convention Center, the main exhibit hall has nine separate single-zoned systems; the main ballroom, three separate systems; several other separate systems supply heating and cooling to other parts of the building.

Left: Escalators in the lobby area descending to the meeting rooms and exhibit hall below, photograph by George Silk.

Project Data

Project: George R. Moscone Convention Center

Location: San Francisco, California

Owner: City and County of San Francisco

Building type: Convention center

Completion date: 1981

Project size: 650,000 sq. ft.

Construction cost: $126,500,000 total project cost with $100,710,000 attributed to actual construction. *See construction cost table for detailed breakdown.*

Structure: Post-tensioned concrete arches spanning 275 ft. supporting precast concrete tees covered by 8-in.-thick slab form roof structure of main exhibit hall; tubular trusses supporting 5-ft.-deep steel girders form roof structure of above-grade entrance pavilion; walls are cast-in-place reinforced concrete; floor is reinforced concrete mat with average thickness of 7 ft.

Earth cover: 95 percent of exterior wall area is earth covered, entrance pavilion walls are only exposed areas; rooftop is presently earth covered only at perimeter but can support 7 ft. of earth over 90 percent of the area in future development

Insulation: 2-in.-thick extruded polystyrene on roof; no wall insulation below-grade

Waterproofing: Sprayed-on elastomeric membrane on roof; sprayed-on bentonite-based mixture on walls and under floor

Heating system: Three oil-fired boilers supply hot water to coils in several separate single-zoned HVAC systems

Cooling system: Centrifugal chillers supply chilled water to coils in several separate single-zoned HVAC systems

Lighting: Metal halide, quartz halogen, and quartz down lights

Energy Use: 69,000 Btu/sq ft/yr

Electricity	36.3×10^9	Btu (10.64×10^6 kWh)
Diesel fuel	4.2×10^9	Btu (30,000 gal)
Natural gas	$.6 \times 10^9$	Btu (5921 therms)
Total	41.1×10^9	Btu

Note: Energy use figures are for an eleven month period from July 1982 through May 1983. Total energy consumption during this period was 63,230 Btu/square foot. Based on this, annual consumption is estimated to be 69,000 Btu/sq ft/yr.

Heating degree days: 3,042

Cooling degree days: 108

Number of occupants: 24,000 capacity

Occupancy schedule: Variable

Credits

Architect: Hellmuth, Obata and Kassabaum, Inc., San Francisco Office

Associate architect: Jack Young and Associates

Structural engineer: T. Y. Lin International

Mechanical engineer: Hayakawa Associates

Seismic design consultants: GKT Consulting Engineers, Inc.

Lighting and electrical consultants: The Engineering Enterprise

Fire safety consultants: Rolf Jensen and Associates

Landscape architects: The SWA Group

Contractor: Turner Construction Company

Photographs: Peter Henricks and George Silk

Construction Costs for Moscone Convention Center

Excavation	$2,020,000
Dewatering	600,000
Shoring	1,570,000
Foundations & structures mat	22,670,000
Exhibit hall tees and arches	12,270,000
Exterior walls	1,970,000
Beams and slabs	15,030,000
Structural steel	1,820,000
Electrical	6,160,000
Sound and audio	1,260,000
Radio and television	210,000
HVAC	5,060,000
Plumbing and toilets	3,820,000
Fire protection	2,120,000
Elevators, escalators	1,370,000
Food service	680,000
Glass and glazing	2,090,000
Rolling doors	290,000
Ornamental metal	1,090,000
Carpentry, millwork	360,000
Acoustic ceilings, walls	1,340,000
Drywall lath and plaster	2,760,000
Operable walls	1,340,000
Painting	560,000
Granite	890,000
Ceramic tile	290,000
Carpet	520,000
Graphics	630,000
Finish hardware	230,000
Hollow metal	210,000
Subtotal	$91,230,000
General conditions, contingency, misc.	9,480,000
Total	$100,710,000

Minnesota Correctional Facility

Oak Park Heights, Minnesota

Architect: Winsor/Faricy Architects
Correctional consultant: Gruzen and Partners

Set into a ravine on a sloping 160-acre site, the Minnesota Correctional Facility at Oak Park Heights demonstrates a number of the unique advantages underground buildings offer. In addition, the 400-inmate maximum security prison for men illustrates some innovative trends in the design of correctional facilities. Although a prison is a very specialized function, many of the concepts of site design, security, and energy conservation demonstrated in the Oak Park Heights structure may be applied to other building types.

By placing the 330,000-square foot building into the sides of a 30-foot-deep ravine, the complex fits into the contours of the land and, most importantly, is not visible from the adjacent highway to the west or the nearby residential community. Almost completely earth covered on the exterior walls, the prison extends around the perimeter of a large interior courtyard; all windows face into this central area. Only the relatively small administration building on the west side of the courtyard extends above grade and is visible from the highway. The site slopes downward to the east, permitting on-grade access to the sunken courtyard at the lowest point.

The underground design also contributes to energy conservation and a high degree of security. In addition to placing the 30-foot-high exterior walls in contact with the more moderate earth temperatures, setting the building below grade shields it from the severe winter winds on this open site. In terms of security, the surrounding earth berms provide a significant barrier around the building perimeter, and the entire complex and sunken courtyard area can be seen from above without guard towers.

A goal in designing the Minnesota Correctional Facility was to provide maximum security in a humane environment. Part of the current philosophy in rehabilitating inmates is to provide as normal an environment as possible, easing the transition back to society. By facing the building inward, the environment viewed by the inmate is a normal one of buildings and outdoor spaces, not fences and guard towers. Some places in the complex provide views of the river valley and surrounding countryside.

In order to improve security, safety, and control while allowing the inmates a degree of freedom, seven separate residential complexes, each housing 52 people, were built. Connected by a corridor on the lower level, the seven units contain private rooms on two levels with views of the courtyard. The cells open onto a wide, corridor-type commons or day space with food service, study activities, meetings, and indoor recreation. Each residential complex has its own outdoor recreation court, and the large central space is used for scheduled activities such as baseball and football games.

Located on the level above the residential complexes are work areas, education spaces, and other support functions. A corridor on this level permits visitors and staff to move around the complex without crossing through the residential areas. The main entrance and administrative offices are located on the highest level in a small building mass that projects above grade in the southwest corner of the complex. In this core area of the facility, the main control center, gymnasium, chapel, 42-bed

Opposite: Aerial view of Minnesota Correctional Facility, photograph by Saari and Forrai.

medical center, kitchen, and other support functions are located on various levels.

Unlike most building types, a correction facility is not entered and used by the public. In addition, a prison is generally considered undesirable by those living near it; thus, minimizing its visibility from the outside is considered an asset. On the other hand, it is the residence of several hundred people for whom a somewhat normal environment is desirable. With these unique concerns in mind, three aspects of the exterior form of the Minnesota Correctional Facility must be considered: its impact on the passerby or neighbor, its impact on the inmate, and its impact as a work of earth-integrated architecture.

Clearly, reduced visibility and awareness of the complex are achieved by its placement below grade. The entry and administrative structure above grade is necessary, but its reduced scale compares favorably with the conventional images of huge building masses, walls, fences, and guard towers. Viewed from within the central courtyard, the complex includes features that create both a normal and interesting environment for the inmate. Building forms are staggered, reflecting individual units, window openings vary in size and placement, the brown brick adds texture and warmth, and the central courtyard is mostly grass rather than hard surface. The building design as a whole demonstrates how to set a massive building discreetly into the landscape without compromising exposure to the

*Above: View from within the central courtyard.
Below: Grade level view from outside the complex illustrating the low profile of the building.*

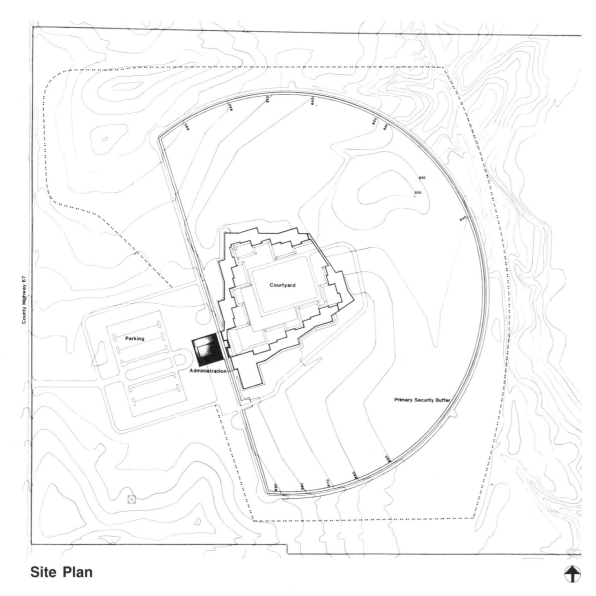

Site Plan

outside. In fact, similar site design concepts could be applied to housing, hospitals, hotels, or other functions. Two missing elements would integrate the building even more with the site and soften some of the hard edges of the complex: a completely earth-covered roof and more extensive landscaping. Although considered, neither of these alternatives proved practical for the prison—earth cover on the roof was simply too costly, and trees or shrubs can interfere with sight lines and thus compromise security. Nevertheless, for a different function under different circumstances, an excellent building and site integration could be achieved.

Special Design Concerns

Some of the special design concerns associated with underground buildings in general are not applicable to a prison. Most notably, concerns over entering from grade and descending to lower levels are not relevant. In addition, many devices typically used to bring natural light into windowless spaces— multistory interior atriums, glass walls, and skylights—are not desirable for security reasons. In spite of these limitations, there was a concern over eliminating any claustrophobic or oppressive spaces, in keeping with the rehabilitation philosophy of creating a normal environment.

Although almost the entire perimeter of the building is earth covered, the long, extended layout of the building, with all spaces facing into a large central courtyard, provides access to natural light and view for a majority of the complex. Every cell has a narrow window facing into the courtyard; larger windows provide light and view into work and education areas on the upper level. Spaces typically requiring no exterior exposure, such as the gymnasium, are placed against the earth rather than along the courtyard. Although the day spaces are on the interior of the building, separated from the courtyard by the cells, some natural light and view is provided through windows because of the staggered arrangement of the plan. In addition, the day spaces have higher ceilings than the cells, and balconies from the upper level of cells overlook the commons space, providing some spatial variety. Interiors are mainly exposed concrete and masonry surface, with bright colors on doors, carpet, and graphics painted in the corridors.

Building Technology and Costs

Although the building was set into a natural landform, 1.3 million cubic yards of earth had to be moved during excavation. The basic structure is a rigid steel-reinforced concrete frame supporting 6- to 10-inch-thick floor and roof slabs. Since the lateral earth loads on the 30-foot-high back wall were unopposed by lateral forces on the courtyard side, a unique approach was used to resist these forces. Placed at intervals of 20 feet along the retaining wall are counterforts—massive triangular concrete bulwarks. At an earlier stage of design, placing earth over the roof was considered, but it not only proved to be expensive but would have required additional columns, which would interfere with sight lines in the spaces below.

Within the complex a number of sophisticated devices and systems are used to control security, fire safety, and building HVAC operation. In the main control center, three computers monitor all

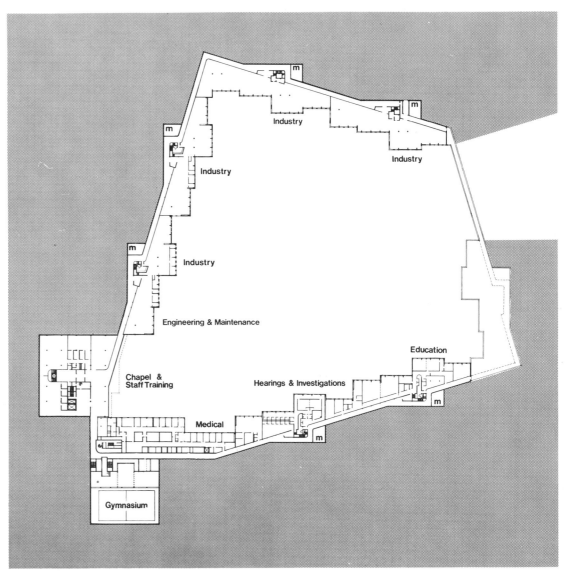

Floor Plan—One Level Below Grade

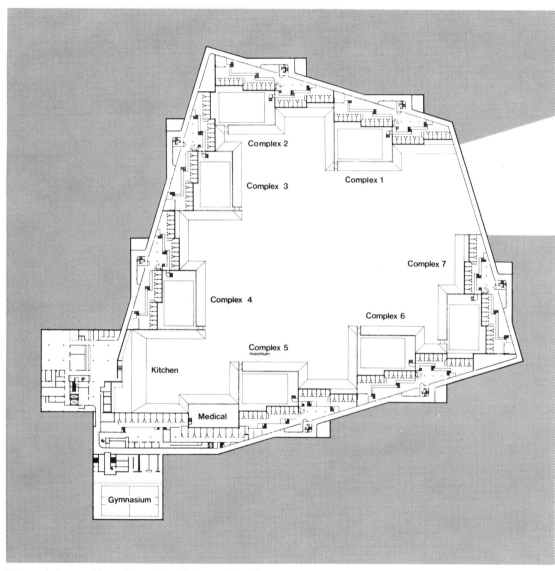

Floor Plan—Two Levels Below Grade

activities in the building, and television surveillance is used extensively. Laminated security glass, ranging from 2 to 8 plies, encloses the control center and other security areas around the building.

The total construction cost of the Oak Park Heights facility was $30.6 million, which is approximately $93 per square foot. Construction costs for a correctional facility are difficult to compare to other types of buildings. Many special and expensive systems, materials, and details are required for security reasons. With regard to the underground placement of the building, the architect has identified two costs that are directly attributable to the below-grade design: the extensive excavation ($1,223,744) and the counterforts required to retain the earth ($500,000). In attempting to compare this facility with an equivalent one above grade, these additional costs would have to be balanced against additional exterior finishing above grade, differences in energy costs, perhaps the construction of guard towers, and the value of reduced visibility underground.

Energy Use Considerations

In addition to placing the structure below grade, the designers of the Minnesota Correctional Facility have employed a number of other energy-efficient concepts in the building. The HVAC system is designed to reclaim internal heat generated by people, lights, and machines with a pipe coil system in the return air vents and kitchen exhaust. When auxiliary heat is required, it is provided by electric boilers using a heat pump. In off-peak hours water is electrically heated to 105°F and stored in two 25,000-gallon tanks for times when demand is the greatest. During summer, cold water is stored at night for daytime use. This system takes advantage of lower electric rates during off-peak hours and is designed for future conversion to solar heating once such a system becomes feasible.

Actual energy use for the building was 97,550 Btu/sq ft/yr during a period from May 1982 to May 1983. While this figure may appear high compared with other building types, it actually is quite efficient considering the facility is operated twenty-four hours per day and requires unusually high electrical use for lighting and security systems. It should be noted that the building was only partially occupied during the period that energy use was measured. It is estimated that total annual energy use will increase by 5 to 20 percent once the building is fully occupied.

Project Data

Project: Minnesota Correctional Facility

Location: Oak Park Heights, Minnesota

Owner: Minnesota Department of Corrections

Building type: Maximum security prison for men

Completion date: 1982

Project size: 330,000 sq. ft.

Construction cost: $30,631,275

See construction cost table for detailed breakdown.

Structure: Cast-in-place reinforced concrete frame; roof and floor are reinforced concrete slabs ranging from 6 to 10 in. thick; exterior walls are 8-in. cast-in-place reinforced concrete; counterforts are placed 20 ft. on center along 30-ft.-high earth retaining wall.

Earth cover: 90 percent of perimeter walls are earth covered (about 50 percent of total exterior wall area); no earth cover on roof

Insulation: 4-in.-thick polystyrene board with 1-in.-thick vermiculite board on roof; 2-in.-thick extruded polystyrene on exposed walls to a depth of 8 ft.

Waterproofing: Glass-reinforced asphalt on below-grade walls; loose-laid EPDM single-ply membrane on roof

Heating system: Electric hot water boilers, air system with dual-duct variable air volume and single-duct constant volume; water warmed by heat reclaimed from kitchen exhaust; return air is stored in two underground storage tanks

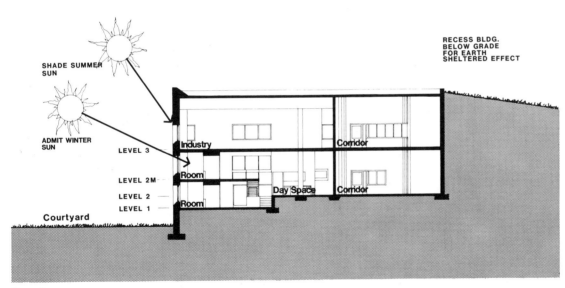

Section

Cooling system: Centrifugal chiller with two 25,000-gal. storage tanks; 420 cooling tons

Lighting: Fluorescent fixtures with security lenses; high-pressure sodium fixtures

Energy use: 97,550 Btu/sq ft/yr

Electricity 32.2 x 10^9 Btu
(9.43 x 10^6 kWh)

Note: Energy use is for period from May 1982 to May 1983. The building was only partially occupied during this period. Energy use is expected to increase by 5 to 20 percent when the building is fully occupied.

Heating degree days: 8,159

Cooling degree days: 585

Number of occupants: 400 inmates plus 250 staff (average during daytime)

Occupancy schedule: 168 hours per week; 52 weeks per year

Credits

Architect: Winsor/Faricy Architects, Inc., St. Paul, Minnesota

Correctional consultant: Gruzen and Partners

Structural, mechanical and electrical engineer: Kirkham/Michael and Associates, Inc.

Construction manager: McGough Construction Company

Photographs: Saari and Forrai Photography, exteriors; James A. Gallop, interiors

Construction Costs for Minnesota Correctional Facility

Site excavation	$1,229,744
Site utilities	43,280
Reinforcing steel	732,815
Concrete structure	5,787,932
Masonry, misc. metal, etc.	9,272,479
Elevators	180,046
Mechanical	5,109,180
Electrical	2,318,156
Electronic sec. equip.	545,500
Inst./elec. sec. equip.	249,264
Building security system	166,141
Fence security system	111,628
Security fence	374,702
Food service equipment	552,224
Lath and plaster	533,887
Tilework	113,690
Site drainage	53,745
Bituminous, paving	239,375
Concrete curb and walks	61,175
Vinyl asbestos tile	62,931
Painting	277,033
Acoustical tile	131,630
Millwork	261,281
Carpeting	9,414
General conditions	838,928
Communications equip.	219,751
Equip. and furnishing	973,910
Industry floor	139,395
Radio building	42,039
Total	$30,631,275

Above: Commons area of a typical residential complex. Below: Public lobby area with control center enclosed in glass, photographs by James Gallop.

Appendices

A: Life Safety and Fire Protection in Underground Buildings

B: Below-Grade Waterproofing

Appendix A:

Life Safety and Fire Protection for Underground Buildings

The inaccessibility of underground structures results in some unique fire safety concerns. Primary among these are the venting of smoke and gases from fires, the evacuation of occupants, and the handicaps to fire fighting. Although these problems are fundamental in all fire protection, their solution in relation to underground structures is more complex and has not been fully addressed in any single standard.

If a fire breaks out, aboveground buildings can usually be vented directly to the outdoors. Fire departments carry forcible entry tools that help them break through walls and roofs, open locked doors, break out windows, and the like. The opening up of the building may turn out to be quite time consuming and difficult at a time when speed is important—but at least the exterior of the building is accessible. The earth sheltered building, on the other hand, is not readily accessible to the fire department. The roof of an earth sheltered building may be exposed and therefore accessible, but even in this case, the exterior walls will typically be buried. An exception is the building that is earth sheltered on three sides, with a fourth side open to the outside air. This building design may, however, still pose an unusual fire suppression problem because of the lack of cross-ventilation and the fact that the building can be approached from only one side.

The inaccessibility of underground structures requires more than the partial fire protection facilities that might suffice in an aboveground building where dependence is placed on public fire service.

Consequently, the major portion of this appendix will be concerned with the life safety provisions of building codes and other reference documents. As a basis for understanding life safety codes as they relate to earth sheltered buildings, these issues will be introduced by a description of fire and smoke behavior in underground or windowless structures and a discussion of more specific building design requirements.

Throughout this appendix, references to the applicable codes or guidelines will be made at the beginning of each section. The following abbreviations will be used:

UBC—Uniform Building Code [A.1]
LSC— National Fire Protection Association Life Safety Code [A.2]
FPH —National Fire Protection Association Handbook [A.3]

Smoke Development and Movement

Applicable guidelines: FPH 2-25, 2-27, 2-28

The confinement of a fire within a space interferes with the dissipation of heat, gases, and smoke, so that the radiative feedback to the seat of the fire is greatly enhanced and initial burning rates increase. As contrasted with outside fires, an enclosed environment is underventilated, resulting in the following possible conditions:

- Under partially ventilated conditions within a partially enclosed area (such as a room with open doors and windows), carbon dioxide will first be produced until ceiling temperatures reach 1,200° to 1,500°F. Beyond this temperature, the carbon dioxide reacts with free carbon to produce carbon monoxide. Although this reaction is endothermic, it is a prolific source of carbon monoxide. Oxygen/Carbon monoxide ratios of between 3 and 1 will form lower flammability mixtures, depending on the prevailing carbon dioxide concentration.

- Under sealed, nonventilated conditions, almost the same general chemical conditions exist except that the oxygen concentration is much lower. Together with the prevailing carbon dioxide concentration, this prevents ignition of the carbon monoxide at the lower flammable limits. Instead, the oxygen/carbon monoxide ratio is much lower, and levels of 0.06 to 0.07 constitute the upper flammable limit. Under these conditions improper ventilation can cause an explosion known as "blow-back."

Below-ground and windowless spaces create significant ventilation problems. Oxygen reduction causes inefficient combustion, resulting in fires that generate dense smoke and carbon monoxide. High temperatures often occur because of the heat buildup that results from inadequate heat venting. Fire department access is limited; moreover, potential access locations are also avenues of escape for heat, smoke, and gases, some of which ignite when mixed with greater amounts of oxygen. Proper engineering design of ventilation systems to operate under typical fire conditions is essential for spaces such as these.

Smoke and fire gases are airborne products of combustion. Even at levels that reduce visibility to nearly zero, however, the concentration of these products is not sufficient to influence materially the overall movement of the atmosphere. Consequently, insofar as the physical movement is concerned, a smoky atmosphere usually moves in a manner similar to normal air having the same characteristics of temperature and pressure. Natural air movement in a building is influenced by a number of factors. The pressures and buoyancy created by the heat of the fire generate movement. This movement is modified by such factors as stack effect, wind pressures, the building geometry and its barriers (such as walls and floors), and ventilation practices. This natural air movement may be significantly affected by the operation of mechanical air-handling equipment in the building. In addition, the sprinkler system will have a cooling effect on the smoke and fire gases. All of these factors combine to make the prediction of smoke movement in a large building a highly complex problem.

Research on the problem of smoke movement in buildings has been conducted by a number of organizations, including the National Research Council of Canada and the American Society of Heating, Refrigerating and Air-Conditioning Engineers' Technical Committee 5.6 on Control of Fire and Smoke.

During a fire in a confined space (such as a room of a building), the atmosphere in the room is a mixture of smoke, fire gases, and air. As noted, a smoky atmosphere and a normal atmosphere usually behave essentially the same (except when the sprinkler system is engaged) with regard to movement. As the fire grows, both the pressure and the temperature increase. The volume of gases in a room could increase by a factor of three or more if unconfined. Every cubic foot of fresh air introduced into the burning space is expanded by this factor before it is displaced as a smoky mixture. As the hot gases move away from the fire, they cool rapidly, thus contracting to their original volume. But, even though the displaced gases eventually cool to the ambient temperature, the effect of the expansion during fire conditions is a net increase in volume of displaced smoke of approximately twice the volume of the spaces involved. Although this quantity of expanded air and smoke is substantial, it is often less significant than the quantity of air that moves through a building during a fire.

Building geometry and space arrangement significantly influence the movement of smoke and heat. Consequently, smoke and heat ventilation reflect design objectives and realistic physical behavior. Design features incorporated into above-grade buildings may be totally inappropriate for structures below ground or without windows.

A fire in a lower floor will emit smoke and heat that will usually travel upward—at least for a while. Occupants can therefore be safely relocated to a level one or two stories below the fire floor. In an underground building, as the occupants try to leave the building they must travel upward and approach that area within the building where the heat and smoke is most likely to gather. It is most unlikely that they would go deeper into the building and below the fire floor. The situation is quite different from that with which most designers are familiar [A.4].

Air Handling and Smoke and Heat Venting

Applicable guidelines: FPH 2-28, 2-29, 2-30, 6-105

The following general principles apply to the effective use of air-handling systems for pressurization:

- *Negative pressures:* A negative air pressure should be obtained in the fire/smoke area by the shutdown of air-supply fans and diversion of return air directly to outside.

- *Positive pressures:* A positive pressure should be obtained in adjacent areas by the shutdown of return air fans and by using 100 percent outside air.

- *Windowless buildings:* In windowless buildings corridors should not be used in lieu of ducts for air handling. Separate fan and duct systems should be used for each fire area.

Smoke venting is used to alleviate smoke and heat buildup in an underground or windowless building by exhausting smoke and fire gases from the building. The current trend in fire fighting, however, is to provide venting only after the fire is out. Storage buildings may require extensive venting facilities, whereas buildings with low fire loading, noncombustible construction, and automatic sprinklers may be cleared of smoke through the ventilation system provided for normal changes of air.

Vents are most applicable to large-area, one-story buildings lacking adequate subdivision. They are also useful in windowless and earth sheltered buildings. Vents are not a substitute for automatic sprinkler protection.

Where vents are used on windowless buildings, an area of openings near the ground at least equal to the area of the vents must be provided, or the vents will not function effectively. Vents will also not function in earth sheltered buildings unless provision is made for air to enter the burning compartment near floor

level. Fresh air falling through the layer of hot smoky gases will itself become heated and smoky.

In below-grade areas where gravity venting is not feasible, power ventilators can provide positive heat and smoke venting. If venting is initiated only to clear the smoke after the fire, then power ventilators will be more suitable.

In large, high spaces, smoke can be exhausted with roof-mounted fans to a height of only 50 to 60 feet. If smoke becomes cool, wet, or heavy because of the operation of the sprinkler system and the ceiling is higher than 55 feet, air must be mechanically introduced at the floor level in order to remove the smoke through the vents. The supply air should be directed vertically, roughly in line with the exhaust fans. The supply should equal 75 percent of the exhaust [A.4].

Wall Openings and Fire Department Access

Applicable guidelines: FPH 5-3, 6-11, 6-92; LSC 9-2.12

Access to a building for manual fire fighting must be made easy. Normally the usual entrances to a building provide satisfactory access for fire fighters; but in underground buildings this may not always be the case. A fire in these spaces often becomes excessively smoky. In addition, heat buildup is usually more intense because heat venting is inadequate. Fire fighters must therefore often attack fires in these spaces in the face of the heat and smoke.

Spaces in which adequate fire fighting access and operations are restricted should be provided with effective protection. A complete automatic sprinkler system with a fire department connection is probably the best solution to this problem. The Fire Protection Handbook and the Life Safety Code recommend that automatic sprinklers be considered a requirement for life safety in

windowless buildings and underground structures. In a conventional building, windows provide access to fresh air and persons in the building can see fire department rescue operations and are therefore less subject to panic. Windows also provide access to the fire department for rescue and fire fighting. When windows are absent, extra precautions such as automatic sprinklers are required.

Building code requirements for wall and opening protection are also provided to limit fire spread through exterior wall openings. They apply to exterior walls close to a property line and also to walls bounding an interior court.

Requirements for fire access indicate that only underground spaces with at least one exterior side exposed above the adjacent ground level are not required to have an automatic fire-extinguishing system, and then only if the maximum distance to the open side from any point within the building is less than 75 feet. Such a narrow configuration may also make the interior more accessible to the reach of hose streams. The term automatic fire-extinguishing system includes sprinkler systems as well as other automatically operated fire-extinguishing systems such as inert gas systems. Automatic fire-extinguishing systems can often be justified on their own merits—they greatly increase life safety and decrease potential fire damage, hence decreasing insurance premiums significantly. In fact, these systems can often be justified economically on the basis of reduced insurance premiums alone.

Sprinklers

Applicable guidelines: UBC 3802, LSC 16-4.2, NFPA 1018-1.6

Automatic fire-extinguishing systems will often be mandatory for large underground buildings, since such structures will fall into one of the categories in Section 3802 of the Uniform Building Code for locations where such systems are necessary. These locations include any story, basement, or cellar where the floor area exceeds 1,500 square feet and where less than 20 square feet of opening entirely above the adjoining ground level is provided for each 50 lineal feet of exterior wall on at least one side of the building. Automatic fire-extinguishing systems are also required when any portion of a basement or cellar is more than 75 feet from required openings. Such a system is always required in basements and cellars larger than 1,500 square feet of Groups A and E occupancies (assembly and educational occupancies).

The Life Safety Code requires windowless and underground areas occupied by 100 or more persons to be equipped with complete automatic sprinkler protection as well as emergency lighting. This code also requires complete automatic sprinkler protection in any type of construction where a place of assembly is located below the exit level.

The Life Safety Code requires that underground buildings, structures, and areas with combustible contents, interior finish, or construction have automatic smoke-venting facilities in addition to automatic sprinkler protection.

Even after actuation of a sprinkler system, where ordinary combustible materials are present, smoke development will significantly increase until the fire is brought under control. Consequently, sprinkler systems without smoke activation begin operating too slowly. A smoldering low-heat fire can develop a significant, even deadly, amount of smoke before the sprinkler operates. During a test involving a chair padded with foamed latex, the entire test facility—approximately 10,000 cubic feet—was completely smoke-clogged from ceiling to floor without activating the sprinkler system [A.4]. A quicker response than that provided by sprinklers alone is clearly needed.

Smoke detection devices can provide this quicker response. To eliminate false alarms, smoke control equipment and alarms should be actuated by two smoke detectors rather than one. Smoke detection devices do not by any means preclude the use of sprinklers. Indeed,

sprinklers are the primary method by which the fire can be controlled.

Refuge Areas

Applicable guidelines: FPH 6-87, 6-88, 6-105

Maximum division of areas limits fire extent and severity and provides areas of refuge for occupants. Temporary refuge areas, stairwells, and elevator shafts are often the principal areas where pressurization and barriers may be utilized effectively. The Federal Building in Seattle, Washington (a mostly above-grade building), for example, utilizes exhaust of the fire floor combined with physical barriers and pressurization of spaces above and below the fire to confine the smoke to the fire area and to protect the occupants in refuge areas within the building.

A great amount of experimental and theoretical work has been conducted in recent years in the field of smoke movement. The National Research Council of Canada has been a leader in this respect. Experimental studies, such as the Henry Grady Fire Tests and others, are valuable references for quantitative verification [A.5, A.6].

The experimental studies cited above demonstrate the feasibility of pressurizing stairways to ensure smoke-free conditions. From a theoretical viewpoint, the magnitude of pressures need be only slightly greater than the pressure of the smoky atmosphere. From a practical viewpoint, a positive pressure of 0.05 to 0.10 inch of water will enable pressures to be maintained, even with as many as three stairwell doors open.

In tall buildings the stairwell pressure required might be large enough to prevent doors from being opened. To alleviate this problem, separate compartments within the stairwell, approximately five floors in height, have been proposed. Each compartment would have its own pressurization fan. In this configuration, fan

capacity can be reduced considerably. In addition, pressures can be reduced significantly and a fan failure in one segment would not seriously impair the effectiveness of the entire system.

For the safety of the occupants, every level of a windowless or earth sheltered building should be divided into two or more separate areas to provide safe places of refuge within that level. Each such area should be on an independent air supply and exhaust system. The separation between areas is critical. A possible configuration might locate a vestibule between adjoining areas, with the vestibule vented as would be required for a mechanically operated smokeproof enclosure. If pipe or conduit goes through the separation wall that establishes the refuge area, penetrations must be tightly caulked to prevent passage of smoke. The use of listed and tested transition devices is suggested. Ideally, there should be no ducts through that wall. Other penetrations should be limited to the connecting horizontal exit.

Access to Exits

Applicable guidelines: FPH 6-95, 6-97

Required exits and fire department access will be a major layout determinants for earth-covered structures or large basements. They will also be a major cost factor for facilities located well below the surface in mine locations, because shafts will be required at intervals to meet the exit distance requirements for most types of occupancy. Maximum distances to exits or enclosed stairways range from 150 to 400 feet, depending on the type of occupancy and protection systems employed. The major means of increasing maximum exit distances are to provide up to 100 feet of the exit path to an enclosed stairway (or exterior exit) within a fire-protected corridor and to provide an automatic fire-extinguishing system for the building.

The access to an exit enclosure is that portion of a means of egress that leads to an entrance of an exit enclosure. The access to an exit may be a corridor, an aisle, a balcony, a gallery, a porch, or a roof. Its length establishes the travel distance to an exit—an extremely important factor if the occupants are to avoid exposure to fire during the time it takes to reach an exit. The average recommended distance is 100 feet, but this varies with the occupancy level, depending on the fire hazard and the physical ability and alertness of the occupants [A.3]. The travel distance may be measured from the door of a room to an exit or from the most remote point in a room or floor area to an exit. In those buildings where large numbers of people occupy an open floor area or where the nature of the business conducted makes an open floor area desirable, the travel distance is measured from the most remote point in the area to the exits. Conversely, in occupancies with only a few people in small cutoff areas or rooms (such as hotels and apartments), the travel distance is measured from the door of the room or area to the exits. The only exception to this rule is office occupancy, where because of the character of the occupancy and the low hazard of the building contents, the travel distance is measured from the most remote point on a floor to the exits. In most cases travel distance can be increased up to 50 percent if the building is sprinklered.

A dead end is an extension of a corridor or aisle beyond an exit or an access to exits that forms a pocket in which occupants may be trapped. Since there is only one access to an exit from a dead end, a fire in a dead end between an exit and an occupant prevents the occupant from reaching the exit. While traveling toward an exit in a smoke-filled atmosphere, an occupant may pass by the exit and be trapped in the dead end. Ideally, dead ends should be prohibited; but for purposes of design latitude and effective utilization of space, dead ends are permitted in most occupancies within reasonable limits.

Goal-oriented (dynamic evaluation) exit design is discussed in the Fire Protection Handbook,

although it is not identified in either the Uniform Building Code or the Life Safety Code as an alternate to the more specific exit requirements. The General Services Administration has established such an approach [A.7]; its major goals are:

1. All occupants exposed to the fire environment must be able to evacuate to a safe area within ninety seconds of alarm.

2. A portion of this time, not to exceed approximately fifteen seconds, can be involved in traveling in a direction toward the fire.

3. All occupants must reach an area of refuge within five minutes of downward vertical travel or within one minute of upward vertical movement (because fatigue is judged to be important after these travel times).

A normal able-bodied person walks about 4 feet per second. As congestion occurs, the speed of advance will slow. As a margin of safety, Degenkolb recommends a travel speed of 2 to 2.5 feet per second [A.4]. He points out that when a fire alarm sounds in a school there is no activity at all for fifteen to twenty seconds. If an area should be evacuated within two minutes, and twenty seconds of that period are deducted as the time it takes for people to react, one-hundred seconds are left for the evacuation. At 2 feet per second, this would permit 200 feet total travel distance. Thus, a case has been made for that particular distance. Degenkolb has argued, however, that this distance seems excessive for below-grade buildings with their inherent life safety concerns and recommends a maximum of 150 feet to a place of refuge for this type of building. He also points out that travel distance should not be measured to a stairway enclosure but to a point beyond this bottleneck. This allows for the possibility of reduced exiting speed as stairs become blocked with people or the exit enclosure fills with smoke.

Exit Enclosures

Applicable guidelines: FPH 6-94, 6-97, 6-105; LSC 16-4.2.2.1, 9-5.4.2.4, 9-5.5.2.4

In addition to physical factors, psychological and physiological factors must be considered when planning exits. People cannot be expected to behave logically in the stress of fire conditions. Panic is contagious, and the danger is greater in a large crowd, as in a place of public assembly. Fear, rather than actual fire danger, is the main factor in panic. Fatal panics have occurred where people have mistakenly thought a fire had broken out. On the other hand, where people have had confidence in a building and its exits, orderly evacuations without panic have taken place even though actual danger was present. As long as people can keep moving toward a recognized place of safety, there is little danger of panic, but any stoppage of movement is conducive to panic. Once panic starts, exits may be quickly blocked.

Under fire conditions people will likely try to leave a building through the same opening by which they entered, neglecting alternate means of exit; thus all exits need to be conspicuously marked. It is also important that all exits from a building be used as a matter of daily routine so that occupants will be familiar with them. The Life Safety Code requires that in assembly occupancies the main exit (which also serves as the entrance) be sized to handle at least half of the occupant load.

Fatigue is judged to become important after five minutes of travel in a downward direction or one minute of travel in an upward direction. It therefore becomes a "human factor" consideration affecting design. To alleviate fatigue concerns, stairs could be made more gradual. Instead of 7½-inch rise and 10-inch run stairs, a 7-inch rise with an 11-inch run could be used, significantly reducing the amount of energy a person would have to expend in climbing. Research indicates it takes about 30 percent less energy to climb up the more shallow stairs [A.4].

Recommendations concerning exits from underground buildings that involve upward travel, such as ascending stairs or ramps, are provided for in NFPA No. 101, Life Safety Code. Those recommendations take into consideration the panic that may result when there is no direct access to the outside and no windows to permit fire department rescue and ventilation. These exits must be cut off from main floor areas and provided with outside smoke venting or other means to prevent the exits from becoming charged with smoke.

In educational occupancies there are certain restrictions in the Life Safety Code on floor location and exiting where children are involved. Below-ground day-care facilities would not be allowed more than one story below the ground; moreover, at least one exit would be required to discharge directly to the outside at ground level.

Elevators

Elevators are not exits but, realistically, they may be used to get people out and fire fighters in. A normal person can go down stairs for about five stories before the legs begin to feel the strain and slowing occurs. If people are deep in the ground, they may have to depend on mechanical systems to evacuate them from the place of refuge.

Elevator lobbies could serve as refuge areas if the lobby is pressurized to prevent the entry of smoke. If 0.06 inches of water column is the pressurization to be expected from a fire in a sprinklered building, the lobby would have to be pressurized to about 0.08 inches of water column [A.4]. Further, all elevators should be programmed to return to the grade-level exit floor. This operation is activated by the building smoke detection system.

Voice Communication

A means of communicating with the occupants of the building is essential, but with a supervised sprinkler system in the building, a conventional public address or background music system should be sufficient. The system must have the capability of being preempted by the emergency services. The wiring for such a system should not be required to be in conduit but should be insulated with Teflon or similar material when the wiring is exposed [A.4].

Emergency Power

Emergency power is critical. Electrical power is required not only for lighting purposes but for air circulation and the removal of smoke, for the pressurization of non-fire-involved areas, and for elevator operations. Emergency power should be almost immediate with not more than ten seconds' delay. Degenkolb considers the sixty seconds normally accepted for full operation of standby power to be too long [A.4].

Exit Lighting

Applicable guidelines: FPH 6-101

Exit lighting is particularly important in underground buildings. Lighting intensity should be at least 1 footcandle measured at the floor, preferably provided by lights close to the floor so that they will not be obscured by smoke during a fire. Emergency power for exit lighting is required by the Life Safety Code underground or windowless buildings with an occupant load of more than 100 persons.

Fire-Fighting Equipment

Applicable guidelines: FPH 6-105

Manual fire-fighting equipment, such as standpipe and hose systems and portable fire extinguishers, can provide quick extinguishment of fires when handled by trained personnel who discover a fire in the incipient stage.

Drainage

Applicable guidelines: FPH 6-12, 6-29, 6-105

Drainage of water from sprinkler discharge or from hose streams can be a serious problem in underground structures and therefore requires study in the early planning stages. If provisions for drainage are required for reasons other than fire protection, it may be possible to use only one drainage system for all purposes, provided that it is designed to handle the expected maximum flow.

Watertight floors are important in this respect. Salvage efforts can be greatly affected by the integrity of the floors. Of greater importance is the number and location of floor drains. If interior drains and scuppers are available, salvage teams can remove water effectively with a minimum of damage.

Although gravity-flow drainage is the most reliable means of removing water, mechanical means may have to be used in areas below grade. A waste-removal pump is best, and it should take suction from a screened sump. Electric power for the pump should be supplied separately from the main electrical service so that building power can be interrupted for fire fighting without interfering with the pump operation. Emergency power should be provided for the pump system.

In evaluating the degree of reliability required of waste-pump power supply and controls, it is important to recognize that fire in below-grade areas is difficult to fight and may be of such duration that complete flooding may be a threat. Similarly, complete flooding may become a necessary fire-fighting strategy to prevent structural collapse of a multiple-floored building; therefore, labeled remote control for the sump pump should be available at an accessible location.

In some occupancies ordinary drainage facilities are inadequate since a slight depth of water can be destructive to contents. Large rolls of newsprint paper stored on end, for example, could be badly damaged by a small amount of water because of the absorbency of the paper. A good slope would be a desirable storage feature to limit water spread in such buildings.

Where large amounts of flammable and combustible liquids are handled, provision should be made for their rapid removal into trapped drains in preference to scuppers. Since most combustible liquids are lighter than water and can readily flow to adjacent areas, isolation tactics should be employed.

In large areas protected by deluge sprinkler systems, drains and scuppers could be overtaxed. Sloping floors ending at a trench would be desirable.

Fire-Resistive Ratings

The fire-endurance rating established for various walls, floors, and ceilings has been established by fire testing in furnaces that are operated at a negative pressure or, at best, a neutral pressure. These tests measure the fire endurance of a particular type of construction under similar conditions.

Whether the test furnace is operated at positive or negative pressure, fire-resistive assemblies

have performed quite well in conventional buildings. But it is quite well established that the fire endurance of a type of construction will be significantly reduced when the test is conducted under a positive pressure of considerably less than the 0.10 to 0.12 column inches of water [A.4].

According to the National Bureau of Standards and the Canadian Research Council, the typical pressure buildup may be in the range of 0.10 to 0.12 inches of water column. According to Degenkolb, Irwin Benjamin of the National Bureau of Standards has indicated that when the building is sprinklered, the pressure buildup will be in the range of 0.05 to 0.06 column inches of water.

Degenkolb points out that the Los Angeles Fire Department panel furnace is conventionally run with a positive pressure of 0.045 near the top of the panel, a neutral pressure about one-third up from the bottom, and a slight negative pressure at the bottom of the panel opening. Wall assemblies that have received a one-hour rating in other furnaces have failed after about forty-five to fifty minutes in the Los Angeles furnace. Doors that have received a thirty-minute rating in negative-pressure furnaces and have also survived a hose stream test have difficulty passing a twenty-minute test in a positive-pressure furnace, and that is without adding the hose stream at the end of the fire test.

These fire tests evaluate an assembly under specific fire conditions that do not necessarily resemble real fire conditions in an underground building. It is possible that, where one-hour fire resistance has been acceptable in aboveground buildings, the underground structures with potentially higher positive pressure may require a greater level of fire resistance.

Appendix B:
Below-Grade
Waterproofing

Adequate waterproofing of earth sheltered structures is one of the major concerns of architects, contractors, and clients. Although some people remain skeptical about whether it is possible to provide a completely waterproof structure, competent waterproofing systems are available. But successful waterproofing involves more than simply selecting and installing a reputable product. It requires a comprehensive approach to keeping water out of the building, based on an understanding of all possible sources of moisture. The basic sources of moisture are:

- surface runoff
- water table below grade
- temporary water pressure below grade
- seepage from adjacent land forms
- broken or leaking utility lines
- vapor pressure
- capillary draw

Waterproofing is referred to as a system because maintaining dryness in an earth sheltered structure depends on a combination of layered elements and techniques, rather than on a coating or membrane material alone. Each layer of the system is intended to deflect moisture at a point nearest its source and furthest from the interior of the structure. Successful waterproofing systems comprise three interdependent lines of defense against moisture. The first involves careful site planning and landscaping in order to limit or control the sources of water. The second component of the system is designed to reduce the amount of unavoidable moisture by means of backfilling and drainage techniques. The third line of defense against moisture problems consists of a protected waterproof membrane or coating along with proper flashing at critical places.

Selecting the proper waterproofing for an underground structure may be a difficult task, not only because many waterproofing systems have similar characteristics, but also because new products or new formulations of existing products are constantly appearing on the market with claims of improved performance over existing systems. In this appendix, a wide range of waterproofing methods that could be applied to underground structures are described and evaluated, based on the typical characteristics of seven types of generic waterproofing products. Specific products must be carefully examined to determine to what extent they may differ from these general classifications. The generic categories are:

- dampproofing techniques
- asphalt and pitch built-up membranes
- cementitious materials
- liquid-applied systems
- modified bitumens
- sheet membranes
- bentonite clay products

The following characteristics are discussed for each category of products.

- durability and stability underground
- ability to withstand movement and cracking
- ability to minimize leaks and facilitate repair
- appropriate use
- application considerations
- relative costs

Other criteria for evaluation and comparison, such as type of guarantee, exact cost, and availability of materials and applicators are not discussed because they are too dependent on the specific product used and specific location of the job. In some cases, of course, these factors could be overriding criteria for product selection.

Material in this Appendix is adapted from *Earth Sheltered Residential Design Manual* which contains additional information on below-grade waterproofing and insulation [B.1].

Dampproofing Products

This group of products includes concrete admixtures, polyethylene sheets, and a variety of surface treatments such as epoxy and acrylic paints, simple asphalt and pitch coatings, and cement pargeting that can be applied to concrete and masonry walls. Although commonly used for foundations and basements, these products should not be considered complete and adequate waterproofing systems. The term *dampproofing* actually connotes the prevention of dampness but not full protection from water that may enter the structure. It is important to distinguish between these relatively inexpensive, easily applied products and other systems that use some of the same materials in different ways to yield products with different characteristics and, in some cases, improved effectiveness (see the sections below on cementitious materials, built-up membranes, and modified bitumens).

stability and durability

The effectiveness of two of the most commonly used dampproofing products—asphalt and pitch coatings—is questionable when they are used underground for two reasons. First, asphalt emulsions can tend to re-emulsify in the presence of groundwater over a long period of time and eventually become ineffective. Second, the quality of both asphalt and pitch has deteriorated in recent years. Improvements in the oil refining process have resulted in poorer chemical properties in the asphalt by-product. Similarly, as health standards have caused some of the more volatile substances to be removed from coal tar pitch, a more brittle, less effective product has resulted. It should be pointed out, however, that a great variety of asphalt and pitch products, with potential differences in properties, is available. Naturally occurring asphalts, for example, would not suffer from most of the disadvantages mentioned above.

Because polyethylene is manufactured at a consistent quality, it can serve as a good vapor barrier if it is carefully applied and seams are overlapped. Although clear polyethylene is subject to degradation if it is exposed to the ultraviolet rays of the sun, this is no problem in underground applications. The main reasons that polyethylene is totally inadequate as a waterproofing system are that it is not sufficiently strong or puncture resistant and that it is difficult, if not impossible, to make watertight seams in the field.

Epoxy and acrylic coatings can be tough and adhere well to concrete surfaces. Using concrete admixtures and pargeting with a dense cement plaster can greatly reduce the permeability of concrete. Although some of these dampproofing products can be effective in preventing water from entering the structure and are also relatively stable underground, they nonetheless do not represent a long-term solution to waterproofing because of the drawbacks discussed below.

ability to withstand movement and cracking

Dampproofing products may be integral with the concrete structure (admixtures), very brittle (cement pargeting), or applied in a relatively thin layer bonded to the surface (epoxy paints, asphalt and pitch coatings). In none of these cases does the product have any real ability to respond to movement in the structure or to bridge cracks. Although asphalt and pitch have some softness and flexibility in exposed locations in summertime, they are usually more brittle and subject to cracking when used at consistently low temperatures underground. Since cracks and movement are virtually inevitable in concrete structures, this is the greatest shortcoming of these coatings. Polyethylene, on the other hand, has some ability to bridge cracks and adjust to movement without failing because it is a sheet rather than a coating. In this regard, the clear polyethylene is superior to black polyethylene for underground applications, where it is not exposed to sunlight.

ability to minimize leaks and facilitate repair

Dampproofing products basically have no ability to reseal any punctures, tears, or breaks in the coating. In a soft and flexible state, asphalt and pitch have a limited ability to reseal; however, this quality is irrelevant in the presence of cooler, below-grade temperatures where these materials can become brittle. Most of the products are integral with the concrete or bonded to the surface. Because any leaks that do occur cannot travel extensively under the coating (as they could with a sheet or membrane), they are easier to locate. Water can, however, travel through the structural cracks and voids, which can be extensive in block walls. The problem of localizing a leak is considerably worse with polyethylene, as water can travel easily behind the loose-laid sheet. If the sheet is bonded to the surface, the tendency for water to travel is reduced.

appropriate use

These products are not recommended for any underground application where a complete waterproofing job is desired. They are only appropriate for secondary spaces in which some moisture and dampness can be tolerated or as a vapor barrier.

application considerations

The various coatings can be applied by unskilled labor and are either sprayed, troweled, or brushed on. Specifications for temperature, humidity, and surface conditions vary with the different products. Polyethylene sheets should be overlapped generously to act as an effective vapor barrier.

relative costs

Most of these dampproofing products have relatively low labor and material costs, compared to costs of high-quality waterproofing systems.

Built-Up Asphalt and Pitch Membranes

This type of membrane, which consists of layers of hot-mopped asphalt or pitch alternated with felt or fabric reinforcing that is bonded to the structure, is a very familiar and commonly used product in waterproofing above-grade roofs. Although this system has been used with some success in various underground applications, there are some basic questions concerning its long-term durability below grade, as well as its ability to perform in the same manner that it does under above-grade conditions. Long-term performance is more critical underground because the waterproofing is not easily accessible for the continued program of repair and eventual replacement that is characteristic of built-up membranes above grade.

stability and durability

As stated in the previous section on asphalt and pitch dampproofing coatings, the long-term stability of many such products underground is not reliable. Although the basic built-up membrane is relatively impervious to water and water vapor when first installed, continual exposure to water—which is common underground—can cause deterioration of the asphalt. With respect to the fabric reinforcing, organic felts will eventually rot with constant exposure to water, whereas glass-reinforced fabrics will last much longer.

The normal formulations of asphalt and pitch products suggest that considerable caution should be exercised in using these materials underground. Improvements in oil refining processes in the last twenty years have resulted in a deterioration of some of the asphalt properties that are most important for waterproofing use; hence, asphalt simply is not as high quality a product now as it once was. Good-quality pitch, which is derived from coal tars, is generally a superior, longer-lasting product than manufactured asphalt. Health regulations now require that many of the most

volatile substances in pitch be removed to protect the applicators, however. Removal of these substances has reduced the quality and effectiveness of the pitch by making it brittle at underground temperatures.

ability to withstand movement and cracking

Built-up membranes have mechanical strength that simple asphalt or pitch coatings do not have. Nevertheless, because membranes are relatively brittle and inflexible at the cooler below-grade temperatures, they cannot absorb movement or bridge cracks in the concrete structure.

ability to minimize leaks and facilitate repair

Built-up roofs used on the roofs of above-grade structures are noted for some ability to reseal punctures, primarily because they become soft and flexible when heated by the sun. In the cooler below-grade environment, however, they remain too brittle and inflexible to have very good resealing ability. If a leak does occur, the built-up membrane does not always adhere to the structural surface as well as other waterproofing products that are chemically bonded. Thus, water that penetrates the membrane may be able to travel behind it to some degree, making leaks difficult to locate. Any repairs to the membrane must be made from the outside.

appropriate use

Built-up membranes can be applied to all types of surfaces, including wood, masonry, and precast or poured concrete. Because poured concrete is likely to have fewer cracks than other types of surfaces, it is the best surface for application of built-up membranes, which are unable to absorb movement and bridge cracks. Horizontal surfaces that have a slight slope for drainage are the most typical and best applications for built-up membranes. Although they can be applied to vertical surfaces, such

application is more difficult (particularly when the membranes are applied hot) and requires a very smooth surface. Because these membranes are not continuous flat sheets or roll goods, but rather are built up from smaller pieces in layers, they are better suited to more complex forms than are other sheet goods. The waterproofing can be formed on complicated shapes, curving surfaces, and flashings around penetrations as an integral part of the built-up membrane.

application considerations

Although the basic work of mopping on the hot asphalt can be done by relatively unskilled labor, knowledge, experienced supervision, and proper equipment are necessary to ensure that an adequate job is done. The conditions required for successful application are not as stringent as for many other products. The surface must be relatively clean, dry, and smooth, but some leeway for irregularities exists. The membranes can be applied in a wider range of temperature and humidity conditions as well. Because the membrane may be relatively soft after application, it should be carefully protected from punctures or damage during the backfilling process.

relative costs

Material and labor costs for built-up membranes are moderate compared to costs for other waterproofing products. One advantage of these materials is that, because they are quite familiar and there are numerous applicators, more competitive bidding may be possible.

Cementitious Materials

The various cementitious waterproofing materials, which are sprayed, brushed, or troweled onto concrete surfaces, consist of portland cement and certain organic or inorganic additives. When this mixture is placed on a concrete surface, it comes in contact with moisture and unhydrated cement, causing the formation of crystals in the voids of the concrete. The size of the crystals is such that water molecules cannot pass through, while air and water vapor can. Thus, the concrete can cure properly while maintaining a waterproof surface.

durability and stability

Most cementitious materials are stable underground and compatible with most soil chemicals and conditions. These alkaline materials (pH of approximately 9.0 to 9.5) will resist pH levels between 3.5 and 11—a range that includes most soil conditions. Products that use sodium-based additives to react with the cement in the concrete may be less desirable because sodium is water soluble and could leach out of the concrete over time. In general, however, cementitious products themselves have a long life span.

ability to withstand movement and cracking

The major disadvantage of cementitious waterproofing materials is that they have very little ability to bridge any cracks in the concrete caused by settling, thermal expansion, or other movements. Although very small hairline cracks can be bridged, any larger cracks—which are common in most concrete structures—represent a break in the waterproofing system. Buildings that incorporate precast elements, cold joints, or masonry walls are generally more likely to crack than are monolithically poured concrete structures. Post-tensioned structures in particular resist cracking because the concrete is held in constant compression. Thus, a post-tensioned structure represents the best possibility for successful waterproofing with a cementitious product.

ability to minimize leaks and facilitate repair

As stated above, any leaks that occur with cementitious waterproofings are likely to result from cracks in the concrete structure. Since the waterproofing is integrated within the concrete, water cannot travel behind the waterproof layer as it can when an attached membrane material is used. It can, however, travel within and along any cracks, thereby increasing the difficulty of finding the major source of the leak. Although cementitious materials have no resealing capabilities, they have one advantage if a leaky structure requires repair: these materials can be applied from the inside of a structure, even against hydrostatic pressure. Presumably, application could be done after major cracks were carefully resealed from the inside, although this can merely cause the entry point of water to shift to a new location by migration of water along unsealed portions of the crack.

appropriate use

Cementitious products are limited to use on concrete and masonry surfaces. Basically, a product that can be sprayed or troweled on and actually penetrates into the concrete appears to have certain advantages. It can be applied to complex geometries and curving forms, for example. Also, it can be applied to vertical or horizontal surfaces. Unfortunately, this apparently wide range of applications must be carefully limited to situations in which cracks are unlikely to appear or to result in leaks.

application considerations

Unlike most waterproofing systems, cementitious materials can be applied by relatively unskilled or moderately skilled labor. Another advantage is that they cannot be easily damaged during the backfilling process. The major concerns with regard to successful application of cementitious materials are the condition of the concrete surface, the moisture content of the concrete, and the temperature. Although the concrete surface should not have any major defects (honeycombing, rock pockets, or faulty construction joints), small irregularities are acceptable. In fact, a surface that is extremely smooth may be undesirable because the waterproofing material must be able to penetrate into the open capillary system of the concrete. Surfaces must also be clean and free from concrete form oil, curing compounds that seal the concrete pores, or other foreign matter that could inhibit penetration. Light sandblasting or water blasting may be necessary. Modified cementitious materials that can be applied on concrete block walls are available. Additional surface preparation is usually required for block walls in order to cover cracks and render the surface smooth.

Because moisture is required to form the crystals, newly poured concrete that is damp throughout is the ideal application condition. Under other conditions some prewatering may be required. It is important that the surface be moist, but if it is wet, it will dilute the penetrating material. Cementitious materials should not be applied at temperatures below 40°F. Proper curing depends on the temperature and the reaction of the materials with water. Most cementitious waterproofing materials require air for curing and must be sprayed regularly over a period of two to three days with a misty spray. Therefore, the materials should not be covered immediately by polyethylene. During curing, however, they must be protected from excessive wind, sun, rain, and frost.

relative costs

Because a number of cementitious materials are available, costs can vary widely. In general, however, material costs can be considered moderate and labor costs low to moderate in comparison with other waterproofing systems.

Liquid-Applied Waterproofing Systems

This group of products includes a variety of urethane elastomers, rubbers, and other synthetic compounds that are applied in a liquid form. They typically cure in forty-eight to seventy-two hours to form a single, seamless, membranelike coating that is bonded to the surface of the structure. In general, they can be applied in thicknesses of 15 to 100 mils. (1 mil. = 1/1000 inch); 60 mils. is generally the minimum thickness desirable for underground application. These products are applied in one or more coats by spray, trowel, roller, or brush. The liquid-applied systems included in this category are:

- urethane
- polyisobutylene (butyl)
- polychloroprene (neoprene)
- chloronated polyethylene
- polyvinyl chloride
- polysulfide
- silicone
- acrylic latex

Because of the large number of products and the almost infinite variations possible with some of them, it is somewhat difficult to generalize about their characteristics. This discussion will emphasize the urethane elastomers because they are the most common and most likely to be used underground. The basic properties of the rubbers—butyl, neoprene and Hypalon—are discussed in greater detail in the section below on vulcanized sheets, which is their more common application. Although the specific chemical properties of these liquid-applied materials can vary considerably, they can be evaluated as a group because most of the general characteristics—the ability to withstand movement, and design and application considerations—are quite similar.

stability and durability

The properties that affect the stability and durability of products within this classification of waterproofing systems can vary widely; hence, these characteristics must be carefully examined. Some products can be prepared to suit a particular application, so that they are especially resistant to certain chemicals, to sunlight, or to abrasion, for example. With respect to underground applications, only the urethane elastomers have a reasonable history of use. Although a discussion of the chemical makeup of these products is beyond the scope of this evaluation, some basic points can be made. One-component polyurethane systems are relatively inexpensive and easy to apply but can become brittle and lose adhesion if not applied properly. Two-component systems, although more costly, perform much better. Products based on esters and ethers are also not recommended for underground waterproofing because they were developed to resist abrasion above grade, and may become brittle over time.

One characteristic of liquid-applied membranes that would appear to be an advantage over factory-produced membrane sheets is that they are seamless (seams are usually the weak point of loose-laid membranes and roll goods). Attaining the same levels of stability and durability characteristic of factory-produced materials in a liquid that is cured in the field may, however, be a significant problem. The rather exacting conditions required to produce a plastic or synthetic rubber are difficult to duplicate in the field, given the variations in surface conditions, temperature, humidity, and manner of application. Although these requirements are discussed in detail under *application considerations*, a few key examples are given below in order to illustrate some potential problems with stability and durability in liquid-applied waterproofing.

One concern with the liquid systems is that the use of spray-on applications can seriously weaken the membrane by entrapping air bubbles. Thicker products that can be troweled on are generally more desirable. Some liquids are intended to be applied in a "self-leveling" form. Since it is nearly impossible to build a completely flat, smooth surface, the self-leveled membrane will be thicker in some areas than others. Sections of the membrane that are too thick can blister, adhere poorly, and cure improperly. A final example of application problems affecting product performance is the need for proper curing time. Although urethane elastomers should react and cure slowly, when the time required for curing is incompatible with construction schedules, additives are sometimes included to speed up the curing process. The drawback to this technique is that the decrease in curing time results in a product that may be more brittle.

As noted above, most of the remarks in this section apply specifically to urethane elastomers, although many of the general problems are common to all liquid systems. The more specific properties of the synthetic rubbers are discussed in a later section on vulcanized sheets. Acrylic latex-based products are not recommended below grade because the groundwater can cause the latex to re-emulsify and migrate from the wall. Polysulfides are composed of synthetic rubber that is quite impermeable to water and resistant to chemical attack. They are quite costly and excessively soft; they are not currently manufactured in the United States. Liquid-applied waterproofing systems based on silicone are relatively new and have little history of application. Because of their poor adhesion to concrete and other properties, silicones seem better suited to above-grade, rather than below-grade, applications.

ability to withstand movement and cracking

Liquid-applied waterproofing systems are fully bonded to the structure; therefore, any strain caused by movement and cracking must be taken up by the material lying immediately over the crack. Although these materials have some of the properties exhibited by factory-made membranes—toughness, tensile and shear strength—the capacity of relatively thin, fully bonded materials to bridge cracks is quite limited. Thus, these products are not recommended for precast concrete roofs, which have great potential for movement and cracking, but rather may be more suited to reinforced and post-tensioned poured slabs, in which cracks are minimized.

ability to minimize leaks and facilitate repair

Like most membrane and sheet materials, liquid-applied systems have no ability to reseal punctures or tears. They do have two advantages over sheet goods in minimizing leaks, in that they are seamless and are fully bonded to the structure. Provided that the material has good adhesion, leaks cannot travel under the membrane, making it far easier to locate the source and facilitate repair. But if improper application has resulted in both a leak and loss of adhesion in the membrane, the leak problem can be compounded. After the leak is located, it cannot be easily repaired from the inside with a similar material, because the liquids must be exposed to the air for curing. Punctures and tears can be patched from the outside, however.

appropriate use

Liquid-applied systems will bond to a wide range of structural and insulation materials if the product is correctly formulated to do so. The limitations on the appropriate type of surface are based not on the ability of the products to bond, but rather on their inability to bridge large cracks that may occur during the life of the structure. Therefore, direct application is not advisable on precast roof decks, masonry surfaces, wood decks, or other surfaces that have great potential for movement and cracking. These products are best applied to reinforced and post-tensioned poured concrete slabs, in which cracks are minimized. In

general, the liquid-applied systems are best suited to horizontal surfaces that have a slight slope, although the self-leveling products require a completely flat surface. Some liquid products are formulated to be applied to vertical surfaces, usually in several coats.

Compared to flat sheet membranes and roll goods, materials with good adhesion that can be troweled or sprayed on are more suitable for designs that incorporate complex geometries and curving surfaces. Some question remains, however, as to whether or not the controlled, uniform thickness required for proper curing and the performance of some liquid products can be easily achieved on a complicated shape.

application considerations

Although the actual brushing or troweling on of these liquid-applied materials does not require highly skilled labor, it is very important to use experienced applicators in order to ensure proper surface preparation, control of the application, and adequate curing time. Some products require a primer or masonry conditioner, which can raise labor and material costs. If the materials are not applied in an even thickness, problems can result. Bubbles can form as gases are released during curing, and adhesion can be lost in areas where the membrane is too thick. Improper application can result in irregularities in the coating, especially in corners and around vent pipes. For best results, two coats are often desirable, whereas on vertical surfaces several coats may be required, along with embedment of the fibers into the first coat. One important consideration is that because many of these products release toxic fumes during application and curing, respirators—and in confined areas, good ventilation—are required.

The most critical aspects related to the application of these materials are the preparation of the surface, the air temperature, and the humidity conditions. More than any other type of waterproofing product, the liquid-applied systems require a very clean, smooth, dry surface. All oils must be removed, voids

filled, and any imperfections in the surface smoothed. The concrete structure should be allowed to cure the full twenty-eight days before the waterproofing is applied, to ensure that most of the moisture is gone from the surface. Some manufacturers do not recommend that their products be applied in situations where moisture must evaporate from the concrete surface underneath, because it will cause the waterproofing to blister and lose adhesion. These situations include lightweight concrete decks, which release large quantities of moisture, and concrete over steel decking, where the moisture cannot escape downward from the slab.

Under the best temperature and humidity conditions, curing of a typical membrane may take forty-eight to seventy-two hours, depending on the specific product. Curing of waterproofing that is applied in temperatures below 40°F would take several weeks, whereas application in above 80°F may result in too rapid curing, which can cause brittleness in the membrane. Similarly, if the relative humidity is below 30 percent, the membrane would cure too slowly; above 85 percent humidity, it cures too fast.

After application, the material should be inspected to make sure no voids or bubbles are left in the membrane. Insulation should not be placed over the waterproofing too quickly since some volatile substances given off during curing can attack polystyrene insulation. Like most waterproofing products, the fully cured liquid-applied material should be protected from damage during backfilling.

relative costs

Labor costs are moderate for the application of this group of products. Material costs can vary considerably because of the many types of liquid-applied systems. Generally, material costs range from moderate to high for the best-quality products in comparison to costs of other waterproofing systems.

Modified Bitumens

These materials, often referred to as rubberized asphalt, consist of asphalt combined with a small amount of synthetic rubber, applied to a polyethylene sheet. In some cases, a second polyethylene sheet is placed between two layers of the rubberized asphalt. The material comes in rolls ranging from 3 to 4 feet wide. The strips of rubberized asphalt adhere to the structural surface and are overlapped to adhere to each other.

durability and stability

Since modified bitumens come in factory-produced rolls, they have uniform thickness and quality, although the quality of the asphalt itself can vary. The rubberized asphalt has good resistance to most chemicals found in the soil. Polyethylene also has good stability in underground conditions, where it is not exposed to the ultraviolet rays of the sun. Generally, these materials will not rot or mildew.

Deterioration of asphalt in contact with groundwater is reduced considerably with this system because the polyethylene prevents moisture from coming in contact with the asphalt. In addition, the polyethylene acts as a good vapor barrier. The addition of rubber to the asphalt gives the product tensile strength and stability. The rubber makes the asphalt softer and may reduce its tendency to deteriorate with time. The rubberized asphalt products can last a relatively long time if they are carefully installed in an appropriate situation.

ability to withstand movement and cracks

The tensile strength of the polyethylene and the rubber in modified bitumen materials make them effective in bridging over cracks up to ¼-inch wide. The softness and flexibility of the rubberized asphalt allow for some movement to occur without stressing the product to the point of failure. The ability of the material to bridge cracks without leaking depends on very good adhesion at the seams, as movement usually creates extra stress in these areas. It is probably best not to place seams directly over points where cracking is likely to occur, such as at cold joints or other structural connections.

ability to minimize leaks and facilitate repair

Modified bitumens are intended to be used with a primer that helps bond the product to the structure. Along the overlapping seams, the rubberized asphalt bonds quite well to the polyethylene. Ideally, the material will be completely bonded to the structure, thus preventing any water that penetrates the membrane from migrating. This means that the source of a leak will be easier to find, because the water is prevented from traveling behind the membrane. Completely bonding the material to the structure may be almost impossible under most field conditions, however. Because loss of adhesion can occur for a variety of reasons, modified bitumen products must be very carefully applied (see *application considerations*, below).

appropriate use

Modified bitumen products are versatile in that they can be used on concrete, masonry, or wood surfaces. They are well suited to applications on vertical surfaces where there is no continuous head of water; however, they must be used with more discretion on horizontal surfaces. Because these products have numerous overlapping seams, it is not advisable to use them on flat horizontal surfaces where they could be exposed to ponding. If a modified bitumen product is to be used on a horizontal surface, the surface should be sloped slightly to provide drainage and the seams must be overlapped in a manner similar to shingles on a conventional roof.

application considerations

Successful application of modified bitumens depends on great care in the preparation of the surface and application only under the proper temperature and humidity conditions. Experienced, skilled labor is usually required for successful application. A smooth, clean, dry surface is necessary for good adhesion of the product to the surface. Mechanical grinding may be required on concrete surfaces, but slight irregularities are acceptable. The waterproofing material should be applied only when the surface temperature is above 40°F, because colder temperatures reduce the quality of both the bonding and the seams. Unvented gas space heaters should never be used to warm the surface or the rubberized asphalt because they add moisture, which can cause condensation that may loosen the bond.

Modified bitumens may be incompatible with pitch and certain solvents and sealants. Because membranes are combustible, they should not be exposed to flames, sparks, or temperatures over 100°F. Modified bitumens, like most elastomeric materials, have a high degree of memory, a tendency to return to the original sheet or roll configuration. Therefore, if any wrinkles or voids are created during application and then rolled out, the material will tend to return to the wrinkled state.

During the backfilling process, the waterproofing products should be protected from damage. Insulation can serve this purpose; on uninsulated roofs a layer of sand can be used, whereas some form of protection board is necessary on uninsulated walls. The backfilling operation should occur relatively soon after the waterproofing is installed so that the polyethylene is not exposed to ultraviolet degradation from the sun.

relative costs

Compared to costs of other waterproofing products, the cost of modified bitumen products can be considered moderate or average.

Vulcanized and Plastic Sheets

This classification of waterproofing materials includes various natural and synthetic rubber compounds and plastic that are formed into sheet membranes by vulcanization or other processes. The generic names and chemical compositions of the six major types of sheet membranes are:

- isobutylene isoprene (butyl)
- ethylene propylene diene monomer (EPDM)
- polychloroprene (neoprene)
- chlorosulfonated polyethylene (Hypalon)
- chloronated polyethylene (CPE)
- polyvinyl chloride (PVC)

Most of these materials are available in roll stock or sheets in sizes up to 50 feet wide and 200 feet long, depending on the product. Flexible sheets of PVC are available in sizes up to 80 feet wide and 700 feet long. Thickness ranges from $\frac{1}{32}$ to $\frac{1}{8}$ inches in the vulcanized products and between 10 and 120 mils. for CPE and PVC. They can be seamed at the site, using special cements or solvents, or in the factory to form a single membrane that will cover the entire structure. The membranes can be loose laid or partially or fully bonded to the structure. Some are used for above-grade conventional applications as well as below grade. Some of the products, EPDM and neoprene in particular, are used as flashing materials and are available on rolls as narrow as 12 inches for this purpose. Most of the generic types of sheets are also available in a liquid form that has the same basic chemical composition. Although most of the characteristics of stability and durability are similar for these liquids, the other criteria—such as the ability to withstand movement or facilitate repair and the application considerations—are quite different. For this reason the liquid forms of these products are discussed in the section on liquid-applied systems.

stability and durability

With the possible exception of PVC sheets, the stability of this group is quite good. In addition, the products in this group have among the longest life spans of all the waterproofing products. The high quality control in the manufacture of the sheets results in very consistent products. Generally, these membranes are moderately tough, puncture resistant, and resistant to most chemicals. Soft and flexible, most of these products can be elastic in temperatures ranging from 40°F to 200°F. The vulcanization process helps prevent the stress cracking that can occur when sheet membranes are used on sudden, sharp bends.

Although the membranes themselves have excellent characteristics for underground applications, the presence of seams is always a concern. The vulcanization process gives butyl, EPDM, and neoprene great strength and resistance to permanent deformation under long-term loading. Unfortunately, seams that are made in the field with cold-applied solvents or cements do not always have the same characteristics as the sheet material itself. Seams can be sufficient, however, if they are not located in areas with great potential for movement or stress from other forces. For best results the number of seams should be minimized and application should be done with extreme care by professionals. The sheets can be seamed in the factory into one custom-fit membrane. Although this process guarantees a good bond, the resulting rather large, heavy membrane may be difficult to work with.

Because the six major types of membranes, although similar in many of their general characteristics, also differ in some ways, the key characteristics of each type are briefly discussed below.

Butyl membranes are lightly vulcanized, resulting in high strength, flexibility, and softness. They can be reinforced with nylon and have a high resistance to heat and ozone. Although they are resistant to bacteria, fungi, and most soil chemicals, they should not be exposed to acids, oils, or solvents. The very low permeability of butyl rubber to gas makes it a good vapor barrier.

EPDM is a synthetic rubber that is quite similar to butyl in most respects. It is even more resistant to weathering, chemicals, and the ultraviolet rays of the sun. Like butyl rubber, it can be reinforced with nylon. The sulfur included in its composition provides EPDM with high strength and stability.

Neoprene is a synthetic rubber that has good resistance to chemicals, oils, solvents, high temperatures, and abrasion. It is more sensitive to degradation caused by exposure to the sun than are the other vulcanized membranes, and it can be permeated by water vapor to a greater degree. Generally, neoprene membranes are not used in underground applications as often as are butyl membranes or EPDM. Uncured neoprene is commonly used for flashings because it can be formed into complex shapes in the field when heat is applied to it. Rolls of neoprene flashing material are available in cured or uncured form.

Hypalon is distinguished from the other sheet membranes in a number of ways. Its chemical composition gives it some unique characteristics. Because Hypalon is highly resistant to the ultraviolet rays of the sun, ozone, and high temperatures, it is suitable for exposure above grade. Unlike the other membranes, it can be manufactured in a variety of colors. Perhaps the most important characteristic of Hypalon is its relatively high rate of water absorption—an undesirable condition if it is constantly exposed to water. Thus, it is generally not recommended for use underground.

CPE, which is also quite durable and stable underground, is available as a 20- to 40-mil. sheet laminated to a polyester backing that can be fully bonded to the structure. Seams can be made on site by welding the sheets with solvents, cements, or adhesives, and in the factory by means of an electrothermal process.

If properly done, the seams can have the same characteristics as the sheet itself. This is one of the assets of CPE that distinguishes it from some of the other sheet membranes.

PVC is a well-known plastic. As a raw material, it is hard and brittle. As a flexible sheet material, it is strong, resists tears and punctures, and has resistance to ultraviolet degradation and soil chemicals. A drawback of PVC sheets, however, is that shrinkage can occur. They also can become brittle as plasticizers leach out of the material over time. Some products have additives that slow this process.

ability to withstand movement and cracking

Basically, vulcanized and plastic sheet membranes have excellent properties for bridging any cracks that occur in the structure. They are flexible under a wide range of conditions and have great tensile and sheet strength. Their ability to bridge cracks is affected by the manner in which the membrane is bonded to the structure. Total bonding of the membrane reduces the flexibility of the material over cracks and concentrates the stresses in the small portion of membrane lying directly over the crack. A loosely laid or partially bonded membrane allows for this stress to be dissipated over a greater area, thus reducing the strain on the material. At points where movement is expected, such as at an expansion joint or near seams, it is desirable to leave some extra material to take up any stress that occurs.

ability to minimize leaks and facilitate repair

A vulcanized or plastic membrane has no ability to reseal itself once punctured. Membranes can be repaired with patches from the outside of the structure that are bonded in the same manner as seams, with cold-applied cements. The major drawback of sheet membranes when loose laid is the inability to locate leaks, because water can travel behind the membrane and enter the structure at a point remote from the original source. This is one of the main reasons why membranes are bonded to the structure. Assuming that an excellent job is done, completely gluing down the sheet can prevent water from traveling behind the membrane; however, this technique is costly and reduces the ability of the membrane to bridge cracks. A compromise solution that is often used is a partial bonding of the membrane in a regular grid pattern so that any leaks will be localized in one section of the grid.

appropriate use

Sheet membranes can be applied over both precast and poured concrete surfaces, as well as on masonry and wood. These large, heavy membranes are best suited to horizontal surfaces, which can be completely flat. No slope is required because the membranes can hold standing water indefinitely. Although the material can easily resist water on vertical surfaces as well, application is quite difficult because of the tendency of the heavy sheets to stretch from their own weight, especially in the heat.

Application of a large, flat membrane over complex shapes is not easy. Flat surfaces and simple shapes are the best applications for sheet membranes. Minimizing projections and penetrations through the membrane simplifies the application by reducing the number of seams, flashings, and other field-bonded details, which are always the potential weak points of the system. Of course, if projections and penetrations are required, they can be waterproofed by using flashing materials and specially formed boots, corners, and other accessories.

application considerations

The application of vulcanized or plastic sheet membranes, particularly the seaming and bonding, is quite exacting work and requires experienced, skilled professionals. If the membrane is factory seamed, installation requires experience because the material is so heavy and difficult to adjust. Clean, dry, smooth surfaces that are free of oil and grease are required if the membrane is to be bonded. Because the membranes are tough, the surface can be somewhat irregular without causing damage, although sharp edges and foreign objects should be removed. The membrane materials remain flexible over a wide range of temperatures, but applying vulcanized membranes in extremely cold or hot temperatures is inadvisable. Heat can cause the membrane to expand considerably; when placed in the cooler underground environment, it will contract, causing stresses in the membrane and at the seams.

Before bonding or seaming takes place, vulcanized membrane sheets should be laid out and allowed to relax and return to their original size. If they are stretched during application, greater stresses will result. One advantage of the solvents and cements used with these products is that they are cold-applied—no hot mastic is required. The adhesives can be moderately toxic. After installation but before backfilling, the system should be water-tested for leaks. Field inspection and water-testing are advised to ensure watertight seams; however, pinhole punctures can sometimes occur in the manufacturing process. Although the materials are relatively tough, insulation or other protective materials should be used to protect them from punctures by sharp objects during backfilling.

relative costs

The cost of vulcanized and plastic membranes is higher than that of any other category of waterproofing materials. This high cost is largely attributable to the cost of a very high quality, durable material, although skilled labor is also required. The cost can be affected by the complexity of the job and by the number of seams and flashings required. The cost of labor for a membrane that is fully bonded to the structure is significantly higher than for a loose-laid application.

Bentonite Clay Products

Bentonite (montmorillonite) clay is used in several forms to provide waterproofing on underground structures. This highly plastic clay, which is mined in the western United States, has the unique property of swelling from ten to twenty times its original size when saturated with water. As it dries, it returns to its original volume. This process of expanding and contracting can continue indefinitely without wearing out the material. The bentonite material is applied in a thin layer confined between the structure and the soil. As the clay material comes in contact with water, expansion of the material is restrained, resulting in a gel- or paste-like barrier characterized by a high density and impermeability.

The many types and grades of bentonite clays have different characteristics. The major types of these products use specific clays and are available in the following forms:

- raw bentonite
- bentonite mixed with asphalt
- bentonite contained in cardboard panels
- bentonite mixed with binding agent in a trowel- and spray-grade product
- bentonite mixed with polymers in a spray-grade product
- bentonite mixed with polymers for caulking joints

The materials most commonly used on underground buildings are the spray-on and trowel-on mixtures and the cardboard panels.

durability and stability

The fact that bentonite is inorganic and will not deteriorate means that bentonite-based products in general are characterized by long-term stability and flexibility. They should not be used in highly salinated soils, however, because salt diminishes the swelling action of the bentonite clay. Another concern is that, if bentonite is allowed to dry out completely and then is saturated with water, there will be a slight delay before the clay is activated and expands to seal all leaks. Thus, it may not be advisable to use bentonite in a hot, arid climate subject to sudden downpours. Although bentonite products function effectively when exposed to a continuous head of water, they should not be exposed to running water that could cause the clay to wash off the surface.

Raw bentonite in its dry, granular form is often used for well casings and sealing the bottoms of reservoirs. Although it can be used to waterproof buildings, this use is generally not recommended because the bentonite does not adhere as well with other applications, its application is difficult to control, and it will not work on vertical surfaces. It is a mistake to mix raw bentonite with water so that it can be applied in a pastelike form. After expanding during application, it will dry out later, shrink to its original size and, thus, allow water to leak through because the amount of material is inadequate. Bentonite mixed with asphalt is also unsatisfactory and is not recommended. Although this product has been successfully applied, the asphalt tends to coat the clay particles, thus reducing their activity.

Application of bentonite contained in the voids of cardboard panels results in a very consistent thickness of the raw material. The panels must be very carefully handled during transport and application in order to prevent damage. The biodegradable cardboard is intended to deteriorate as a result of the bacteria in the soil. Problems can occur if the backfill soil does not contain sufficient organic matter to cause this deterioraton. For example, water may penetrate past the bentonite and run behind the cardboard and along the seams between the panels. Bentonite should not be placed between two rigid surfaces or against nonstructural walls and floors where the pressure from clay expansion can cause structural damage. This problem can be alleviated by using a type of cardboard panel that incorporates voids so that the expansion can be absorbed within the panel.

The effectiveness of the trowel-on and spray-on mixtures of bentonite is dependent on good quality control in product formulation and application. Trowel-on applications do not require the high skill level and exacting tolerances needed for applying other waterproofing products. Two types of spray-on products are currently available. The first, which is similar to the trowel-on product, is applied in a pastelike form and must be covered with polyethylene to help cure and protect it. It is partially activated and remains in a gel-like state that can be maintained at 50 percent relative humidity. The second type of spray bentonite is a relatively new product that dries immediately on application. A polyethylene cover sheet is recommended on the second type of spray to contain the bentonite, even though it is not needed for curing.

ability to withstand movement and cracks

Bentonite clay products have excellent ability to respond to movement and cracks in the structure that occur after installation. Because it can expand to many times its original volume, bentonite can bridge cracks up to 1/4-inch wide and fill voids created by movement, provided that these cracks or voids do not provide a large enough path to transmit bentonite particles and wash them through the crack to an interior void. Extra protection can be applied to cold joints or other points where cracking is anticipated by means of bentonite-based caulking or tubes of bentonite that decompose in a manner similar to the cardboard panels.

ability to minimize leaks and facilitate repair

The same expansion capability that allows bentonite to bridge cracks also permits it to reseal any punctures or holes that may be present in the waterproofing. Another important advantage is that if any leaks should occur, they will enter the structure near the source of the leak, thereby making it easier to locate. This benefit results from the full adhesion possible with the trowel-on and spray-on products; the adhesion prevents water from traveling away from the source of the leak, as it can when a loose-laid membrane is used. Water can travel somewhat behind cardboard panels unless they are embedded in a gel that is applied to the surface.

If a leak does occur and is located inside of the structure, it can also be repaired from the inside by injecting bentonite through a small hole in the area of the leak. This type of repair has considerable cost advantages over having to excavate in order to locate and repair a leak from the outside. One drawback of bentonite is that, if waterproofing problems occur, options for future repair or replacement by other products may be limited because the bentonite is difficult and messy to remove.

appropriate use

Generally, bentonite products, particularly in the spray-on and trowel-on forms, are quite versatile in comparison with most other waterproofing systems. They can be applied to virtually all types of surfaces, including poured or precast concrete, masonry, and wood (provided that it is pressure-treated). Both vertical and horizontal surfaces can be waterproofed with these products; there are no special requirements for a sloping surface or fast-draining soil. In fact, these bentonite clay products can perform effectively against a constant head of water. Trowel-on and spray-on systems are well suited to complex geometries. Bentonite can be applied to curving forms, complex penetrations, and on very rough, irregular surfaces such as stone, blocks, or corrugated metal. An important design detail is that because bentonite cannot be exposed above the grade line, it must be covered or protected by a flashing that extends over the material.

The cardboard panels containing bentonite have more limitations than do the spray-on and trowel-on products. They are not recommended for use on block walls unless they are first covered with a cement plaster coat. Generally, there is more concern over their effectiveness

on horizontal (as opposed to vertical) surfaces. Problems with the cardboard not deteriorating as expected seem to occur more often on horizontal surfaces. If the panels are used on horizontal surfaces, a slope is desirable. Finally, the large, flat panels are not well suited for situations involving complex geometries, curving forms, irregular surfaces, or numerous penetrations.

application considerations

Application of each type of bentonite product requires a different level of skill and experience. The trowel-on product can be applied by relatively unskilled labor and is one of the only waterproofing products that could possibly be applied adequately by an amateur. The cardboard panels require a moderate level of skill and experience in order to avoid pitfalls. The spray-on application requires an experienced applicator who has invested in the proper equipment for this application. Because bentonite is a relatively new product, the number of qualified applicators is limited.

Very little surface preparation is required for the spray-on and trowel-on products. Rough, irregular, surfaces such as those of spalled or honeycombed concrete are acceptable. The cardboard panels require a smoother surface unless they are applied with a gel. One of the major advantages of bentonite products is that they can be applied in virtually any temperature and humidity. In addition, they are nontoxic.

A critical element in the successful application of the trowel-on and spray-on products is that an even thickness of material must be achieved. For the spray-on product, a $3/16$- to $3/8$-inch thickness is acceptable depending on which system is used; the trowel-on product requires a thickness of $3/16$ inch, with greater thicknesses at corners and construction joints. The application of these products can be interrupted without leaving any seams or joints that could weaken the material. Because bentonite should not be sprayed over 8 feet high without using scaffolding, it may be necessary to backfill before spraying higher;

thus, application of spray-on waterproofing products may require more than one stage. In the second stage of the application process, it is important not to leave spillage of bentonite on top of the first layer of backfill, so that it cannot interfere with the free-draining of the soil.

Polyethylene and insulation are usually placed over spray-on or trowel-on bentonite. Because the bentonite will reseal around any punctures, nails can be used to hold insulation in place. One of the most important application concerns is to prevent the bentonite from getting wet before backfill takes place. Thus, backfilling must be scheduled as soon as possible after the material has been applied and has had time to cure. Curing time for both the trowel-on product and the most common type of spray-on product ranges from four to thirty hours, depending on temperature and humidity conditions. The polyethylene keeps the material from completely drying out during the curing process. The material is too soft to walk on without damaging it before it is cured; however, a newer type of spray-on product dries immediately and can be walked on and backfilled immediately. Backfilling can also be done immediately when cardboard panels filled with bentonite are used.

During the backfilling process, it is important to protect the bentonite from damage. One concern with bentonite applications is that settling of the earth can drag the insulation down the wall and scrape the waterproofing layer off. Because nails can exacerbate this problem, they are not recommended unless absolutely necessary. Although the polyethylene helps reduce friction, it is most important that the backfill be compacted to minimize settling.

relative costs

The cost of the bentonite products is low to moderate in comparison with the other general types of waterproofing systems. One of the key factors influencing costs with the spray-on product is simply the availability of a qualified applicator.

References

Chapter 1

1.11 Bernard Rudofsky, *Architecture Without Architects* (Garden City, NY: Doubleday, 1969).

1.2 Kenneth Labs, "The Architectural Underground, Part II," *Underground Space*, Vol. 1, No. 2, July/August 1976, pp. 135-156.

1.3 Raymond Sterling, John Carmody, and Gail Elnicky (Underground Space Center, University of Minnesota), *Earth Sheltered Community Design: Energy-Efficient Residential Development* (New York: Van Nostrand Reinhold Co., 1981).

1.4 Malcom Wells, "Underground Architecture," *CoEvolution Quarterly*, Fall, 1976.

1.5 R. K. Maxwell, *Temperature Measurements and the Calculated Heat Flux in the Soil* (M.Sc. Thesis, University of Minnesota, 1964).

Chapter 2

2.1 D. J. Bennett, "Notes on the Underground," *Earth Covered Buildings and Settlements*, F. Moreland (ed.) Proc. Conf. Ft. Worth, TX, May, 1978, Gov. Print. Off. Conf-7805138-P2.

2.2 S. D. Hollon and P. C. Kendall, "Psychological Responses to Underground Structures," *Going Under to Stay on Top: Nonresidential Applications* (Minneapolis: Underground Space Center, University of Minnesota, 1980).

2.3 L. L. Boyer, "Daylighting in Subterranean Spaces," *Going Under to Stay on Top: Nonresidential Applications* (Minneapolis: Underground Space Center, University of Minnesota, 1980).

2.4 Belinda Lowenhaupt Collins (ed.), "Windows and People: A Literature Survey: Psychological Reaction to Environments With and Without Windows." Gaithersburg, MD: U.S. Dept. of Commerce, National Bureau of Standards, Building Science Series 70, June, 1975.

2.5 J. Longmore and E. Ne'eman, "The Availability of Sunshine and Human Requirements for Sunlight in Buildings," *Journal of Architecture Research* Vol. 3, No. 2, May, 1974.

2.6 C. Bitter and J.F.A.A. van Ierland, "Appreciation of Sunlight in the Home," *Proceedings of the Conference on Sunlight in Buildings*, pp. 27-37 (Rotterdam: Bouwcentrum International, 1967).

2.7 P. B. Paulus, "On the Psychology of Earth Covered Buildings," *Underground Space*, Vol. 1 No. 2, July/August 1976, pp. 127-130.

2.8 A. Mehrabian and J. A. Russell, *An Approach to Environmental Psychology* (Cambridge: The MIT Press, 1974).

2.9 S. D. Hollon, P. C. Kendall, S. Norsted and D. Watson, "Psychological Responses to Earth Sheltered, Multilevel and Aboveground Structures With and Without Windows," *Underground Space*, Vol. 5 No. 3, November/December 1980, pp. 171-178.

2.10 F. D. Hollister. *Greater London Council: A Report on the Problems of Windowless Environments*, (London: Hobbs the Printers Ltd., 1968).

2.11 Frank W. Lutz, "Studies of Children in an Underground School," *Underground Space*, Vol. 1, No. 2, July/August 1976, pp. 131-134.

2.12 R. J. Wurtman, "Biological Implications of Artificial Illumination," *Illuminating Engineering*, Vol. 63, 1968, pp. 523-529.

2.13 John N. Ott, *Health and Light, the Effects of Natural and Artificial Light on Man and Other Living Things*, (Old Greenwich, CT: Devin-Adair Co., 1973).

2.14 J. N. Ott, "Effects of Wavelengths of Light on Physiological Functions of Plants and Animals," *Illuminating Engineering*, Vol. 60, 1965, pp. 254-261.

2.15 H. May, "Ionizing Radiation Levels in Energy-Conserving Structures," *Underground Space*, Vol. 5, No. 6, May/June 1981, pp. 384-391.

2.16 Frank W. and Susan B. Lutz, "Interim Report of the Abo Project," Office of Health, Education and Welfare, Contract #OE-3-99-003, January 1964.

2.17 Frank W. Lutz, P. D. Lynch and S. B. Lutz, "Abo Revisited," Defense Civil Preparedness Agency, Contract #DAHC20-72-C-0115, June 1972.

2.18 Elizabeth Wunderlich, "Psychology and Underground Development," *Underground Utilization: A Reference Manual of Selected Works*, Vol. IV, Truman Stauffer, Sr. (ed.), pp. 526-529, (Kansas City, MO: Department of Geosciences, University of Missouri, 1978).

Chapter 3

3.1 R. Thomas Quinn, "Energy Analysis of Harvard's Underground Library," *Earth Shelter Performance and Evaluation Proceedings*, October 16-17, 1981, Oklahoma City, Oklahoma, L. L. Boyer (ed.) (Stillwater, OK: Oklahoma State University, 1981).

Chapter 4

4.1 Donald L. Michelsen, Douglas N. Carter, Robert L. Whitelaw, and James A. McCulley, "Reflection on Terraset School: Increasing Energy Conservation in Earth Construction," *Proceedings of Internationales Sonnenforum*, June 24-25, 1980, Congress Centrum, Hamburg, Germany.

Chapter 5

5.1 Automation Industries, Inc., Vitro Laboratories Division, "Solar Performance Bulletin: University of Minnesota Bookstore, May 1982 through July 1982," Department of Energy, National Solar Data Network.

5.2 U. S. Department of Energy and Booz, Allen and Hamilton, Inc., "Design and Performance Trends for Energy Efficient Commercial Buildings," March, 1982.

5.3 L. L. Boyer and R. W. Roush, "Daylighting Analysis for an Earth Covered Office Building in Sacramento, California," *Proceedings of International Conference on Earth Sheltered Buildings*, L. Boyer (ed.). (Sydney, Australia, Aug. 1983). Available from Architectural Extension, Oklahoma State University, Stillwater, OK.

Chapter 6

6.1. Conversation with Don Woodard, Great Midwest Corporation, June 20, 1983.

6.2. Truman Stauffer, Sr. (ed.), *Underground Utilization: A Reference Manual of Selected Works*, Vol. I-III (Kansas City, MO: Department of Geosciences, University of Missouri, 1978).

6.3. Donna Ahrens, "Going Under Provides a New Industry for Kansas City," *Underground Space*, Vol. 5, No. 1, 1980, pp. 15-24.

6.4. Donald R. Woodard, "Downtown Industrial Park, Kansas City—Commercial Use of Deep Underground Space," *Going Under to Stay on Top: Nonresidential Applications* (Minneapolis: Underground Space Center, University of Minnesota, 1980).

6.5. Joe Roberts, "Kansas City's Big Dig Pays Off," *Construction Contracting*, May, 1979, pp. 55-57.

6.6. Truman Stauffer, Sr., "Energy Use Effectiveness and Operating Costs Compared Between Surface and Subsurface Facilities of Comparable Size, Structure, and Enterprise Classification: A Report." Kansas City, MO, 1979.

Chapter 8

8.1 Vladimir Bazjanac, "Energy Analysis of Benedictine Mission House," *Progressive Architecture*, March, 1981, pp. 104-109.

Appendix A

A.1 International Conference of Building Officials, *Uniform Building Code*, 1979 edition (Whittier, California, 1979).

A.2 National Fire Protection Association, *Life Safety Code 1976: Code for Safety to Life from Fire in Buildings and Structures*, NFPA 101 (Boston, Massachusetts, 1976). (Hereafter referred to as *Life Safety Code*.)

A.3   National Fire Protection Association, *Fire Protection Handbook*, 14th ed., eds. Gordon P. McKinnon, Keith Tower (Boston, Massachusetts, 1976). (Hereafter referred to as *Fire Protection Handbook*.)

A.4   Degenkolb, J. G., "Fire Protection for Underground Buildings," *Underground Space*, Vol. 6, No. 2, September/October 1981, pp. 93-95. Also *Going Under to Stay on Top*: *Nonresidential Applications* (Underground Space Center, University of Minnesota, 1980).

A.5   N. A. Koplon, "Report of the Henry Grady Fire Tests," City of Atlanta Building Department (Atlanta, Georgia, 1973).

A.6   P.R. DeCicco, "Report of the Fire Tests, Analyses and Evaluation of Stair Pressurization and Exhaust in High-Rise Office Buildings" (New York: Baywood Publishing Company, 1972).

A.7   In December, 1979, the GSA document, *Interim Guide for Goal-Oriented Systems Approach to Building Fire Safety*, was discontinued as being too cumbersome. However, chapter 4 of *Building Fire Safety Criteria* (GSA publication PBS P5920.9) contains timed exit calculations and is still in use.

Appendix B

B.1   Ray Sterling, William Farnan and John Carmody (Underground Space Center, University of Minnesota), *Earth Sheltered Residential Design Manual* (New York: Van Nostrand Reinhold Co., 1982).

Index